# Safety, Liberty, and Islamist Terrorism

# Safety, Liberty, and Islamist Terrorism

## American and European Approaches to Domestic Counterterrorism

Gary J. Schmitt, Editor

The AEI Press

*Publisher for the American Enterprise Institute*

WASHINGTON, D.C.

Distributed to the Trade by National Book Network, 15200 NBN Way, Blue Ridge Summit, PA 17214. To order call toll free 1-800-462-6420 or 1-717-794-3800. For all other inquiries please contact the AEI Press, 1150 Seventeenth Street, N.W., Washington, D.C. 20036 or call 1-800-862-5801.

Library of Congress Cataloging-in-Publication Data

Schmitt, Gary James, 1952–
  Safety, liberty, and Islamist terrorism : American and European approaches to domestic counterterrorism / Gary J. Schmitt.
    p. cm.
  Includes bibliographical references and index.
  ISBN-13: 978-0-8447-4333-2 (cloth)
  ISBN-10: 0-8447-4333-X (cloth)
  ISBN-13: 978-0-8447-4349-3 (pbk.)
  ISBN-10: 0-8447-4349-6 (pbk.)
  [etc.]
  1.  United States—Foreign relations—Europe.  2.  Europe—Foreign relations—United States.  3.  National security—International cooperation.  4.  Security, International.  I. Title.
  JZ1480.A54S38 2010
  363.325'16094—dc22

                                                      2010018324

14  13  12  11  10              1  2  3  4  5

*Printed in the United States of America*

# Contents

# Acknowledgments

This book owes its origins to long and fruitful conversations with Reuel Marc Gerecht, my former AEI colleague. Much of the initial spadework for the volume was a joint effort. In particular, the chapter on France owes much to Reuel's insights into French security politics. I would also like to thank Abram Shulsky of the Hudson Institute and John Yoo of the University of California, Berkeley School of Law for taking the time and effort to read the manuscript and provide me with their thoughts and suggestions. In addition, I would like to thank the numerous government officials, scholars, and policymakers from Spain, France, Germany, and the United Kingdom who agreed to share their thoughts on their countries' respective security practices and policies. Allied relations have gone through a particularly rough patch since the Iraq War, but cooperation in the field of intelligence and counterterrorism remains a solid cornerstone of transatlantic ties. Finally, I would like to thank Philipp Tomio, my research assistant, for seeing this project through and providing invaluable research help.

*Gary J. Schmitt, July 1, 2010*

# Introduction

*Gary J. Schmitt*

This volume owes its genesis to several long discussions with a former AEI colleague, Reuel Gerecht. Gerecht, a Middle East scholar and former operations officer with the Central Intelligence Agency (CIA), had lived in Europe for extended periods and had worked Middle East "targets" for much of that time. I, on the other hand, was trained as a scholar in presidential studies and worked in both Congress and the White House in senior positions overseeing the U.S. intelligence community. What struck us both in the wake of the attacks on 9/11 was the general failure to put recommended changes to our domestic counterterrorist efforts into proper historical and comparative perspective. It was as though the United States had never in the past dealt with a security threat on its own soil, or democratic allies had not faced or were not facing similar problems from jihadist terrorists.

This observation led us to publish an initial paper that looked at France's success in meeting its own Middle East terrorist problem and at the possible "lessons learned" for the United States.[1] It also led us to think that a broader set of country studies might be useful; hence, this volume, with chapters on France, Spain, the United Kingdom, and Germany, as well as a chapter detailing the U.S. counterterrorism regime. These individual country studies describe the nuts and bolts of current domestic security laws, institutions, and practices and place those elements in the unique political and historical context of each nation. Each country study also looks at what changes have been made since the attacks of 9/11 and, in the case of the European allies, what changes have followed the bombings in Madrid (March 11, 2004) and London (July 7, 2005). The final chapter draws together these earlier analyses and considers what broader points can be drawn from comparing the counterterrorism practices of the United States with those of other democratic states, while at the same time considering the changes in U.S. laws and practices since 9/11 within the broader sweep of American history.

All too often, the debate in the United States over its post-9/11 policies looks only at U.S. policies and practices, and through the lens of the past three decades. Although stated in different forms, the underlying question derived from this narrowed perspective is whether we have moved too quickly and too aggressively to undo the regulations put in place to keep the American intelligence community under greater control in the wake of the investigations of the mid-1970s into intelligence practices—or, less often, whether we have not moved quickly and decisively enough. Not only does this time-constrained focus do little justice to our own history of dealing with serious domestic security issues, but it ignores the efforts by long-time allies—all of whom have had to deal with serious terrorist challenges in the recent past—to find the proper balance between safety and liberty. If nothing else, being clear about the lines being drawn by other liberal democracies between, say, the right to privacy and the need for surveillance, between law enforcement and intelligence gathering, and between free speech and incitement, makes for a more meaningful and more useful debate here in the United States.

The time is right for such a debate, given the change in the U.S. administration. Certainly, as a candidate and senator, Barack Obama promised to rethink the Bush administration's policies on the "global war on terror," which he described as "dangerously flawed" and as "undermin[ing] the very values we are fighting to defend."[2] As president, he has pointedly characterized the previous administration's decisions as "hasty," "based on fear rather than foresight," and he has criticized its "ad hoc legal approach . . . that was neither effective nor sustainable."[3] Few were surprised then when the new administration moved swiftly and dramatically to distance itself from the policies of the previous White House: on his third day in office, the president issued executive orders to close the detention facilities at Guantánamo Bay, renounced the use of torture, and shut down the CIA's network of secret detention facilities.[4] And while controversial, other decisions by the administration are hardly surprising either, given candidate Obama's rhetoric about Bush administration policies: for instance, the decision to try Khalid Sheikh Mohammed, along with four other detainees associated with the attacks on 9/11, in a federal court rather than before a military tribunal, and to treat the case of would-be Christmas bomber Umar Farouk Abdulmutallab as a criminal matter rather than one involving an unlawful enemy combatant. These changes in policies are significant—if for no other reason than the signal they are designed to send abroad: that the Obama administration will rebalance America's approach to the jihadist threat to be more in line with what allied, especially European, publics believe should be a less warlike, more law-bound approach to counterterrorism. The goal was, as one advisor put it, to change the "mood music" for allies and the Muslim world by recalibrating presidential rhetoric and expanding the use of the criminal justice system in cases of terrorism.[5]

But reality being what it is, there has been less change than perhaps many of the president's supporters, both here and abroad, expected. For example, the Obama administration has not abandoned the option of indefinite detention without (civilian or military) trial for captured members of the Taliban or al Qaeda; it has modified but not eliminated the use of military commissions to try some of those same detainees; it continues to use—indeed, has expanded—targeted killings against suspected terrorists; it has retained the option of rendition, that is, capturing terrorist suspects in one country and then handing them over to the government of another; it has reaffirmed the principle of "state secrets," in which the government can prevent the disclosure of certain information on the grounds that it would harm national security; it has argued against expanding habeas corpus rights to captured Taliban and al Qaeda members under U.S. military control in Afghanistan.[6] And, finally, of course, the president has added—perhaps reluctantly, but added nevertheless—tens of thousands of ground troops to Afghanistan in an effort to prevent the return of the al Qaeda–friendly Taliban.

Many of these policy decisions flow from the fact that the Obama administration sees the nation as still being "at war against a far-reaching network of violence and hatred,"[7] even if it does not wish to call its efforts a "global war on terror." As the president's senior advisor on such matters has put it, the president is "under no illusion about the imminence and severity" of the threat.[8] Moreover, whatever the substantive differences between the Bush and Obama approaches to waging "war" on al Qaeda, it is striking that, so far, those differences have not been about the domestic counterterrorism regime put in place following the attacks of 9/11. One can certainly argue that the Obama administration's decision about interrogation practices and its willingness to Mirandize a would-be terrorist, like Nigerian Umar Farouk Abdulmutallab, cannot help but have an impact on domestic security; but what is notably absent from either the White House or the Justice Department is any suggestion that there should be a wholesale revision of the laws, guidelines, and institutional changes made by the previous team to address the terrorist problem at home.[9]

On the one hand, this is a bit surprising. There were any number of commentators, both here and abroad, who suggested that the post-9/11 changes were an overreaction to the attacks and, to one degree or another, put in danger some basic American liberties.[10] Certainly, the Patriot Act's expedited passage—it was signed into law on October 26, 2001—gave civilian libertarians on both the right and the left much cause for concern. And questions about the government's use of its new authorities—such as the large-scale issuance of national security letters—did nothing to reassure those critics about how those powers would be used.[11]

On the other hand, excepting such things as the increased inconvenience of flying, the vast majority of Americans have not felt any less free, nor have they felt the exercise of their basic civil liberties to have been restricted in any substantial fashion. And what problems appear to have arisen as a result of the government's new powers seem largely to have been exposed by the government's own internal monitoring system or by stories in the press, and then dealt with either by new regulations promulgated within the executive branch or by statutory modifications to previously enacted laws. Reinforcing the status quo is the fact that, since 9/11, the United States has not suffered a similar terrorist attack domestically, while the government has uncovered more than two dozen terrorist plots and has arrested and successfully prosecuted numerous would-be jihadists from all parts of the country.[12] And, indeed, numerous high-profile arrests were made during the new administration's first year in office.[13] At the broadest level, the current domestic counterterrorism regime is still obviously needed and appears, with some well-known exceptions, to be working fairly well. Moreover, when compared with past U.S. "wars," the war against al Qaeda and its affiliated groups has had only the most minimal effect on the daily lives of Americans. In brief, there are good reasons for leaving things alone and for limiting changes, if any, to those necessary to deal with specific problems.

That the Obama administration has not made an effort to overhaul what was put in place after 9/11 is no prediction that it will not do so in the future, especially since it has not gone out of its way to defend the current regime. As some have noted, given what was on the administration's plate as it took office, some issues were bound to be reviewed rather later than sooner. The murders at Fort Hood, the 2009 Christmas bombing plot, and the failed bombing in Times Square undoubtedly make efforts to introduce substantial, liberalizing modifications to the domestic security regime politically problematic in the short term. But still out there in the political ether is the view by many, especially on the left, that Congress and the previous administration overreached and that a more balanced, more nuanced, and more civil liberty–friendly approach exists as an alternative.[14] As one defender of the administration's decision to try Khalid Sheikh Mohammed in a federal court has argued, doing so reflects the judgment that the Justice Department, rather than the Pentagon, should have the "lead role in handling the prosecution of terrorism"; this and similar decisions reflect an intent to bring "the whole approach to handling terrorists back inside the rule of law."[15]

Precisely because the Bush administration's approach to the post-9/11 world was thought to be overly militarized, the so-called European approach, in which law enforcement is at the forefront, has been held up as a model from which much could be learned. It is therefore important that we understand the European model or, more precisely, models—how they compare with the U.S. counterterrorism system, and what useful insights might be drawn from that comparison. Obviously, the four countries analyzed in this volume—the United Kingdom, France, Spain, and Germany—are not the whole of Europe. Nor because of differences in history, political culture, and constitutional structures can they be easily collapsed into a single, distinct European approach to Islamist terrorism. Indeed, one of the "lessons learned" from looking at each country's approach is how difficult it is to say what specific practices, institutions, or laws might be usefully borrowed from one nation and adopted by another.

That doesn't mean, however, that we have nothing to learn from what has—and has not—worked in Europe. For example, a considerable amount of the criticism in the post-9/11 reviews was focused on the need to bridge the gap in the United States between law enforcement and intelligence, so examining how France, the United Kingdom, and others have tried to square this circle is instructive. In the case of France, as I note in a later chapter, a key factor has been the investigative magistrate system, in which a few long-serving officials based in Paris have the capacity to draw on intelligence, police, and judicial authorities in terrorist investigations and prosecutions. As for the British, whose situation is analyzed by Tom Parker, the once relatively distinct line between intelligence collection by MI5 (the United Kingdom's domestic intelligence service) and the collection of evidence for use in court by the police has been substantially altered: MI5 works much more closely now with the Metropolitan Police to develop usable evidence earlier in an investigation, and new units in London and elsewhere, in which police and intelligence officials work side by side, have been established to promote a more seamless investigative effort.[16]

Neither of these models is directly applicable to the United States. The French *juge d'instruction* exercises powers, as the name suggests, that overlap the executive and judicial spheres—something our separation of powers system would not tolerate. As for the British, the closer integration of local law-enforcement and intelligence efforts is not burdened by the fractionalization present in the American law enforcement community—a community consisting of over fifteen thousand separate police and sheriff departments and forty-nine state police agencies.[17] But the fact that both countries have had to develop means to overcome the divide between intelligence and police work is an important reminder of the permanence of the issue itself.

What is especially noteworthy when one steps back and looks at the countries under review here is not that their laws, practices, and institutions are more sensitive than America's to the need for balance between civil liberties and security, but that all four have been so forward leaning in their approach to the jihadist threat. This is especially true for France and the United Kingdom; but even in Spain, where (as Rafael L. Bardají and Ignacio Cosidó note in their chapter) the government is reluctant to acknowledge the threat the country faces, laws and practices are not lax. To the contrary, arrests have skyrocketed in recent years, and Spain's pre-trial detention practices continue to be criticized by human rights groups. And while Germany remains the most hesitant of the countries under review to reset its intelligence and police powers (as Eric Gujer shows in his chapter on the German experience), the reality is that the trend line since 9/11 has been to create, step by step, a capacity within its police and intelligence agencies to prevent terrorist crimes.

Indeed, the larger conclusion one takes away from this cross-country analysis is just how much the United States and its liberal democratic allies are in the business of "preemption"—either principally at home, as in the case of European states, or both at home and abroad, as in the case of the United States. Although most European countries avoid the notion that they are "at war" with al Qaeda and argue that they have retained a "rule of law" approach to dealing with that threat, in fact the laws governing their counterterrorist practices and institutions are no less aggressive than those found in the United States—and, in many cases, are more aggressive. France, Germany, the United Kingdom, and Spain have all dealt with terrorism in the past, but each recognizes, if at times quietly and only within government circles, that the nature of the danger posed by al Qaeda and its allies is of an order of magnitude far greater. The damage done and lives lost because of the Basque separatist group Euskadi Ta Askatasun (ETA), the Irish Republican Army (IRA), and Germany's Red Army Faction (RAF) pale in comparison with the lethality of the strikes on New York, the Pentagon, Madrid, and London. But the key point here is not that these allied states have "gone off the rails" when dealing with a terrorist threat that is uniquely dangerous; rather, it's that each (and this includes the United States) remains firmly liberal and democratic by any sensible measure. Certainly, trade-offs have been made between individual liberties and security. But if we take the broad view—stepping back from today's debates and looking both at our own history and at what other democratic states are doing—we are struck by how minimal those intrusions on our liberties have been, given the threat we face. The idea that "Americans [have] let fear of terrorism stop life" is simply not accurate.[18]

This conclusion hardly means that everything that has been put in place since 9/11 has been correct, or that there is no need for a continuing debate over precisely what authorities the government needs (or doesn't) to address the jihadist threat. Yet it does strongly suggest that both the United States and its democratic allies have done a reasonable job of addressing that threat while maintaining core freedoms.

# 1

# United Kingdom:
# Once More unto the Breach

*Tom Parker*

The British authorities disrupted the first al Qaeda plot against the United Kingdom in November 2000. Sixty-seven British nationals died in the September 11 attacks. In 2005, al Qaeda affiliates bombed London, claiming fifty-two victims. Two other major attempts to bomb the capital, in July 2005 and June 2007, failed only because of poor execution by the groups involved.

Outside the United Kingdom, twenty-six British tourists were killed in the 2002 Bali bombing and eleven more in the 2005 bombing of Sharm el-Sheikh in Egypt. In 2003, the British consulate in Istanbul was leveled by a car bomb and a number of staff killed, including the consul-general. Other British civilians have been killed in Iraq, Madrid, Saudi Arabia, and Qatar. Inside the United Kingdom, Glasgow Airport has been attacked; and the British police have disrupted plans to manufacture the nerve agent ricin in a London suburb, uncovered the so-called gas limos plot, and preempted an alleged conspiracy to bomb international flights originating from Heathrow Airport. Suffice it to say, Britons have every reason to take the threat from al Qaeda very seriously indeed.

Of course, terrorism is not new to Britain; it has been a factor in British life for 140 years. Police on the British mainland have confronted terrorism in myriad forms since 1867, when Irish Fenians planted a bomb outside Clerkenwell Prison.[1] London suffered its first coordinated terrorist attack at multiple locations in 1883, and the capital's transport infrastructure was repeatedly attacked between 1883 and 1885.[2] Terrorist suspects today are still often charged under the Explosive Substances Act 1883, a legacy of this campaign.[3]

In the twentieth century Britain has faced anarchist violence, home-grown Marxist terrorists, two mainland bombing campaigns by Irish Republicans in 1939–1940 and 1972–1996, and three IRA campaigns in Northern Ireland in 1939–1945, 1956–1962, and 1969–1998. Animal rights activists have planted more than a hundred incendiary devices around the country, and Scottish nationalist extremists have been responsible for forty-seven terrorist-type attacks, mostly involving letter bombs. Welsh nationalists have been linked to more than 180 arson attacks. Foreign terrorists were responsible for eighty serious terrorist incidents in the United Kingdom between 1975 and 1995 and caused the deaths of three hundred people.[4] The worst of these incidents, the bombing of Pan Am Flight 103 over Lockerbie, Scotland, in December 1988 by Libyan intelligence officers, killed 270 and remains the most serious terrorist attack against the United Kingdom to date.

The British response to terrorism at home has drawn on half a century of experience in counterinsurgency warfare gained while disengaging from fractious colonial outposts such as Palestine, Malaya, and Cyprus.[5] Britain's approach to such conflicts emphasized the primacy of the political, the importance of intelligence gathering, and the need for interagency coordination.[6] It was this approach that Britain turned to in confronting the greatest domestic security challenge faced by successive British governments in the twentieth century: what the British euphemistically have dubbed "the troubles" in Northern Ireland. And it is Britain's approach to "the troubles," in turn, that has served as the foundation for efforts to combat al Qaeda. How the Irish model evolved, and how it has been adapted and augmented to address the newer and more deadly jihadist threat, is the subject of this chapter.

## Northern Ireland

The British Army was deployed to Northern Ireland in August 1969. In the decades that followed, a counterterrorism doctrine slowly evolved that drew upon all arms of the government to support an integrated approach ultimately grounded in the law enforcement paradigm. But this approach was far from a forgone conclusion in 1969.

During that first summer of rioting and sectarian violence in Northern Ireland, the local police force, the Royal Ulster Constabulary (RUC), had abandoned any pretense of impartiality. Although the army was supposedly sent in to act "in aid of the civil power," in reality it rapidly became the lead security agency in the province.[7] The army initially found itself interposed between the two warring communities, striving to at least appear, in Prime Minister Harold Wilson's words, "firm, cool and fair."[8]

In June 1970 a Conservative government led by Edward Heath took power in London, and the role of the British Army began to change from neutral arbiter to security partner of the Unionist government.[9] This shift in policy from peacekeeping to counterinsurgency[10] was soon cemented by the army's aggressive house-to-house search through the Catholic area of Belfast in early July, which left five locals dead. In the words of one Belfast politician, the army succeeded overnight in turning the mood of the Catholic working class "from neutral or even sympathetic support for the military to outright hatred."[11]

In the face of escalating violence and the first British military casualties, the government introduced internment—open-ended detention without charge for suspected terrorists—in August 1971. Crippled by poor intelligence, the initial operation was a fiasco, with the main players in the Provisional IRA (PIRA) avoiding detention and only 18 of the nearly 1,600 people interned in the fall of 1971 eventually charged with a criminal offense.[12] The introduction of internment further alienated the Catholic population, as did the news that some of the internees had been subjected to coercive interrogation techniques. This alienation was made complete on January 30, 1972, when British paratroopers fired on an anti-internment protest in Londonderry, killing fourteen demonstrators and wounding twenty-eight.[13]

As nationalist resistance hardened and the death toll continued to rise, the army redoubled its efforts. In July 1972 the army deployed thirty-one thousand troops to retake Catholic-controlled "no-go" areas in Londonderry and Belfast, a move accompanied by a vast increase in the number of house and vehicle searches.[14]

Increased military activity did reduce the Provisional IRA's freedom of movement and significantly degraded the organization's operational capability.[15] But tactical success came at a strategic cost. There is considerable testimony from members of the Provisional IRA describing how the ubiquitous presence and hostility of British soldiers patrolling nationalist neighborhoods generated a constant stream of new recruits for the organization.[16]

The negative impact of military operations on the political situation was not lost on the British government. Prime Minister Edward Heath's cabinet began casting around for meaningful political initiatives less than a week after the imposition of internment. By December 1971 London was forced to conclude that defeating the IRA as a "precondition" for political progress was no longer a viable goal, and a new objective emerged, that of dampening down the conflict to "an acceptable level" of violence while new political avenues for resolving the conflict could be explored.[17]

In early 1974 a new Labour government began a sweeping review of security operations in Northern Ireland, which led to a shift away from classic counterinsurgency doctrine and back to an internal security model[18] that placed criminal justice and local policing—rather than military operations—at the heart of a new counterterrorism approach in the province, what would become known as "normalization, criminalization, Ulsterization."[19] The essence of this new approach was that counterterrorism policies should depart from societal norms and values as little as possible.

The Birmingham pub bombings of November 1974, which left twenty-one people dead and 145 injured, prompted additional innovation on the British mainland.[20] The government responded by introducing the first piece of national counterterrorism legislation since the Second World War.[21] The Prevention of Terrorism (Temporary Provisions) Act 1974 entered into law within eight days of the bombings and ushered in another new concept that would also become closely associated with counterterrorism in the United Kingdom: "temporary permanence."[22]

Like normalization, the concept of temporary permanence had at its heart the idea that the current emergency would eventually pass and that society and the legal infrastructure of the state would then return to the status quo ante. This belief was captured in the Prevention of Terrorism Act, which was initially subject to biannual parliamentary review.[23]

The first Prevention of Terrorism Act introduced to the wider United Kingdom the powers of proscription (designating a terrorist organization illegal), created a power of exclusion to restrict travel between Northern

Ireland and the mainland for designated individuals, and expanded the period of police detention without charge from forty-eight hours to seven days in terrorist-related investigations. In a perfect illustration of the spirit of normalization, the only organizations that could be proscribed under law were those associated with the political situation in Northern Ireland.

Other institutional norms developed out of operational failures. After the publication of the 1979 Bennett Committee Report on the forcible extraction of confessions in police custody, the policy of securing convictions on the basis of confessional evidence lost much of its viability. The RUC turned its focus instead to obtaining "accomplice evidence" from terrorists in custody, the so-called supergrass system that relied on informants.[24] Between November 1981 and November 1983 at least twenty-five informants provided leads that led to more than six hundred individuals on both sides of the sectarian divide being charged with terrorist offenses.[25]

Yet thirteen of the twenty-five retracted their testimony in 1983 before going to court, resulting in the collapse of three hundred cases.[26] Equally damaging, the British Court of Appeal also overturned more than fifty successful convictions that rested on such testimony.[27] The supergrass system had been able to flourish in the jury-free Diplock courts, introduced as a response to jury intimidation in the 1973 Northern Ireland (Emergency Provisions) Act, but could not stand up to the level of scrutiny brought to bear by the higher British courts. Discredited, the supergrass system was abandoned in 1985.

A major consequence of the supergrass system's collapse has been a change in how evidence is sought. British prosecutors are now loath to rely on the testimony of informants alone, and there is an additional institutional aversion in the intelligence community to risking an important human asset, especially one with potential long-term access, for the sake of an individual case. As a result, the authorities currently favor using intelligence assets to monitor operations until they are sufficiently far advanced that the police can be confident of recovering enough evidence at the point of arrest to support meaningful criminal charges.

This period also saw a reconceptualization of how best to employ military force against the Provisional IRA. Between 1976 and 1987 a standing force of approximately 150 British Special Forces soldiers were deployed to Northern Ireland to conduct intelligence-led operations against PIRA and its socialist rival, the Irish National Liberation Army (INLA). During their deployment British Special Forces killed thirty PIRA and two INLA members, typically by laying ambushes at weapons caches or interdicting an active service unit (as PIRA's cells were called) in the field.[28] Six innocent bystanders were also killed in the course of these operations.[29]

The involvement of Special Forces troops in counterterrorist operations was not confined to the province of Northern Ireland. On March 6, 1988, a Special Air Service (SAS) team shot dead three members of the Provisional IRA active service unit in Gibraltar, claiming that they had adopted an aggressive stance when challenged. There was widespread criticism of the SAS's failure to apprehend three unarmed suspects without loss of life, and their families took the case to the European Court of Human Rights. In September 1995 the court narrowly ruled in a 10-to-9 majority decision that the PIRA team had been "unlawfully killed."[30]

Clearly, even this reconceived use of military force was problematic. As Louise Richardson has noted, real or perceived missteps by the British Security Forces—allegations of a shoot-to-kill policy, the "inevitable accidents" that result from deploying soldiers in a civilian setting, and a series of miscarriages of justice associated with police investigations on the British mainland—only served to blacken Britain's international reputation and undermine British claims to legitimacy in Northern Ireland.[31] As a consequence, a well-developed awareness exists across the political spectrum in Britain of the potential pitfalls of deploying military units—whether regular army or Special Forces—in a civil setting.

## A Period of Transition

The 1990s were marked by three major developments that affected British counterterrorism doctrine and practice: the increasingly high-profile role of the Security Service (MI5) in counterterrorist operations; the success of the Northern Ireland peace process; and the government review of existing terrorist legislation headed by Lord Lloyd of Berwick, which led to significant changes in British law.

Prior to 1985 none of the work of the British intelligence or security agencies was done on a statutory basis.[32] The government disavowed the very existence of both the Security Service and its overseas counterpart, the Secret Intelligence Service (SIS). Such an arrangement became increasingly untenable. The *Spycatcher* debacle of 1987–1988, in which the British government tried unsuccessfully to prevent the publication of a memoir by former MI5 officer Peter Wright, made a mockery of the government's refusal to admit the existence of the Security Service. With two pending cases involving alleged Security Service investigations before the European Court of Human Rights promising further embarrassment,[33] Margaret Thatcher's government surrendered to the inevitable and introduced the Security Service Act in 1989. The act is brief and the service's mission is stated simply: "The function of the Security Service shall be the protection of national security and, in particular, its protection against threats from espionage, terrorism and sabotage, from the activities of agents of foreign powers and from actions intended to overthrow or undermine parliamentary democracy by political, industrial, or violent means."[34]

It is important to note that the Security Service has never held executive powers. When executive action is called for, it falls to other government agencies to move things forward: for example, the Home Office may seek to deport terrorist suspects, the Foreign Office may refuse entry visas, and the police and the Crown Prosecution Service pursue criminal charges.[35]

In 1989, primacy in Irish terrorism-related intelligence activities still rested with the Royal Ulster Constabulary in Northern Ireland and with the Metropolitan Police Special Branch (MPSB) on the British mainland.[36] The Security Service's primary focus was on counterintelligence and countersubversion.[37] However, MI5's role changed dramatically in 1992. The end of the Cold War had meant a much-reduced requirement for a national countersubversion and counterintelligence capability, and the Security Service accordingly embraced counterterrorism as its new primary mission.[38] On May 8, 1992, Home Secretary Kenneth Clarke announced that the Security Service would take the lead in collecting intelligence on Irish terrorism on the British mainland.[39]

The Security Service immediately moved to address long-standing complaints that MPSB had not been effectively channeling intelligence to its regional counterparts and that there was little coordination between the different regions. MI5 provided the United Kingdom's fifty-plus regional special branches with a secure communications system, and began to distribute regular briefing papers on relevant topics. A Regional Special Branch Conference was instituted to further boost cooperation and information exchange. The Security Service participated "jointly" with MPSB in training new Special Branch officers recruited from around the country.[40]

Between 1990 and 1994, the proportion of MI5's resources devoted to counterterrorism doubled.[41] The result was an increase in the number of preemptive disruptions of terrorist activity. Security Service operations led to twenty-one convictions for terrorism-related offenses between 1992 and 1999.[42]

Although relations between MI5 and MPSB were strained as the former assumed its new role, this was, for the most part, only a short-term phenomenon. Contrary to persistent press reporting of rifts between the Security Service and the Metropolitan Police, the two agencies continued to work closely together on a daily basis. For instance, surveillance crews from both organizations routinely worked alongside each other on the same operational targets, and officers from each agency served on temporary attachments with the other agency's investigative sections. Methodologically, the Security Service did have to adjust its operational procedures to ensure that intelligence could, if necessary, be admitted as evidence in criminal proceedings.[43] This process was enshrined in statute with the adoption of the Regulation of Investigatory Powers Act 2000.

A number of factors finally led to the Provisional IRA's declaration of a "complete cessation" of military activities on August 31, 1994. Brendan O'Leary and John McGarry have attributed PIRA's desire for peace to the growing perception of a "hurting stalemate" and the realization that there could be no military solution to the conflict.[44] PIRA's public standing was also badly damaged by two high-profile operational blunders in 1993 (a bomb placed outside a McDonald's in Warrington in March which killed two young children, and an attack in October on a Belfast chip shop that took nine innocent lives[45]), resulting in an upsurge in support for the peace movement in Northern Ireland. These factors—facilitated by the growing security partnership between London and Dublin—combined to allow peace proposals to gain traction.

The Provisional IRA ceasefire held until a breakdown in negotiations over arms decommissioning led to a temporary resumption of hostilities from February 1996 to July 1997. The British government stepped in with a nuanced formula—that PIRA would "address" rather than actually carry out decommissioning—which allowed the parties to move forward. The peace process culminated in the Good Friday Agreement of April 1998. As Louise Richardson has noted, the British learned from their Northern Ireland experience the importance of engaging terrorists—in order to learn how they operate, understand their grievances and priorities, and ultimately influence their internal dynamics.[46] The Good Friday Agreement was possible because the British had learned these lessons well; it has survived for a decade despite the best attempts of rejectionist groups like the Real IRA and the Continuity IRA to undermine it.[47]

In December 1995, as the Northern Ireland peace process began to gather momentum, Lord Lloyd of Berwick was asked to conduct an inquiry into the need for specific counterterrorism legislation should a lasting settlement be achieved. The Lloyd review differed from previous public inquiries in that his mandate included all British counterterrorism legislation and took into account for the first time Britain's hardening judicial and political obligations under the European Convention on Human Rights and the International Covenant on Civil and Political Rights.[48] His report would lay the groundwork for an overhaul of British counterterrorism legislation.

Lord Lloyd had no doubt that the terrorist threat to the United Kingdom would not evaporate with peace in Northern Ireland. He noted that Britain was "particularly liable" to be caught up in foreign struggles because of "the number of communities of foreign nationals" who had settled, and sought sanctuary, in the United Kingdom. Lord Lloyd also identified "a worrying trend towards the use by terrorists of more and more deadly methods." He noted that past emergency legislation had done "some damage to the United Kingdom's international reputation in the field of human rights," and he enumerated the instances in which the European Court of Human Rights had found against the United Kingdom and the criticisms leveled by the United Nations Human Rights Committee and Committee against Torture.[49] He recommended disbanding the Diplock court system of jury-free trials,[50] removing the power of internment from the statute books, and withdrawing the power of exclusion.[51] He nevertheless judged as sound the basic proposition that countering terrorism's "exceptionally serious threat to society" required "special offenses and additional police powers."[52]

To meet Britain's needs moving forward, Lord Lloyd advocated that counterterrorist measures be consolidated into a single, permanent act covering both Great Britain and Northern Ireland. He recommended, *inter alia,* introducing a new offense of conspiring in the United Kingdom to commit a terrorist act abroad, the use of telephone intercept material at trial, and a reduced sentencing scheme along the lines of the *penititi* initiative, used successfully by the Italian authorities against the Red Brigades, to encourage cooperation from terrorism suspects.[53]

Although John Major's Conservative government did not implement Lord Lloyd's recommendations, the new Labour government of Tony Blair in 1997 quickly moved to debate the introduction of permanent counterterrorist legislation and drew heavily on the recommendations of Lloyd's report. Home Secretary Jack Straw told the House of Commons: "Like Lord Lloyd, the Government envisage that some existing powers will be confirmed and placed on a permanent footing; that some will be strengthened; and that others will substantially be changed."[54]

The power of internment was withdrawn from the Northern Ireland (Emergency Provisions) Act 1998.[55] The power of exclusion was also dropped.[56] In November 1998 the government passed the Human Rights Act to "give further effect" to the rights and freedoms detailed in the European Convention on Human Rights (ECHR) by enshrining them in British law.

The Criminal Justice (Terrorism and Conspiracy) Act 1998 introduced four new powers: the opinion of a police officer would henceforth become admissible as evidence of membership in a terrorist organization; courts would be allowed to "draw inference" from a suspect's refusal to answer questions during a police investigation into a proscribed organization; assets used to further the cause of proscribed organizations could now be confiscated on conviction; and, finally, as Lord Lloyd had recommended, conspiring to commit terrorist or other serious crimes abroad would now be an offense in Britain.[57]

To bring British electronic and human surveillance practices in line with the ECHR, Parliament passed the Regulation of Investigatory Powers Act 2000 (RIPA). Part I of RIPA authorized the home secretary to issue warrants for the interception of communications. Under the law, warrants for surveillance, either electronic or physical, must meet the standard of being both "necessary" and "proportionate" for collecting information "in the interests of national security," "for the purpose of preventing or detecting serious crime," or "for the purpose of protecting the economic well-being of the United Kingdom."[58] Part II of RIPA introduced formal regulations for "human intelligence" operations, such as source recruitment and handling.

On the other side of the equation, RIPA required communications service providers to maintain a "reasonable interception capability" in their networks. It also permitted any public authority designated by the home secretary to access "communications data" without a warrant. These data include the source, destination, and type of any communication, such as mobile phone location information and Web browsing logs. Part III of RIPA allowed senior law enforcement officials and members of the judiciary to demand that users hand over the plaintext of encrypted material, or in certain circumstances decryption keys themselves.

An omnibus Terrorism Act (TACT) was finally introduced by the Labour government in 2000 and entered into force in February 2001. British law does not contain a specific offense of terrorism analogous to treason or piracy. Instead, terrorist organizations are designated by executive order through the power of proscription. Under the Prevention of Terrorism Act 1989, the power of proscription was limited to organizations "connected with the affairs of Northern Ireland."[59] TACT extended proscription for the first time to international terrorist groups. As of December 2009, there were forty-five proscribed international organizations, including al Qaeda, ETA, November 17, Hezbollah, the Tamil Tigers, and Hamas.[60]

TACT also enhanced police powers to "stop and search" persons or vehicles in designated areas, without specific cause; and it permitted detention without charge for an initial forty-eight hours in connection with terrorist-related offenses, with possible extension to seven days subject to judicial review. Most crucially, it also created new criminal offenses such as inciting terrorist acts, collecting or holding information useful to those involved in acts of terrorism, and seeking or providing terrorist training either at home or abroad. With the passage of the Terrorism Act 2000, the doctrine of "temporary permanence," which had underpinned the legislative approach to the terrorist threat of British governments for more than twenty-five years, was finally retired.

## 9/11 and Its Aftermath

More British lives were lost on September 11, 2001, than in any other terrorist attack in British history. Consequently, the British government reacted strongly to events in New York, Pennsylvania, and Washington, introducing new legislation, expanding police powers, strengthening cooperation between different security agencies, and formulating a coherent strategy for dealing with the al Qaeda threat.

The Anti-Terrorism, Crime and Security Act 2001 (ATSCA) was the first concrete manifestation of the government's hardened approach. Although ATSCA created new penalties for crimes aggravated by racial or religious hatred and permitted the freezing of a suspected terrorist's assets at the outset of an investigation (rather than after conviction), the act's primary purpose was to prevent terrorist suspects from using political asylum laws to block their detention in or removal from the United Kingdom. Where deportation was not possible, it allowed foreign nationals suspected of involvement in terrorism to be detained indefinitely.[61] There was no obligation to charge such detainees with an offense. The power to indefinitely detain a terrorism suspect rested with the home secretary, although his decision could be challenged on points of fact and law at the Special Immigration Appeals Commission.[62] On the same day that ATCSA was brought before Parliament, Home Secretary David Blunkett laid a Human Rights Derogation Order in respect of article 5 of the European Convention on Human Rights, which prohibits detention without trial. Britain was the only European country to enter a derogation from the convention as a result of the September 11 attacks.[63]

From its inception ATCSA proved controversial. The House of Lords made seventy amendments to the original bill, although most were subsequently reversed in the House of Commons.[64] Particularly contentious was the fact that habeas corpus rights were not extended to the ATCSA detainees.[65] Detainees challenged the law in British courts, and the case reached Britain's highest court of appeal, the House of Lords, in 2003. The Law Lords were asked to consider the nature of the threat facing the United Kingdom; whether ATSCA represented a necessary and proportional response to that threat; and whether by its nature ATSCA was unjustifiably discriminatory. In December 2004 the Law Lords ruled, by an 8-to-1 majority, in favor of the ATSCA detainees.[66]

The government responded by rushing the Prevention of Terrorism Act 2005 (PTA) through Parliament, which introduced the use of control orders. The home secretary is empowered by the PTA to apply to the courts for writs to confine subjects (including UK citizens) to house arrest or to restrict their movements and access to them. In exceptional circumstances the home secretary can authorize a control order on his own authority subject to judicial review within seven days. As of June 2009 thirty-eight individuals have been subjected to control orders under the PTA.[67]

In addition to the potential threat posed by foreign nationals and asylum seekers, the government sought in 2002 to address the threat posed by naturalized British citizens with links to international terrorist groups. Under the Nationality, Immigration and Asylum Act 2002, a British citizen engaging in activities "seriously prejudicial to the vital interests of the United Kingdom" may be deprived of citizenship or status by order of the home secretary, so long as this would not leave the individual in question stateless. This power was used for the first time in April 2003 to withdraw British citizenship from the controversial London-based Muslim cleric Sheikh Abu Hamza al-Masri.[68]

In the aftermath of the September 11 attacks, there was increasing integration of British law enforcement and intelligence operations. The police and Security Service continued to work closely on a wide range of counterterrorism targets, with police special branches around the country providing the vital "two-way linkage" between the "bobby on the beat" and the national agencies.[69] Working together on an "unprecedented scale" during Operation Crevice, MI5 and police disrupted a plot to use homemade explosives manufactured from ammonium nitrate to attack civilian targets in London and Kent.[70]

Under the provisions of the Terrorism Act 2000, the police arrested 544 suspects between September 11, 2001, and January 31, 2004.[71] In 2001–2002, the Security Service devoted 23 percent of its total operational capacity to the Islamic terrorist threat, but by July 2005, the figure was 56 percent. The SIS and Government Communications Headquarters operational effort against the Islamic threat also rose "significantly."[72]

In 2002 the British government adopted a new "core strategy" for countering international terrorism, known within government circles by the appellation CONTEST.[73] The strategy is divided into four principal strands: prevention, pursuit, protection, and preparedness.[74] Prevention consists of addressing structural problems that may contribute to radicalism (such as racial discrimination and inequality); the goals are to deter those who facilitate terrorism and extremism by restricting the space in which they can operate, and by engaging them in "the battle of ideas." Pursuit takes the form of intelligence gathering, law enforcement, and international cooperation. Protection revolves around hardening targets and strengthening border security. Preparedness emphasizes forward planning and first-responder training. CONTEST is explicitly conceived as a holistic strategy that aims to mobilize all arms of government acting in concert.[75] Of particular note is that the use of military force is scarcely addressed in the strategy document: the government declares itself willing in principle to use military force, in accordance with international law, for counterterrorism purposes when nonmilitary tools cannot achieve its goals, but recognizes that there are "considerable challenges" to doing so.[76]

In June 2003 the Joint Terrorism Analysis Center (JTAC) was established in the headquarters of the Security Service. JTAC is a freestanding entity reporting to the director general of MI5 and comprised of representatives of sixteen government departments and agencies. It establishes threat levels, issues threat warnings, and distributes reports on terrorist activity and trends. On the whole, it has received a positive reception as a cross-agency, integrated assessment center.[77]

In November 2004 Parliament passed the Civil Contingencies Act introducing "a single framework for civil protection in the United Kingdom." The act was the culmination of a four-year-long review process started in December 2000 following (of all things) widespread rural flooding.[78] In addition to outlining forward-planning responsibilities for first responders and "co-operating bodies," the act also made provision for a range of emergency powers that could be activated in the immediate aftermath of a major incident, such as the power to requisition, confiscate, or destroy property; to prohibit movement in key areas or compel evacuation; and, if necessary, to deploy the armed forces. These powers would be available for a maximum of thirty days, subject to review after seven days by both houses of Parliament.[79]

## 7/7 and Its Aftermath

In June 2005 the Joint Intelligence Committee warned that Western governments could not be confident of identifying preparations for attacks and predicted a successful attack in the United Kingdom within the next five years.[80] The committee was proved right, not once, but twice, in the space of just one month. On July 7, 2005, fifty-two civilians were killed and seven hundred injured in four simultaneous rush-hour suicide bombings on London Transport. A copycat attack two weeks later failed when the detonators used by the bombers did not ignite. Three of the bombers responsible for the first attack were second-generation British citizens of Pakistani descent, and the fourth was a British national of Jamaican origin who had lived most of his life in Huddersfield.[81] The failed bombers came from Somalia, Eritrea, and Ethiopia; all were in the United Kingdom legally, and three were naturalized British citizens.

The government responded rapidly to the attacks. At a Downing Street press conference on August 5, 2005, Prime Minister Tony Blair announced a twelve-point action plan to strengthen counterterrorism operations.[82] The Terrorism Bill, introduced in the House of Commons on October 12, 2005, made it a criminal offense to offer "direct or indirect encouragement" to commit acts of terrorism, to disseminate terrorist publications, or to prepare terrorist acts, and it extended the powers of proscription to include organizations that "promote or encourage" terrorism even if they stop short of actual involvement in terrorist acts.[83]

On November 9, 2005, the government introduced an amendment to the Terrorism Bill proposing that the maximum period of police detention without charge for terrorism suspects—which had already been increased from seven to fourteen days under the Criminal Justice Act 2003—be increased to ninety days. The proposal was made on the recommendation of the Metropolitan Police, who argued that international terrorism's potential for mass casualties required earlier intervention than was previously the operational norm, and that this fact, coupled with the fact that terrorist investigations often necessitated inquiries overseas, made it impossible to complete a thorough pre-charge investigation within the fourteen-day window previously allowed.[84]

The government proposal was greeted with hostility in the House of Commons, and the measure was rejected by 322 votes to 291, with forty-nine members of the Labour Party rebelling against their leadership. This was the first defeat for Tony Blair's Labour government.[85] However, Parliament endorsed an amendment permitting an extension of detention without charge to twenty-eight days, subject to judicial review.[86] The amendment was incorporated into the Terrorism Act 2006 along with the other elements of the Terrorism Bill detailed above.

In one of the last major initiatives of his premiership, Tony Blair announced in March 2007 that he would be dividing the responsibilities of the Home Office between the existing department and a new Justice Ministry to allow the home secretary to concentrate more fully on the terrorist threat.[87] An Office for Security and Counter-Terrorism was created within the Home Office to take on overall responsibility for the CONTEST strategy. A new Ministerial Committee on Security and Terrorism to be chaired by the prime minister was also established by the reorganization, supported by a new subcommittee focusing on counterradicalization. The changes took effect on May 9, 2007.

Following the abortive attack on Glasgow Airport in June 2007, the new British prime minister, Gordon Brown, announced his intention to seek legislation allowing the detention of terrorism suspects for up to fifty-six days without charge—making clear that he would be as tough on terrorism as his predecessor.[88]

In January 2008 the Brown government introduced the Counter-Terrorism Bill, which, among other measures, sought to extend pre-trial detention to forty-two days. This proposal was ultimately defeated in the House of Lords by 309 votes to 118. The pre-trial detention period for terrorism-related offenses remains twenty-eight days, although Home Secretary Jacqui Smith told the House of Commons that the government has prepared a Counter-Terrorism (Temporary Provisions) Bill to introduce a forty-two-day detention period "if and when the need arises."[89]

Elements of the bill that survived to comprise the Counter-Terrorism Act 2008 included the authorization of post-charge questioning for terrorist offenses;[90] the creation of a terrorist offenders database and monitoring regime similar to that used for sex offenders; and language making it an offence to elicit, attempt to elicit, or publish information relating to a member of the armed forces, a constable, or the intelligence services that might be useful to a terrorist. In an unrelated measure, a compulsory biometric identity card was also introduced in November 2008 for foreign nationals from outside the European Economic Area and Switzerland.[91]

## More Resources, More Coordination

The July 2005 bombings seem to have intensified a trend, already in progress at the time, of more funding and more staffing for counterterrorist organizations in the United Kingdom, though the struggle to match resources to the scope of the problem is ongoing. Talking to an audience at Queen Mary University of London in 2006, Dame Eliza Manningham-Buller, then director-general of MI5, explained that the service was struggling to handle the increase in casework.[92] The Intelligence Service Committee had reported in May 2006 that at the time of the July 2005 bombings the service was pursuing approximately 800 "primary investigative targets" (as compared to 250 in 2001),[93] and by November 2006 this figure had doubled to 1,600.[94] In November 2007 the new incoming director general of MI5, Jonathan Evans, stated that 2,000 suspect individuals were now believed to pose a "direct threat to national security and public safety."[95] And this in an environment in which, according to the Parliamentary Intelligence and Security Committee, "an intensive operation, for example into imminent attack planning, can consume almost half of the Security Service's operational and investigative resources."[96] As Dame Eliza dryly observed in her lecture: "We are faced by acute and very difficult choices of prioritization."[97] Parliament's Intelligence and Security Committee similarly noted: "We have been struck by the sheer scale of the problem that our intelligence and security agencies face and their comparatively small capacity to cover it."[98]

The revelation that two of the July 7, 2005, bombers, Siddeque Khan and Shazad Tanweer, had been noticed in the course of a 2004 surveillance operation involving an essentially unrelated Islamist group, and that no further action had been taken because other inquiries were deemed more pressing, led the Intelligence and Security Committee to conclude: "If more resources had been in place sooner the chances of preventing the July attacks could have increased."[99]

The point was not a new one, and both security budgets and staffs have been steadily increasing since 2001. In January 2006 the home secretary announced that an additional £446 million would be made available to the police specifically for countering international terrorism and domestic extremism,[100] and in April 2006 the Security Service suspended its work on organized crime targets to focus more resources on counterterrorism.[101] The total Single Intelligence Account allocation has risen from £1,313.7 million in the 2004–2005 financial year to £1,553 million for 2007–2008, with 73 percent of the additional funding going to the Security Service.[102] The staff of MI5 in 2006 numbered 2,800. By 2008 the Security Service was twice the size it was in 2001.[103] By 2011 the overall security budget is expected to rise to £3.5 billion.[104]

In addition to increases in funding and staffing, the July 2005 attacks inspired further institutional reforms geared toward creating ever more integrated operations. In October 2006 New Scotland Yard merged the Metropolitan Police Special Branch and the Anti-Terrorist Branch to create a new Counter Terrorism Command with a staff of 1,500. The new command united the Metropolitan Police's counterterrorism intelligence and evidence-gathering operations and marked the doubling of the force's counterterrorist capability since September 11, 2001.[105] The Counter Terrorism Command presents a single point of contact for international partners in counterterrorism matters, simplifying liaison channels, and the head of the Counter Terrorism Command serves as the United Kingdom's national coordinator for terrorist investigations. Regional Counter Terrorism Units have been established in London, Manchester, Birmingham, and Leeds, along with smaller Regional Intelligence Cells in Wales, the East Midlands, and the South West.[106] And MI5 has opened eight regional offices across the United Kingdom based in local police buildings.[107]

In a lecture delivered in April 2007, the head of the Counter Terrorism Command, Peter Clarke, testified to the progress that had been made in interagency cooperation: "The police and Security Service now work together in every case from a much earlier stage than would ever have happened in the past," and setting joint objectives and devising investigative strategies have become "the daily routine." He further noted that "sometimes, the barriers between the various Special Branches and MI5 were lower than within the police itself."[108] He concluded: "It is no exaggeration to say that the joint working relationship between the police and MI5 has become recognized [globally] as a beacon of good practice."[109]

In April 2008 the government took additional steps to improve the security of Britain's borders by merging the Border and Immigration Agency, UK Visas, and the port of entry functions of HM Customs and Excise to form the UK Border Agency.[110] The merger created a single customs and passport checkpoint for visitors to Britain. UK Border Agency and police analysts now work together in the national e-Borders Centre (e-Boc) to screen, check, and risk-assess passenger data in advance of travel so that potential threats can be identified prior to an individual's arrival in the UK.[111] The Association of Chief Police Officers has gone even further, recommending the creation of a national border police force to work alongside the UK Border Agency at British ports.[112]

## Londonistan and Liaison Partners

Yet another consequence of the bombings of 2005 has been increased outreach by the UK government to minority communities within its borders, in particular to Muslims. Britain has somewhere between one and a half and two million Muslim citizens, and a million live in London alone. Britain is also home to approximately 1,500 mosques, many of which are influenced by the conservative Deobandi school of Sunni Islam with its origins in Pakistan.[113]

As part of its outreach efforts, the British government provides consular and other support services to British Muslims making the pilgrimage to Mecca, has passed legislation making discrimination on the grounds of faith illegal, and holds monthly meetings at New Scotland Yard to address matters of concern to local Muslim communities.[114]

Following the bombings of July 2005, Home Office ministers launched the Preventing Extremism Together (PET) initiative in consultation with Muslim community leaders from nine major British cities. One notable PET success has been the establishment of the Scholars' Roadshow program, in which "influential mainstream Muslim scholars" engage audiences of young British Muslims in theological discussion; by November 2007 an estimated seventy thousand people had attended the road shows.[115] Another important initiative to come out of PET has been the establishment in June 2006 of the Mosques and Imams National Advisory Board, which has already published a good-practice guide for mosques.[116] In November 2007 the board proposed a ten-point code of conduct to "actively combat all forms of violent extremism" within the Muslim community and "promote civic responsibility."[117]

British constabularies are also making increased efforts to recruit civil-ian Police Community Support Officers from minority communities to act as a bridge to local families. There are currently 3,500 neighborhood police teams operating around the country, and in 2007 £70 million was allocated to community projects dedicated to countering violent extremism.[118] How-ever, despite considerable investment in the "community intelligence" approach, results to date have been disappointing. Almost all of Britain's successful counterterrorism prosecutions in the past five years have had their origins in intelligence received from liaison services overseas, the intel-ligence services, or technical attacks.[119]

Foreign liaison services also play an important role in British counter-terrorism. The former director-general of the Security Service, Dame Eliza Manningham-Buller, has stated publicly that MI5 has links to one hundred services worldwide.[120] The Security Service enjoys excellent relations with most of its European Union counterparts, with MI5 liaison officers stationed in the major European capitals and in Europol.

The bilateral relationship with the United States is undeniably the United Kingdom's most important intelligence partnership. In the words of Sir John Scarlett, chief of SIS, "the global resources of CIA, FBI, and NSA are vast . . . The UK Agencies' long-developed relationships with US intelligence agencies give them vital access to US intelligence and resources. It is neither practical, desirable, nor is it in the national interest, for UK agencies to carry out [counter-terrorism] work independently of the US effort." Signals intel-ligence exchange between the U.S. National Security Agency and Govern-ment Communications Headquarters is especially strong, and Britain is by far the greater beneficiary of this relationship in terms of shared traffic.[121]

In September 2005 Dame Eliza testified publicly about two cases in which liaison relationships with nontraditional allies have borne substan-tial fruit.[122] The director-general cited the cases of Djamel Beghal and Mohammed Meguerba. Beghal was detained in 2001 in the United Arab Emi-rates, where he confessed to knowledge of a plot to mount terrorist attacks in France. This information was shared by the United Kingdom with the French authorities and led to the disruption of the plot, one of whose targets was the United States Embassy in Paris, and to the subsequent conviction of Beghal in France. As for Meguerba, he was detained in December 2002 in Algeria, where, under interrogation, he provided the local authorities with intelligence of an imminent plot by Islamic extremists to deploy a "poison" (later identified as ricin) in London. Acting on this information, British Police were able to make a number of arrests in January 2003.

A further insight into the close operational relationships MI5 has developed with its European partners was provided by the successful conclusion of Operation Samnite in 2002. The Security Service learned that the Real IRA was seeking a rogue state to sponsor its operations, and MI5 officers posing as representatives of the Iraqi Intelligence Service met with members of the Real IRA in Dublin, Slovakia, Austria, and Budapest before triggering an arms sting that resulted in the arrest and subsequent conviction of three of the organization's members.[123] Operation Samnite was the first MI5 operation in which evidence was gathered entirely overseas and would have been impossible to mount without the active support of local liaison services, especially those in Slovakia.[124]

On the law enforcement front, perhaps the most important liaison development has been the introduction of the European Arrest Warrant, a fast-track extradition procedure that was introduced after the September 11 attacks through the mechanism of a framework decision made under article 34 of the Treaty of European Union. The expedited warrant procedure was first used successfully after the July 2005 London bombings to extradite would-be suicide bomber Hussain Osman from Italy.[125]

But all is not simply rosy when it comes to liaison relations. One of the major ethical dilemmas that Britain's counterterrorism establishment has wrestled with has been the reported mistreatment of detainees, or complicity in mistreatment, by allied nations.[126] Two operational practices in particular—extraordinary rendition and targeted assassination—have raised difficulties for the British intelligence community.[127]

The British authorities have been forced to become increasingly circumspect in their dealings with U.S. partners for fear of breaching the human rights protections enshrined in British and European law, a fact Dame Eliza Manningham-Buller acknowledged in testimony before the Parliamentary Intelligence and Security Committee in 2007: "We certainly now have . . . greater inhibitions than we once did."[128] The SIS now seeks "credible assurances" that any action taken on the basis of intelligence provided by UK agencies would be "humane and lawful";[129] according to SIS director John Scarlett, when such assurances are lacking, "we cannot provide the information."[130]

A related problem has arisen in connection with the British government's introduction of aggressive new grounds for deportation in the wake of the July 2005 bombings. London seeks to address the principle of non-refoulement by asking for diplomatic assurances under a bilateral Memorandum of Understanding that the receiving state will respect deportees' fundamental human rights on their return.[131] Yet, as Amnesty International has argued, such diplomatic assurances are of suspect reliability and are ultimately unenforceable.[132]

Britain has also not been squeamish about benefiting from intelligence volunteered by states known to employ coercive interrogation methods. In a September 2005 statement to the House of Lords, Dame Eliza affirmed the value of detainee reporting even in circumstances in which the UK agencies did not know "the location or details of detention." She added that it could "damage cooperation and the future flow of intelligence" to inquire too closely into the circumstances in which such intelligence had been obtained.[133] And while in December 2005 the Law Lords ruled that material gathered overseas by means of torture would be both inadmissible as evidence in British courts and contrary to five hundred years of British legal tradition,[134] the Law Lords stopped short of placing a positive burden on the prosecution to prove that evidence had not been obtained by torture.[135]

## Conclusion

Britain has been on the frontline of the War on Terror for the past forty years. By trial and error, a coherent counterterrorist doctrine has evolved that rests on three pillars. The first, in the words of Lindsay Clutterbuck, an academic with extensive counterterrorism experience as a serving officer in London's Metropolitan Police Service, is that "policy, strategy, operations, and tactics are firmly anchored in the criminal justice system."[136] The past decade has admittedly seen a substantial growth of executive powers[137] and intelligence capacity, but the overriding ethos remains one in which the terrorist threat is seen first and foremost as a law enforcement problem.

The second, derived largely from Britain's experience in Northern Ireland, is that coordination among the agencies of government be maximized.[138] And, indeed, perhaps the greatest single strength of the British counterterrorist establishment is its collegiality, which underpins a degree of interdepartmental cooperation unrivaled elsewhere in the Western world.

The third is that the War on Terror is as much about projecting values as force.[139] "Communities defeat terrorism" has been the mantra of the commissioner of the Metropolitan Police, Sir Ian Blair,[140] and since 2001 Britain has devoted substantial resources to community outreach both at home and abroad—although admittedly there does not appear to be any quantifiable operational benefit from this approach.[141]

One final asset of the British system, albeit one not always appreciated by those in power, has been the assertiveness of both judicial and legislative oversight mechanisms, which have often served to check the more utilitarian impulses of those charged with the public's protection. As Louise Richardson has noted, "There continues to be a healthy and admirable public debate in Britain about the way a democracy needs to balance the conflicting claims of security and liberty in the fight against terrorism."[142]

The fact that there has been a healthy debate in Britain does not, of course, mean that a perfect balance between liberty and security has been struck, or that this balance will never change. Only time will tell. But it does mean that the legitimacy of the government's efforts in this area is solidly grounded with the public and less open to the vicissitudes of unforeseen events. Thus the British government has positioned itself to carry out its struggle with Islamist terrorism for the long term—making the British people more secure, not less.

# 2

# France:
# In a League of Its Own

*Gary J. Schmitt*

By all accounts, the al Qaeda attacks on September 11, 2001, shocked public opinion in France. But for French citizens and the French government, 9/11 was not the watershed event that it was for the vast majority of Americans. France had been dealing with terrorism within its borders for some time, and as far back as 1994 had even faced the possibility of a scenario similar to 9/11 (in which a hijacked passenger plane would be used as a missile against a Paris building or target).[1] Accordingly, the attacks on the World Trade Center and the Pentagon did not have an immediate impact on French counterterrorist thinking or practices. But subsequent attacks in Karachi, Yemen, Madrid, and London[2] motivated French authorities to reflect on the precise character of the threat posed by Islamic terrorism and the changes in French laws and policies that might be required to address it. For France, it had become increasingly difficult to ignore that the threat posed by this new brand of Islamist terrorism was hitting closer and closer to home.

The product of this reflection was the French government's 2005 white paper on public security and terrorism.[3] Over a hundred pages in length, the white paper is a wide-ranging evaluation of French counterterrorism policy. Although the document begins by noting that the problem of terrorism is nothing new for the French, it goes on to argue that today's threat is different in some key respects.[4] In particular, al Qaeda's ambitions are sweeping—both in the casualties the organization aims to inflict and the

31

political goals its leaders hope to achieve.[5] In addition, this brand of Islamic terrorism has made the most of globalization and the revolution in communications technology, allowing groups to develop flexible organizational structures and a unique ability to hide, plan, and conduct operations.[6] The French government's assessment is "that the threat to our country has never been so great"—quite a statement for a country that has been dealing with terrorism for many years and sees sangfroid as the epitome of virtue.[7] Clearly, the French government needed to update its ability to meet its main mission: the prevention of attacks and the security of its citizens.

Update, but not fundamentally change. The white paper emphasizes that the "terrorism prevention system in place" in France "is sound and has proven its effectiveness." Although the need "to continue to adapt this system" to current realities remains, the overall assessment is that France has "the means to identify the most dangerous individuals, to neutralize those who are planning to act, and to monitor groups that might be at risk."[8]

In short, the unique threat posed by al Qaeda and its affiliated groups has led the French to reform their approach to counterterrorism but not overturn it. As I will suggest below, their approach may seem relatively aggressive by American standards; but it is generally accepted by the French—and generally seen as successful, by the French themselves and by others. From the vantage point of Paris and elsewhere, the judgment is that the French government is on top of the problem.

## The French System

Although France's ability to combat terrorism at home is now recognized around the world for its effectiveness, this has not always been the case. To the contrary, it was the French government's failure to protect its own population in the mid-1980s and mid-1990s that gave rise to the current system.

As already noted, France has been no stranger to the problems of terrorism. In modern times, it has had to deal with attacks from partisans involved in the war in Algeria, as well as from Palestinian groups, radical leftists, Basque and Corsican separatists, and terrorists with ties to and support from Middle Eastern states. Yet in many cases, France's response to these threats left much to be desired. For much of the 1970s and 1980s, the government's approach to Middle Eastern terrorist groups was largely one of benign neglect. A de facto bargain took shape: the French government would not interfere with those groups' use of French territory as something of a safe haven if, in return, the groups would leave France itself alone.

The problems that arose with this approach were multiple but coalesced around two seemingly insurmountable issues. The first issue, reflecting divisions within the various movements and Middle Eastern states themselves, was that the terrorist groups themselves were not of one mind. The French government's "neutrality" with respect to these divisions was not always seen by the various entities and factions as acceptable; one couldn't be a friend to all without angering some. The second problem was that, given the complexities of Middle East statecraft, it was impossible for France to avoid making choices in its own policies (for example, support for Chad, intervention in Lebanon, or backing Iraq in the Iran-Iraq War) that wouldn't anger another state or terrorist organization in turn. By the mid-1980s, the French game of turning a blind eye to Middle Eastern terrorist groups in France itself had come to an end as attacks within France became more frequent. By 1986, when a series of bombings targeting Paris's public spaces (stores, official buildings, trains, etc.) nearly brought the city to a halt, the French public was ready for authorities to reevaluate the government's approach to counterterrorism—indeed, was demanding that it do so.[9]

The government's interim response was to begin random identity checks, tighten visa requirements for non-Europeans, increase reward monies for useful antiterrorist tips, institute bag searches in public buildings and stores, put more police on the street, and increase from one day to four days the period in which a terrorist suspect could be held without charge.[10]

If one element of the new strategy was to flood the streets with police and security officers,[11] France certainly had the assets to do so. Among the lead elements and agencies, there was the Direction de la Surveillance du Territoire (DST), France's domestic intelligence service; the Direction Centrale des Renseignements Généraux (RG), the antisubversion branch of the national police; the Gendarmerie Nationale, a military police largely responsible for small towns and rural areas; and the Police Nationale, a police force covering France's larger cities. France also had a special branch for border and immigration control and antiterrorist units within both the

Direction Centrale de la Police Judiciaire and the Paris police. However, this wealth of police and intelligence capabilities was poorly utilized, went largely uncoordinated, and was marred by long-standing bureaucratic suspicions and rivalries.[12] To take just one example of overlapping mandates, the DST's task was to prevent and counter threats to French domestic security directed by foreign powers or entities, while the RG's broad mission was to collect intelligence within France that helps defend the "fundamental interests of the state."[13] In theory, the RG would focus on terrorism that originates internally, and the DST would be concerned with terrorism generated from outside France's borders but aimed at France. But of course, the terrorism mission was not so easily divided, since much of the Muslim-related terrorism France faces is generated from afar but involves radicalized French nationals or individuals who have immigrated to France.

To begin to address the problem of inadequate coordination, in 1984 the French government established within the Interior Ministry an anti-terrorist coordination unit called Unité de Coordination de la Lutte Anti-Terroriste (UCLAT). This office collects and collates information supplied by a wide swath of agencies, including the Ministries of Interior, of Defense, and of Finance; in theory, it can then provide a more strategic approach to the terrorist threat than in the absence of such coordination. As noted by Shapiro and Suzan:

> Previously, no single service had specialized in terrorism and thus no one was responsible for assembling a complete picture from the various different institutional sources, for assuring information flows between the various agencies, or for providing coordinated direction to the intelligence and police services for the prevention of terrorism.[14]

UCLAT was unique in the sense that it was the precursor to what other countries would do, particularly after 9/11, and it was uniquely needed in France because of the myriad array of French police and intelligence units involved in counterterrorism.[15] Although the office cannot in practice force agencies to share information, and, presumably, like similar offices in other countries, faces the day-to-day challenge of managing interagency coordination, it was a significant first step in the French effort to reduce competition among the various police and intelligence agencies and to increase the government's overall ability to deal with the terrorist problem.

The next problem the French addressed was that terrorist investigations and prosecutions were being handled in a serendipitous fashion. Cases were being given to whatever prosecutor happened to be available and then tried wherever the incident itself might occur. This meant prosecutors typically had only a passing knowledge of the terrorist organizations whose members they were seeking to bring to justice, typically lacked working ties to the intelligence and police involved in the case, and, as a result, were almost always conducting investigations after a terrorist act had taken place. It was largely an ad hoc arrangement when it came to terrorist investigations and prosecutions. French officials concluded that a more centralized investigative and prosecutorial system was needed if they were to stay on top of a threat portfolio that was increasing in danger and complexity. To address that requirement, the French government centralized investigations and prosecutions in the Tribunal de Grande Instance de Paris (trial court of Paris). And, in so doing, it laid the cornerstone to what has become the most distinctive (and, over time, perhaps the most important) element of the French counterterrorist system.[16]

Since 1986, all investigations of terrorist crimes or terrorist conspiracies, no matter where they might have occurred or are underway, are now referred to a small handful of investigative magistrates (*juges d'instruction*) in the Paris trial court. Not only do these *juges* specialize in terrorist cases, they often specialize in distinct categories of terrorism (Islamist, Corsican separatist, anarchist, etc.).[17] Their task is to conduct an impartial investigation, determine whether a crime has been committed and, if so, recommend that French prosecutors bring formal charges against the accused. In carrying out their mandate, the investigative magistrates have broad powers and may open an investigation, order wiretaps, issue warrants and subpoenas, order the detention of suspects for days without charge, and extend internment for years pending completion of an investigation. In addition, they have the authority to follow leads internationally, if that is where a case involving a French national takes them.

The *juges d'instruction* are in many ways the linchpin of France's current counterterrorism prowess, allowing the French to move from intelligence collection, to investigation, to prosecution, as they harness France's enormous police and intelligence resources. Their effectiveness results from a distinctly French combination of administrative statutes and, just as important, personal working relations. The *juges d'instruction* do not have, for example, the formal authority to command French domestic intelligence to do their bidding. Those assets still reside under the formal authority of the minister of interior. But because such long-time magistrates as Jean-Louis Bruguière and Jean-François Ricard showed themselves able to handle sensitive information effectively and in a politically neutral manner, the leadership of the DST at that time came to value the ties with the *juges* and created a specific unit tasked with assisting them—in effect allowing the DST officers to move relatively seamlessly from collecting intelligence to taking part in a judicially authorized investigation.[18] In practice, this meant the *juges d'instruction* could employ DST assets and direct operations in terrorism cases literally from start to finish. The intelligence–law enforcement divide was in effect gone. In the words of one investigative magistrate, "We can pass easily from intelligence to the judicial part . . . It's a great advantage of efficiency . . . because [it allows] an intelligence agency working under cover to take its judicial police 'hat,' do a *proces-verbal* [report for a magistrate]," and then quickly arrest a suspect.[19]

Today, the magistrates and their offices are in key respects *the* repositories of counterterrorism information in the French government. Bruguière, France's most famous *juge d'instruction,* stayed on the counterterrorism beat for over twenty-five years and could overwhelm his interlocutors with details and insights that come only from long-standing first-hand experience. These magistrates have become virtually their own counterterrorism intelligence services. As Olivier Dutheillet de Lamothe, a member of the French Constitutional Council, has remarked:

> This centralization and specialization have proved in practice very effective. It turned out that the personality of the specialized investigating magistrates . . . was a decisive factor in the success of a certain number of cases. One of the secrets to the effectiveness of counter-terrorist action is the personal bond between the various actors, especially policemen and magistrates. The . . . counter-terrorist magistrate [is] both a judge and in permanent contact with the police, [and thus accumulates] great personal knowledge and experience in such matters.[20]

The office has no American parallel, and the range of its powers, which combine in one person some of the authorities normally reserved for both executive and judicial branch officials, seems to be unique even within Europe; the *juge* appears as a hybrid of intelligence official, prosecutor, and judge, although technically he wears none of those hats. The investigative magistrate system was designed to create impartial investigators who were politically neutral, acted neither as prosecutor nor defender, and were capable of assessing whether a crime had been committed. In practice, the informal and formal authorities they have been able to wield, in conjunction with the broad set of laws pertaining to terrorism within which they have to work, have made them the sharp end of a very effective French counterterrorist system.

The political class in Paris has grown comfortable with the independence exercised by the investigative magistrates in the area of counterterrorism. In part, this is a product of the statist tradition in France. And a cynic might say that this reflects the political sensitivity of the terrorism portfolio—better that magistrates handle the potential blowback from these cases than elected officials. But it is also an acknowledgment of how effectively and professionally the *juges d'instruction* have conducted themselves when it comes to counterterrorism since 1986.[21]

On the other hand, the investigative magistrate system more generally has not fared as well when it comes to public opinion. In early 2009, President Sarkozy announced his intention to do away with the system of investigating magistrates and replace it with a more "adversarial," "Anglo-Saxon" system in which a government-appointed prosecutor carries out criminal investigations, defense lawyers are given earlier access to evidence and their clients, and the whole proceedings are supervised by an independent judge.[22] To date, only the broad outlines of what the reforms might entail have been put forward.[23] Opposition to abolishing the current system has come from both the left and right, principally on the grounds that it would require putting decisions about investigations in the hands of the government; in the past, this practice led to charges that political considerations weighed more heavily than the evidence in deciding whether investigations should go forward.[24]

As yet, there has been little detailed commentary on how this change might be applied to, or affect, French counterterrorism efforts. For instance, there has been no suggestion that key counterterrorism laws, such as the law governing "association" with terrorists (discussed below), will be altered. But other suggested changes—such as giving judges, not government investigator-prosecutors, say over police wiretapping and tightening up rules regarding precharge detention of criminal suspects—if applied to counterterrorism cases are bound to alter how those cases are handled. More fundamentally, France will have shifted subtly but surely the current presumption that, when an investigative magistrate has completed his investigation and brought the matter to trial, the defendant is probably guilty. By creating a more adversarial system in which state prosecutors and defense lawyers are involved in cases much earlier, and defense teams are given more and earlier access to the government's evidence, the reverse will presumably hold. If these reforms are made and applied to the counterterrorism field, then, new ties will have to be established between prosecutors, police, and intelligence officials. At the moment, in the words of one French official, "there is a very good anti-terrorist system in France—but it relies on people,"[25] and given the relationship now existing between the investigative magistrates and the intelligence and security agencies, a decision to do away with the *juges d'instruction* will undoubtedly have an impact on the effectiveness of French counterterrorism efforts—at least in the short run.

The current French counterterrorist system is enhanced by the scale of its domestic police and intelligence efforts. As noted above, until the 2008 reform which combined the DST and the RG into one organization,[26] the main services involved in domestic counterterrorism were the DST, the RG, and the Direction Centrale de la Police Judiciaire (DCPJ), the detective element of the French national police. (The DCPJ and the Paris police conduct terrorist investigations with specialized units.) Combined with elements from within the customs bureau and the Finance Ministry, France deploys a formidable number of "boots on the ground" domestically. This has allowed French security elements to develop an extensive human intelligence network within France's Muslim community. French security officials will also often cut deals with petty criminals or possible deportees if they will become informants.[27] As one French police official remarked, French authorities have been able to stay ahead of terrorists in part by bringing to bear the whole of the French police effort (tax, customs, health, intelligence, and judicial) on the semilegal enterprises terrorists use to support themselves. They overwhelm a target with a range of investigative techniques.[28]

France's long history of dealing with subversive groups at home appears to have made French citizens more tolerant than other democracies of relatively invasive domestic security practices and laws. As noted earlier, police do not need a specific, crime-related predicate to search personal belongings on the streets or in stores, or to conduct random identity checks. And since 1881, France has had a law on the books that prohibits "speech" of any sort that incites or condones terrorism,[29] which makes it possible, among other things, to monitor closely French mosques. Nor do French authorities have to meet a "probable cause" threshold to use wiretaps or electronic surveillance. Whether a *juge d'instruction* or a designated senior official within the government authorizes such surveillance, the standard is that the collection technique be deemed reasonably necessary for carrying out an investigation or conducting an intelligence operation. In short, the issue is not whether there is already evidence of individual criminality to justify further collection, but whether the surveillance will potentially provide information needed in counterterrorism investigations to prevent an attack. And by and large, this decision lies with the investigative magistrate and senior interior officials.

In the wake of a 1990 ruling by the European Court of Human Rights determining that France's electronic surveillance practices violated article 8 of the European Convention on Human Rights,[30] a new law was passed in 1991 designed to give increased oversight to those practices.[31] Wiretaps issued by *juges* are limited to four months, although they can be renewed. "Administrative" wiretaps—that is, those authorized by France's executive agencies—must be reported to the Commission Nationale de Contrôle des Interceptions de Sécurité (CNCIS). The commission (whose three members are appointed, respectively, by France's president, the president of the Senate, and the speaker of the National Assembly) ensures that the government's intercept practices are within the law, investigates complaints of abuses, issues an annual report on the government's electronic surveillance practices, and, should it question the legality of any particular intercept, recommends to the prime minister that the surveillance be ended. These recommendations, however, are not binding on the government.

While the French government's wiretapping practices have not gone without criticism,[32] by far the most controversial aspects of the French counterterrorism regime are preventive sweeps and long-term incarcerations of terrorist suspects.[33] In the past, French investigative magistrates have ordered the mass roundup of individuals suspected of having ties to a terrorist network. These sweeps have resulted in the detention of scores of individuals, in one case netting more than 130 suspects.[34] Under French law, the magistrate can order on his own authority the pre-trial detention of individuals for up to four days (and possibly six in some circumstances) before they are either brought before a judge to be charged, or released. And while in police detention, suspects have limited access to lawyers and may be questioned without a lawyer being present.[35]

The sweeps serve two purposes, according to French officials. The first is simply to disrupt whatever plotting may be going on and to put the networks on their back foot. "Kicking the anthill" (*coup de pied dans la fourmilière*), the magistrates believe, undermines a network's operational cohesion and its ability to provide logistical support to its members. In addition, the sweeps provide investigators with the time and opportunity to gain a more precise picture of the network through more focused interrogations and searches of homes and computers. Even if many of those rounded up are not eventually charged, the result of the sweeps, French authorities believe, is to provide more pieces of the puzzle than they otherwise would have.[36]

As for the practice of detaining suspects for lengthy periods before they are formally charged with a crime or tried, French law offers fairly broad justifications: a lengthy detention is permissible in order to prevent a suspect from being coerced by accomplices, to preclude the possible destruction of material evidence, to ensure a suspect does not disappear upon release, or simply to prevent a crime. Beyond the four (or six) days of detention, the investigative magistrate may also request that, upon being charged, suspects be remanded into pre-trial custody for initial periods of four months to one year, with extensions possible for up to four years. The specifics depend on the nature of the terrorist-related crime involved.

The one check on the decision to remand a suspect into pre-trial detention or to extend detention is that, since 2001, a separate "liberty and custody judge" rules on the motion. However, as some have noted, the evidentiary standard for keeping someone in detention is not especially difficult to meet. Nor have the judges shown much of an inclination to question the judgment of the investigating magistrates. According to a 2006 National Assembly report, the judges have sided with the magistrates nine out of ten times.[37] Presumably, the very fact there is an independent review will incline magistrates not to push for detentions that, on their face, seem unreasonable. On the other hand, as one judge conceded, decisions are influenced by the fact that the detentions involve possible terrorists. As one judge remarked: "We're afraid to let people go free and to make a mistake. I don't give myself the same freedom of evaluation that I take in other cases. In ordinary criminal cases, I stick to what the investigators have already found. In terrorism cases, I ask myself, what might they still find?"[38]

The law that allows the French investigative magistrate to employ these practices as fully as they have is the 1996 legislation that made it a crime to associate with terrorism in any of its facets (*association de malfaiteurs en relation avec une entreprise terroriste*).[39] The law's intent is to criminalize any and all preparatory acts (associative, logistical, financial, etc.) that might support terrorist efforts. Because of the law's broad reach, and the fact that it applies even where no specific terrorist act is underway, the magistrates have been able to use it to support arrests and detentions that disrupt plots before they come to execution. An interview that Human Rights Watch conducted with French counterterrorism prosecutor Phillipe Maitre makes clear how the law is being used:

> Maitre explained that the association de malfaiteurs statute criminalizes the preparatory acts that are the furthest from the actual commission of a terrorist act. Drawing three concentric circles on a piece of paper, Maitre identified the central circle as the terrorist act, the surrounding circle as direct complicity—acts that immediately and directly contribute to the commission of the crime—and the outer circle as any and all acts, no matter how removed in time and space, that have contributed to a terrorist enterprise. Even if these acts themselves are not crimes, "the mere fact of having participated in an enterprise is punishable behavior. When it comes to terrorism the consequences are so serious that any behavior that revolves around this objective is criminalized."[40]

According to the French government's own numbers, of the 358 individuals in prison for suspicion or conviction of terrorism in 2005, well over 80 percent were being detained under the 1996 law's strictures.[41]

## Changes Since 2001

French officials and national security analysts point with pride to the fact that after the attacks of 9/11, there was no need for a wholesale reordering of the French domestic counterterrorism regime. As the French government's 2005 white paper notes, the government and citizens of France had every reason to believe that this was one area in which France could claim to have the effective lead among the West's democracies.

Nevertheless, it is not entirely accurate to suggest that the attacks on the World Trade Center and the Pentagon had no impact on French counterterrorism laws and practices. While the Patriot Act—America's most immediate legislative response to the attacks—was enacted in the last week of October 2001, the French government was hardly any less expeditious in passing new legislation. On November 15, 2001, the law "on everyday security" was passed to increase French capabilities to combat terrorism.[42]

Not as sweeping as the Patriot Act, the French law did expand the government's authorities and did so with an eye toward taking account of what was then known about the planning, funding, and operations behind the 9/11 attacks. The French police were given expanded powers to search vehicles, check personal identification, and inspect personal luggage and cargo traveling by plane or ship—all in the name of what the law called preventive security ("*assurer préventivement la sûreté*"). In addition, the law gave the police increased access to files of ongoing judicial procedures and investigations. Recognizing the terrorists' unprecedented use of the Internet to communicate, the law mandated that Internet service providers store certain categories of technical data (name, addresses, log-on information, etc.) on customer activities for up to one year; it also required that the government have access to encryption keys and put increased restrictions on encryption software's use. Finally, the law expanded the crime of terrorism to include activities related to its financing, whether the handling of funds or assistance in raising monies.

The year 2002 appeared to be no less dangerous than 2001, with terrorist attacks in Tunisia, Pakistan, and Indonesia resulting in French deaths. There was also a suicide attack on a French oil tanker off Yemen and an attempt to bring down an Air France flight between Paris and Miami. Finally, there were threat letters against France from the Algerian Salafist Group for Preaching and Combat (known today as the al Qaeda Organization in the Islamic Maghreb) and bin Laden's own November 12, 2002, communiqués which made clear that France had been and would remain a target of terrorism. In May 2003, an attack in Morocco by an al Qaeda–affiliated group left scores dead, including four French citizens; and in September, an al Qaeda cell leader was arrested in the midst of planning an attack on the French Cultural Centre in Yemen. Then, in late February 2004, bin Laden's deputy, Ayman al-Zawahiri, threatened the French government for its proposal to ban the wearing of head scarves by female students and, more generally, for France's secularism.

The French government responded in part with the passage of two laws (one in March 2003 and the other in March 2004), which, while not simply focused on counterterrorism, did enhance counterterrorist efforts principally by increasing a variety of police powers.[43] The 2003 statute (dealing with internal security) set out the authorities and guidelines for vehicle searches, the use and sharing of information from domestic and international criminal files and data banks, and the increased penalties for trafficking in dangerous materials and substances, while providing for new authorities to monitor harbors, airports, and roadways. The 2004 law (the so-called Perben II Law, named after then–justice minister Dominique Perben) moved in the same direction. It extended the time the police could hold someone in custody without charge, and extended the delay before an individual might have access to a lawyer to seventy-two hours after initial detainment in terrorist-related investigations. The law also broadened the circumstances in which the police could conduct investigations using infiltrations, mail covers, wiretaps, and nighttime raids. And, finally, the law introduced into the French penal code new offenses pertaining to the manufacture of explosives or biological weapons and to organizing a terrorist group. Only a few days later, on March 11, the Madrid train bombings occurred, killing nearly two hundred commuters and wounding nearly two thousand.

The next major piece of French domestic security legislation was passed in January 2006.[44] It was enacted following the July 7 terrorist attack against London's public transport system, in which coordinated suicide bombings on three underground trains and a bus killed fifty-two people and injured some seven hundred. Although the Madrid and London bombings caused far less damage and far fewer casualties than the attacks of 9/11, they took place in the capitals of countries that bordered France. For French officials, it seemed possible, perhaps even likely, that Paris would be al Qaeda's next "ground zero."

Unlike the two broader laws put in place in 2003 and 2004, the 2006 statute was explicitly directed at enhancing French counterterrorism tools. Seeing the utility of CCTV (closed-circuit television cameras) in solving the London bombings, the 2006 law greatly expanded the possible use of video surveillance within France wherever large numbers might gather, be it a street, a store, or even a place of worship.[45] Although there is a process for authorizing the placement of the cameras, in times of emergency the police may do so at their discretion or when sizable crowds are expected for an event. The law also permits French authorities to monitor cars and trucks on French roads by employing automatic devices to read license plates and take pictures of drivers for the broad purpose of fighting organized crime and preventing terrorist attacks. The new statute provides for freezing of terrorist-related assets, increases penalties for terrorism, makes possible revocation of French citizenship after a terrorist conviction, authorizes intelligence agencies' access to government databases (passports, driver's licenses, visas, etc.), and upgrades airport and border security. And, finally, the law expands police access to Internet and telecommunications data by requiring that not only Internet service providers but also cybercafés and Wi-Fi hosts retain data on users, and by allowing the police to obtain these data without a judicial order "in order to prevent acts of terrorism."[46]

On the operational side, the French government in 2003 updated its national security alert and crisis-management system (Plan Vigipirate), which entails a "whole of government" approach (including the use of the military) to prevent attacks, secure critical infrastructure, protect the population, and, when necessary, provide emergency relief. In place since the early 1980s, the alert system hit code red after the Madrid and London bombings, meaning that specific measures were taken to protect key institutions and people, set up relief and response efforts, and allow authorities to curtail or ban various activities, such as athletic events at which large crowds might gather. Then, in early 2005, the Interior Ministry ordered the establishment of "regional hubs to fight radical Islam." The hubs, initially led by the RG, but consisting of all law enforcement and intelligence agencies, are intended to keep track of Islamist proselytizing and fundraising and, where necessary, disrupt nascent terrorist cells. Since 9/11, more than a dozen imams have undergone deportation proceedings for preaching in a manner that ran afoul of French law, and numerous Islamic places of worship have been closed for similar reasons.[47]

## Conclusion

Although much of the French elite and general public believe that America's "war on terror" is the wrong response to Islamic extremism, and probably counterproductive, the French government's 2005 white paper on terrorism makes clear that the French military has a role to play in countering terrorism. In the most likely instance, the paper states, the armed forces can be used in "peace restoration or stabilization missions," thereby helping to eliminate the "havens" from which terrorists might recruit and operate. Or, as was the case after 9/11, French forces might take "part in counterterrorism operations," as they did "in Afghanistan and the Indian Ocean under American command." However, the white paper does not confine the military's role to acting after an attack or in the face of a failing state. It also envisions the use of French forces for "pre-emptive action" when and where a "clear and established threat" is seen.[48]

But again, the French position is that these are exceptional measures and the problem of jihadist terrorism does not require France to be put on a war footing. Accordingly, there is no need for "recourse to emergency legislation" or for "curbing" the "most essential daily liberties." From the government's perspective, the French system of specialized institutions and laws is "not an extraordinary system" in the strictest sense of the term and falls within the guiding principles of democratic governance and the rule of law.[49]

Whether the French counterterrorism effort is called "extraordinary" or not, there is no question that the government's approach to domestic security is unique. This is due, in part, to France's own history and political culture. Since the time of the French Revolution, the country and its successive governments have had to deal with a variety of internal threats and subversive movements. By the habit of history, the French public has come to accept that the state will have strong domestic policing and intelligence capabilities. It is this element of France's political culture that has laid the foundation for today's effective counterterrorism system.

Moreover, according to Jean-Louis Bruguière, until recently France's most famous *juge d'instruction*, the fact that France relies on civil law gives it an advantage over nations that rely largely on common law, such as the United Kingdom or the United States.[50] "Every government has an obligation to react to the threat," he explains. "But the common law system is too rigid, it can't adapt because its procedural laws are more important than the criminal laws at the base, and the procedure depends on custom so it doesn't change easily. The civil law system is more flexible because it functions according to laws voted by parliament and can react faster."[51]

Since the system is understood to have been effective in curtailing the attacks and bombings that once plagued the country, and because the investigative magistrates in cases of terrorism are largely seen as being "above" politics, the French public continues to give considerable leeway to the more intrusive elements of the country's counterterrorism system. Although there is discussion and debate within France about whether the system is too intrusive,[52] at the moment, domestic critics of the French system appear to be in the minority.

Observers outside of France are struck by the ability of the French to concentrate the combined resources of the state so quickly. Relying on a range of methods—from wiretaps and other forms of electronic interception to substantial physical surveillance and preventive detentions—magistrates and their allied police and intelligence services can rapidly monitor, harass, and paralyze those they suspect of terrorist activity. As the French white paper on domestic security and terrorism states: "To be effective, a judicial system for counterterrorism must combine a preventive element, whose objective is to prevent terrorists from acting, and a repressive element, to punish those who commit attacks as well as their organizers ·and accomplices. The French system follows this logic. But its originality and strength lie in the fact that *the barrier between prevention and punishment is not airtight.*"[53] Indeed, the *juges d'instruction* and French laws have largely demolished this wall.

As noted at the start, the French government believes that it has devised an effective counterterrorism system and that it is on top of the problem. If we compare France with other European states, we have little reason to doubt that claim. That is undoubtedly why, in the wake of the attacks on 9/11, the U.S. government decided to set up its principal counterterrorism liaison office in Paris—and remained there in spite of the acrimony that arose between Washington and Paris over the Iraq War. In the domestic fight against terrorism, France was (and remains) in a league of its own.

# 3

# Spain:
# From 9/11 to 3/11 and Beyond

*Rafael L. Bardají and Ignacio Cosidó*

The events of September 11 had an immediate impact in Spain, as they did throughout the world. Sadly accustomed to mourning the victims of ETA, the Marxist Basque-separatist terrorist group,[1] Spanish society felt an immediate and intense solidarity with the victims of the atrocities in New York and Washington.

Nevertheless, once the initial emotions and sympathies had passed, a growing division emerged in Spain regarding the way in which the Spanish government should understand and respond to Islamic terrorism. On the one hand, Prime Minister José María Aznar argued that the threat of jihadist terrorism could not help but affect Spain in its capacity as a Western country, an ally of the United States, and a member of the Atlantic Alliance. Others, principally on the Spanish left, believed that American policies in the Middle East, including support of Israel, were in some sense partly responsible for the attacks. In fact, this segment of Spanish public opinion was more concerned about the United States' possible reaction to the 9/11 attacks than about the possibility that similar attacks might occur elsewhere in the world. This sentiment was captured in the front-page headline of the leading Spanish daily on September 12, 2001: "The World Waits Nervously for the US Reaction."

Spanish opinion was muted on the early American and coalition effort to eliminate al Qaeda bases in Afghanistan and remove the Taliban from power there. Because the initial military operations were executed rapidly and successfully, causing little collateral damage, and because they were clearly connected to removing a group that had sponsored the attacks on New York and Washington, the war in Afghanistan generated little criticism in Spain. However, as the Bush administration began to put in place a more comprehensive strategy for addressing the Islamist threat, Spanish opinion was far more mixed.

Spain's own experience with terrorism colored its views of the U.S. response to September 11. Madrid's practice was to treat the threat of ETA largely as a police and criminal matter, thereby laying the burden of Spanish antiterrorism policy on the shoulders of the police and intelligence services; as a result, Spaniards were slow to appreciate the new, larger threat posed by Islamic terrorism, and the real and potential ties of terrorists to states possessing or developing weapons of mass destruction. They were similarly confounded by the logic of the United States' aggressive counterterrorism strategy, and especially the decision to go to war with Iraq in order to remove Saddam Hussein from power. Hence, after an initial period of Spanish solidarity with the United States, public opinion in Spain gradually turned to criticism as the Bush administration came to define the emerging international security challenges as a "global war on terror."

The Spanish government at the time was unable to combat this point of view. While José María Aznar had made clear his determination to use whatever legal means were at his disposal to defeat terrorism domestically, he also believed that the threat posed by transnational Islamic terrorism would require military measures beyond Spain's borders. The former was certainly popular with Spaniards, but the latter was running against public opinion. Over ninety percent of the Spanish population was against the Iraq War and, with national elections in 2004 pending, the war and Aznar's support for it became a highly charged issue that the opposition Socialist Party hoped to exploit in order to regain power.

Against this backdrop, on the morning of March 11, 2004, the jihadists struck. As Spain and the world would later learn, thirteen backpack-bombs had been placed on local trains headed to Madrid at rush hour. The result: nearly two hundred dead and nearly two thousand injured.

This shocking blow was delivered barely three days before the general election of March 14, and was understood not as part of the broader global jihadist threat posed to the West but as a direct consequence of the government's policies with respect to Iraq: if Spain had been bombed, it must have been because the government supported the war. As a result, once the new government announced the withdrawal of Spanish troops from Iraq, the majority of the public became confident that Spain would no longer be a target of Islamist-inspired terrorism.[2]

This view still prevails. It explains why, after six years and various attempted jihadist terrorist attacks on Spanish soil, Spanish citizens still believe that the country is relatively safe from Islamic terrorism.

The current government has taken only modest steps to deal with a jihadist threat. Even though it has acted to detain numerous would-be Islamic terrorists, it has also attempted to downplay its counterterrorism efforts. Trapped by its own rhetoric from 2004, the government can neither acknowledge the possibility that Spain remains a prime target of the jihadists nor allow the reality of another attack to call into question its stated view that the real target was only Spanish support for the war. This has led the government to adopt a policy of detaining suspected Islamic terrorists before it can obtain sufficient evidence either to proceed to an actual trial or to convict. As a result, many of those detained on suspicion of being Islamic terrorists end up being released before their case even reaches the courts due to a lack of evidence, and are acquitted at trial or convicted for lesser crimes.[3] Lacking the necessary tools to deal with the terrorist threat confidently, the security services are inclined to follow a strategy of ending investigations early in order to ensure no attacks occur, even at the risk of ultimately losing cases in court. In short, Spain's security services by and large are attempting to make do with the authorities and resources they have at hand. But there are real concerns that these may not be sufficient and that the Spanish government will not be able to protect the country from another March 11–like attack.

## Policing the Threat

The principal institutions for combating terrorism in Spain are the National Police (Cuerpo Nacional de Policía), the Civil Guard (Guardia Civil), and the National Court (Audiencia Nacional). The National Police and the Civil Guard are the two main security bodies in Spain, with the former primarily focused on Spain's urban areas and the latter deployed in the rest of the country.[4]

Under Spanish law, the police and guard have law enforcement responsibilities that overlap, as well as ones that are unique to each organization. They share the antiterrorism mission, however, operating under the auspices of the Ministry of Interior and at the direction of the state secretary for security.

Regardless of where in Spain a terrorist act takes place or is planned, all terrorism-related cases are investigated by and tried before the National Court.[5] Established in 1977 and given special security features, this court allows Spanish authorities to investigate and try cases without being unduly affected by local political and social pressures. (Such pressures had been a particular problem in processing cases in the Basque country involving terrorism by ETA.) The court is composed of six examining magistrates who lead the investigations, along with six trial courts, each presided over by a panel of three judges. The crimes adjudicated under the National Court are not subject to trial by jury. Because ETA has been active over so many years, the court and the magistrates have built up a body of experience in handling terrorism investigations and trials.

Spain does not have a specific antiterrorism law. Instead, it treats terrorism as an aggravated form of crime, folding into the penal code and organic statutes various measures that deal with terrorism and with the government authorities responding to it.[6] And while the Spanish constitution sets out a series of rights for Spain's citizens involving judicial procedures, length of detentions, the inviolability of the home and private communications, the constitution also provides for their modification by duly enacted law in cases involving terrorism.[7]

Perhaps the two Spanish laws that have generated the most discussion in recent years are the laws on suspect detentions and the practice of holding suspects "incommunicado."[8] In the first case, under Spain's Code of Criminal Procedure, suspects who have been detained by the police must normally be brought before a judge within seventy-two hours. However, where terrorism is involved, the court may authorize that someone be held for an additional two days before being formally indicted. Once suspects have been charged, an investigative magistrate may, with the approval of the court, keep them in custody for up to four years while preparing the case for trial. The code also allows terrorism suspects to be held "incommunicado" (in solitary confinement) for five days while in initial police custody. During this five-day period, there is no public notification of the suspect's arrest, no communication by the suspect with anyone on the outside, and no right to a lawyer of his own choosing. Instead, the court provides the suspect with a court-appointed lawyer and, if requested, a court-appointed examining doctor.[9] If the magistrate believes that public knowledge of the arrest and indictment may compromise his investigation, he may extend the solitary confinement for five more days while the suspect is in pre-trial detention. Once a suspect is charged and the solitary confinement is lifted, the court may reimpose that status for three more days when the investigation so warrants.

As for searches of private dwellings and the interception of communications conducted without the consent of the owner or knowledge of the individual, the government is required to obtain the approval of an investigative magistrate (*juez instructor*) from the National Court. In the case of a physical search, there must be clues that evidence connected to the investigation or prosecution will be found within; mail openings, wiretaps, and other methods of interception can be ordered if there is reason to believe that they will provide information related to a case. The magistrate conducting the investigation is authorized to make that judgment. However, under the law, there are exceptions made for bypassing the finding requirement, allowing the police (in the case of a search) or the top officials in the Ministry of Interior (in the case of an interception) to act in an emergency or under exceptional circumstances. In both cases, though, the decision to bypass the finding requirement must be transmitted immediately to the relevant magistrate.

There has been some controversy about Spain's laws regulating government interception of communications. Spain's Constitutional Court, for instance, has stated that there is a need for more "adequate regulation" of intercept practices. It noted in particular that the European Court of Human Rights had previously cited Spain for failing to specify with more exactness the offenses that could justify an intercept, for failing to set some limit on the number of extensions that a judge may grant for continuing the activity, and for failing to clarify regulations concerning the control and future use of material gathered by the intercepts.[10]

There are two other pre-3/11 laws of note. The first, passed in 2000, makes it a crime to extol terrorists or terrorism through speech or other forms of public expression. The law also punishes any acts that have the effect of discrediting or showing disrespect for the victims of terrorist crimes or their family members.[11] The second measure, passed in 2003, establishes the Commission for Monitoring the Funding of Terrorist Activities.[12] The commission, a specialized administrative body, is empowered to freeze funds thought to be supporting terrorist-related activities. The decision to take that step, however, does not carry with it a determination that an actual crime has been committed. The commission, which coordinates its activities with the investigative magistrate and the court, is tasked with preventing terrorist acts, not adjudicating complicity.

### Policing the Threat after 3/11/04

The principal response to the atrocities of March 11 on the part of the current government in Spain consisted of strengthening the police forces entrusted with combating terrorism. Specifically, the government increased the number of intelligence units attached to the National Police Force and Civil Guard, bringing the total number of agents working within this field to six hundred.[13] The increase in personnel has not always been accompanied, however, by a corresponding modernization of the units' equipment. The government has also expanded the number of Arab translators working for the police, although here too deficiencies still exist.

The government's second measure has focused on enhancing police coordination. To this end, a National Counter-Terrorism Coordination Center (CNCA) was established shortly after the bombings, in May 2004. The CNCA is under the supervision of the Ministry of the Interior and is manned by personnel from the National Police, the Civil Guard, and Spain's intelligence service, and it is designed to boost the integration of their databases and enhance the processing and evaluation of terrorist-related intelligence. In addition, the government also created a new office, the Directorate General of the National Police and Civil Guard, headed by a senior interior official, to provide a unified command for the police and the guard.[14]

However, there are doubts about how effective these steps have been. The low administrative rank of the CNCA director has turned the center into a "study group" more than an effective arm of the government; it lacks the capacity and the mandate to effectively manage and coordinate counterterrorism operations on the part of the state's security forces. And while the directorate "sits on top" of the guard and the police, both organizations retain their specific authorities, responsibilities, and structures. The fact is, Spain's police intelligence services remain reluctant to share information with each other, which makes it difficult to achieve a more integrated effort.

The government has also increased support for the Spanish National Intelligence Center (CNI), the body that has the legal authority in Spain to carry out both domestic and foreign intelligence-gathering tasks.[15] This agency's budget, which comes within the Ministry of Defense's allocation and is classified, has reportedly increased from €157 million in 2004 to €255 million in 2009—a substantial increase in its resources.[16] Islamic terrorism is undoubtedly one of the organization's priorities.

Despite the mixed results of some of the changes made to Spanish police and intelligence services, overall the increased attention to the jihadist threat, combined with the growth in resources and the general professionalism of the forces themselves, has resulted in the arrest or detention of a number of suspected terrorists. Among the main operations that have been carried out by the security forces are the following:

- Operation Tigris. On June 15, 2005, eleven people were arrested in Catalonia. The detainees, most of whom were of North African origin, were seeking to recruit fighters for Iraq.

- Operation Sello II. In January 2007, individuals allegedly linked to the atrocities of March 11 were detained in Catalonia, and a network for delivering terrorist recruits to Iraq was broken up.

- Operation La Unión. In 2005, suspects were detained in Málaga, La Unión, and Ceuta.

- Operation Duna. In 2006, Various proselytizing networks preparing recruits for terrorist attacks were disbanded in Ceuta.

- Operation Tala. On February 5, 2007, Mbark El Jaafari, a Moroccan accused of links to al Qaeda and the al Qaeda Organization in the Islamic Maghreb, was arrested in the town of Reus (Tarragona). Since May 2006 the network to which he belonged had been recruiting volunteers in Morocco and Algeria to be delivered to Iraq or trained and brought to Europe and North Africa. According to the police investigation, El Jaafari sent some thirty-two volunteers to Iraq.

- On January 19, 2008, fourteen individuals were detained in Barcelona for membership in an Islamic terrorist cell that was apparently planning a major attack on the city's public transport system. Eleven of the fourteen were eventually convicted of being members of a terrorist group.

As a result of such operations, more than three hundred Islamic terrorist suspects were detained by the Spanish security forces between 2004 and 2008.[17] After France, Spain is the European country with the highest number of detainees. That is not only a sign of the success of Spanish police in preempting acts of terrorism, but equally important, a reflection of the presence and activity of Islamic terrorist groups in Spain.

In addition to the new resources and new institutional arrangements designed to combat terrorism in the wake of the March 2004 bombings, the Spanish government has enacted three measures designed to improve relevant legal mechanisms. On the whole, these new laws are modest in reach and importance.

The first new measure, passed in October 2005, amended the Spanish penal code's treatment of crimes committed with explosives. The new measure was intended to tighten controls over explosives available for legitimate commercial activities by making the persons and institutions in charge of them more directly accountable and by increasing the penalties and sentences for failure to comply with the new security norms.[18]

The second measure, passed by the Spanish Parliament in late May 2006, sought to make Spain's laws consistent with its role as a member of the European Union's Eurojust system and previous decisions taken by the European Council.[19] Taken as a whole, the council's directives are designed to enhance the exchange of information and operational cooperation on terrorism matters between the member states' security and judicial bodies and the relevant European Union (EU) institutions.[20]

The third measure concerned the storage of electronic communications data by telecommunication companies. This law requires companies to store for one year the "traffic" and "connection" data generated or processed by their customers and spells out under what conditions they would be obligated to provide those data to the government.[21] The law does not apply to the content of the communications.

## The European Framework

The existence of ETA—the only surviving Marxist-Leninist separatist group in Europe, and one that had killed hundreds over the years—led the Spanish government, especially under the premiership of Aznar, to become the champion of European counterterrorist cooperation. Nevertheless, Spain's initial attempts to create an appropriate penal definition of terrorist crimes, with a view to devising an instrument for police cooperation and for facilitating the extradition of terrorist detainees among the countries of the European Union, were frustrated by the general indifference of the majority of the EU members.

This changed after September 11. The attacks, which were carried out by individuals who had lived, traveled, and plotted in Europe, generated a new appreciation among Europeans about the seriousness of the threat. After September 11, and especially after the bombings of March 11, 2004, a number of important measures were introduced throughout the EU, piloted in both cases by Europol[22] and Eurojust.[23]

With the appointment of Gijs de Vries as the European coordinator for counterterrorism after the March 11 attacks in Madrid, the EU implemented various initiatives, such as maintaining and sharing a list of terrorists and terrorist organizations. It also set up a team of counterterrorism experts within the heart of Europol, established a shared definition of the crime of terrorism as well as guidelines for setting sentences related to acts of terrorism, and launched a crackdown on terrorist financing.

Nonetheless, Vries was not optimistic about the effectiveness of the new EU initiatives, since Europol's underlying authority was insufficient to carry out the tasks given to it. To fortify EU counterterrorism efforts, he believed, it was essential for the member states to ratify pending legal conventions that underpinned Europol's authority and its capacity to conduct cross-border operations. He also thought member countries needed to show a greater degree of political energy in implementing the measures already agreed to. Vries, who stepped down from his post in 2007, clearly thought that there was a gap between the urgency expressed at the political level by the European Commission and the actual response on the part of bureaucrats within the member states.[24]

The Islamic terrorist threat within the EU is not receding; it persists and may well be growing. The attacks in Madrid in 2004 and in London in 2005, the failed attempts in Germany in 2007 and in Spain in 2008, along with the nearly 200 arrests of suspected Islamist terrorists throughout Europe in 2008—all make clear that the threat to Europe remains significant.[25] In May 2005, an internal report produced by Europol offered a concise account of the terrorist threat faced by the twenty-five members of the EU and testified to al Qaeda's ongoing desire to act within the union's borders and to influence European policies.[26]

Subsequent Europol reports reinforce the seriousness of the problem. In 2007, Europol noted that in the previous year, a total of 706 terrorist suspects had been arrested in fifteen European countries; half the suspects were linked to Islamic terrorist groups. Spain, France, and Italy were the countries that detained the largest numbers of suspected Islamic terrorists. It is interesting to note that the majority of the suspects arrested in these three countries were originally from Algeria, Morocco, and Tunisia, and that all of them were affiliated with terrorist organizations in North Africa, mainly Salafist groups.[27] The 2008 and 2009 reports have similar findings.[28]

Given that Islamic terrorist activities often are transnational, international organizations such as Europol have a particularly important role to play in implementing effective police counterterrorism measures, especially in the timely exchange of information. European legislatures and the EU also need to harmonize the penal sentencing that follows from cross-border, multiparty investigations. Yet it appears that, except for emergency situations and cases in which high-level political pressure is exerted, the Europeans have had difficulty in multilateral information sharing; bilateral exchanges, which allow for more direct and immediately rewarding reciprocity, seem easier to achieve.

Today we find ourselves in a global society within a post-9/11 security system; hence military, political, economic, environmental, social, and personal realms must interrelate more intimately and efficiently than in the past. A series of multilateral and bilateral counterterrorist measures has arisen out of the new international architecture with the aim of preventing or responding to terrorist acts. The challenge today resides in developing institutions and mechanisms that are effective in combating large-scale terrorism. In the long term, it will be necessary to introduce structural changes that gradually shape a more clearly defined domestic European security system, one that transcends today's generally informal, largely bilateral system of police and judicial cooperation. Within this new context, it would seem logical to create a European public prosecutor's office with its own investigation department in order to act throughout the entire EU.

### The Threat Today

Al Qaeda has never clearly claimed responsibility for the attacks of March 11, 2004. Nevertheless, bin Laden and his supporters have repeatedly made Spain a target of their declarations and speeches. Sometimes they did so in order to threaten the Spanish for sending troops to Afghanistan.[29] At other times, it was within the context of al Qaeda's ambition to recreate the caliphate from al-Andalus (the Iberian Peninsula) to the Philippines.[30] Al Qaeda has also made direct references to the two Spanish cities in North Africa (Ceuta and Melilla), which it wants "liberated" by the global jihad movement.[31]

Al-Andalus, which has long been a symbol of the past splendor of the Islamic world, has now become a focal point of radical Islamic rhetoric. Spain is being targeted because it was under Moorish occupation for eight centuries and because the expulsion of the Moors in 1492 coincided with Islam's long period of historical decline, a process that the jihadists seek to reverse. The number of references to al-Andalus has increased sharply on Islamic chat rooms and Web sites, and children attending schools run by Hamas and Hezbollah are taught that the "reconquest" of this region is inevitable.[32]

Yet this rhetoric has not been accompanied, at least as far as we know, by a greater degree of activity in Spain on the part of the central al Qaeda movement. In spite of the fact that, prior to September 11, various members of the cell that attacked the Twin Towers were on Spanish soil (without our knowing exactly where or for what reason), the individuals detained over the last few years, including those found responsible for the events of March 11, have not been members of al Qaeda, or have only loose links to the organization. Presumably, international pressure on al Qaeda has helped keep its members at bay.

As is often noted in these matters, however, it is always hard to know what you don't know. The case of Mustafa Setmariam Nasar, who is better known by his jihadist alias of Abu Musab al-Suri, is a chilling reminder of this fact: the author of al Qaeda's most detailed operational manual, the official sponsor of the Hamburg cell that eventually attacked the United States on 9/11, and the promoter of numerous "sleeper" cells, Nasar lived in Spain for an entire decade, where his plans were undisturbed and his movements unchecked. It is thus hard to feel assured that al Qaeda does not have Spain in its sights today.

The more apparent threat posed to Spain comes from the al Qaeda organization in the Islamic Maghreb, an organization that has emerged from the merger of various Islamic groups in North Africa and that was called the Salafist Group for Preaching and Combat (better known under its French initials, GSPC) until 2006. Its alignment with al Qaeda was sanctioned by bin Laden's second-in-command, Ayman al-Zawahiri, in September 2006. Since then, various attacks have occurred in Algeria and Morocco, while Spaniards and Frenchmen residing in the region have been threatened, and local staff of European oil companies killed.[33]

Another source of risk for Spain from the jihadist movement originates from terrorists who spring from Spain's own soil, principally among the growing number of Muslim immigrants. Indeed, the majority of the plots that have taken place on Spanish soil have been linked to Islamic radicals residing in Spain, and only on a couple of occasions have they received directions from elements outside Spain.

One must bear in mind that immigration is a relatively new trend in modern Spain. In 1996 there were little more than three hundred thousand immigrants on Spanish soil. Today, the immigrant total in Spain is over five million (out of a total Spanish population of 45 million).[34] A significant number is Muslim and, of this group, Moroccans make up the largest share.

However, over and above numbers, there are other factors that must be borne in mind when addressing the threat posed by Muslims living in

Spain. Muslim immigrants coming to Spain tend to be increasingly young, and the Spanish police report that many of them arrive having already been exposed to radical ideas in their homelands. The spread of the Islamist movement in Morocco, for example, means that immigrants are increasingly aware of the fundamentalist agenda, potentially more reluctant to accept integration into Spanish society, and, as a consequence, more susceptible to rapid radicalization on Spanish soil.

In November 2007, the Spanish Interior Ministry released a survey on the attitudes of the Muslim population in Spain. The government highlighted the fact that more than 80 percent of the respondents said they were satisfied with their place and role in Spain. However, some 5 percent indicated that they understood the reasons why Muslims would turn to terrorism, and 2 percent believed that terrorism itself was justified.[35] On the one hand, the percentage of Muslims with Islamist sympathies might be lower in Spain than in other European states such as Great Britain. On the other hand, if the math is correct, then more than fifteen thousand Muslims residing in Spain could potentially be manipulated by the jihadists and enlisted into their ranks.

## Conclusion

The 2004 election of Rodríguez Zapatero and the Socialist Party entailed a significant change in the Spanish government's foreign, security, and counterterrorism policies. Concerning foreign and security issues, Zapatero made clear from day one that his government would distance itself from the United States' "war on terror" and marked that change in policy by withdrawing Spanish troops from Iraq and inviting the rest of the allies to do so, too. The new government has opted for emphasizing European over transatlantic ties. And toward countries with terrorist ties, like Syria and Iran, Zapatero's administration has been far more willing to follow a policy of engagement than Aznar's.

The current Spanish government's counterterrorism policy is guided by the view that Islamic terrorism is not a major threat to the nation. Counterterrorism is not a priority on the government's public agenda; other issues, such as world poverty and climate change, are considered much more important. Under Zapatero, the battle against Islamic terrorism has been defined—as historically the fight against ETA was—as a police matter: one that can and should be fought using the traditional instruments of domestic security and ultimately addressed through political dialogue and negotiation.

Only time will tell whether this change in strategy will protect Spaniards from a ruthless, uncompromising jihadist threat that is both home grown and global—and one that, if plots and jihadist rhetoric are any signs, sees Spain as a target no less than it did before March 11, 2004.

# 4

# Germany:
# The Long and Winding Road

*Eric Gujer*

In the age of global Islamist violence, some Europeans are already asking whether there might be a way of negotiating with some Muslim terrorists. In fact, Germany has a record of taking just this approach. In the 1990s, for example, the German government sent a high-ranking official from the federal domestic intelligence service (Bundesamt für Verfassungsschutz, or BfV) to meet with emissaries from the Kurdish terrorist group PKK, and reached a mutual understanding with them. The extremists agreed not to attack targets in Germany, and the law enforcement agencies refrained from pursuing the Kurdish activists living in Germany's large Kurdish communities. As a result, the Federal Republic became an important logistical base for the PKK, and Germany considered itself immune to PKK-related terrorism.

Around the same time, French authorities accused their German counterparts of not investigating Algerian extremists hiding over the border in Germany. Given the lax German regime of internal security, which by 2001 was well known among militant Muslims, Hamburg was definitely not a bad choice for Mohammed Atta to begin planning for his own role in the global jihad. In fact, on September 11, 2001, Germany was living in the past. To the degree Germans worried about terrorism at all, the focus was on domestic threats, such as the Rote Armee Fraktion (Red Army Faction, or RAF). The RAF had traumatized German society. In the thirty years of its existence, RAF attacks had resulted in the death of sixty-two persons. As RAF violence reached its peak in the autumn of 1977, Germany had had enough, and the authorities hit back hard. Although the government never declared a formal state of emergency, the Bundestag, Germany's federal parliament, did adopt emergency laws in only five days' time, including a measure that barred RAF prisoners in Stuttgart's Stammheim Prison from all outside contacts, even with lawyers and relatives.[1] With more vigorous counterterrorism measures in place, the German state reduced the menace and, by 1998, could declare that the RAF was no longer a threat.

Yet even before the RAF had been thoroughly dealt with, popular support for the state's aggressive investigative techniques and broad police powers began to wane. A majority of Germans, it appeared, wanted to see law enforcement agencies constrained. During the *Deutscher Herbst* (German Autumn)—the period in late 1977 when terrorist attacks against German targets were at their worst—a new atmosphere of angst emerged in response to the state's perceived violation of citizens' rights. Germany's history—the memories of two dictatorships on German soil and their secret police forces, the Nazi Gestapo and the Communist Stasi—has produced a profound nervousness among Germans about the dangers of a too-powerful executive authority. In particular, German society still harbors a suspicious attitude toward intelligence agencies and all state action that may intrude on civil liberties. There is little public acknowledgment about the need for domestic intelligence services, let alone the need for German agencies to exchange information with the likes of America's Central Intelligence Agency or the British Secret Intelligence Service. The German public views the intelligence community not as a defender of freedom but as a threat to it.[2]

This seemingly enduring schizophrenia within German society, the bouncing back and forth from worrying about the government's ability to handle terrorism to worrying about the powers being wielded by the government, is no less evident when it comes to Islamist violence in Germany. After a botched bomb attack or a foiled plot, political parties and the media are prone to urge more intrusive action. When two Lebanese students placed defective explosive devices on regional trains in 2006, for instance, politicians and the press worried endlessly about the deficiencies in German counterterrorism. The same happened in 2007 after German authorities thwarted a terrorist attack on American facilities at Ramstein Air Base. In Germany and Turkey, police arrested two German converts to Islam and two men of Turkish origin who together had managed to acquire detonators and two hundred gallons of a concentrated hydrogen peroxide solution, a key ingredient in homemade bombs. "This would have enabled them to make bombs with more explosive power than the one used in the London and Madrid bombings," Jörg Zierke, chief of the federal criminal police, the Bundeskriminalamt (BKA), told an audience.[3] Yet, as sure as the ocean's tide, concerns recede and German public opinion reverses itself; citizens once again begin to see aggressive law enforcement agencies, not Islamic terrorists, as the greater menace to civic well-being.

Indeed, a kind of "don't ask, don't tell" attitude now prevails toward terrorist threats. When the Ministry of Interior warned of the potential risks of nuclear, biological, and chemical agents in the hands of extremists, the ministry was widely accused of threat mongering. But the possibility of weapons of mass destruction (WMD) in the hands of terrorists deserves serious debate and deliberation.[4] The German federal government obviously takes such a threat seriously; it provides local offices of its homeland security agency with detection and decontamination equipment, it prepared for possible use of WMD by terrorists before the 2006 World Cup, and it stores sufficient amounts of vaccines to inoculate the whole of Germany against certain viruses. Nevertheless, counterterrorism is not a policy issue that either the German public or its politicians have generally wanted to discuss in public. Indeed, counterterrorism remains a vexed issue in Germany, where an uncertain legal regime, a blurring of state and federal responsibilities, and an idealistic public uncomfortable with a strong security regime have impeded the effort to prevent and punish Islamist violence.

### Germany's Islamist Threat

There is less anxiety about terrorism in Germany than elsewhere in Europe or in the United States. As of 2009, not one Islamist plot has been carried out successfully there. The situation in the less affluent quarters of Berlin, Hamburg, or Cologne is less tense than in Pakistani-heavy "Londonistan" or the North African ghettos of the Paris suburbs. The vast majority of Muslim immigrants in Germany come from Turkey; they tend not to be religious, or else they practice the state-controlled form of Islam established by the secular Turkish Republic. It is not hard to understand, then, why before 9/11, religious groups enjoyed an exemption from prosecution under German laws that made it a crime to engage in speech designed to incite hatred or violence against parts of the population.[5]

Following 9/11, however, some radical Turkish and Arab Islamist organizations were banned, and Germany's domestic intelligence services intensified the surveillance of mosques.[6] Suddenly Germans had to confront the fact that jihadists had been living and plotting in their midst. Eliminating the religious exemption to the hate law did not provoke heavy criticism from within the Muslim community because only a few groups and religious centers were affected, but it did spark a debate about the treatment of Muslim immigrants within Europe and Germany. Previously, Germany had rejected the idea that it could be a nation of immigrants, or even a nation partially consisting of immigrants, and it had largely ignored the difficulties of Turkish laborers in Germany. Now the federal government hosted national "summits" with representatives of immigrant and Muslim organizations. Despite some complaints about the xenophobic overtones of some of the discussion, the new public debate did signal a new awareness within Germany of its largest religious minority.[7]

Europe's failure to integrate the second and third generation of Muslims into society, either economically or socially, is arguably one of the main reasons for radicalization of young Muslims and the growth of violent forms of Islam on the continent.[8] But who exactly are the Muslims now living in Germany? Germany's Turkish community consists of 2.7 million people. They do not appear to be any better integrated than other alien communities in Europe, but the Turkish brand of Islam is substantially different from that practiced by other European Muslim groups. With twenty-six thousand followers, the largest Islamist group in Germany is the Turkish Milli Görüs, which does not propagate a violent interpretation of Islam,[9] and relatively few Turks in Germany have been identified as members of violence-inclined groups. The times are changing, however. Two of the four arrested "peroxide plotters" were Turks who had long resided in Germany. And in March 2008, a twenty-eight-year-old Turkish citizen, born and raised in the small Bavarian town of Freising, killed two U.S. soldiers in a suicide attack in Afghanistan. It is worth noting here that a growing number of Germans are converting to Islam—many becoming adherents of the ultra-orthodox

Wahhabi or Salafi branches of the faith.[10] These Muslims have their own mosques and imams, separate from the Turkish religious centers.

In 2004, it was reported that German law enforcement was investigating more than 270 Muslims—Germans and non-Germans alike—who were thought to be planning terrorist crimes or who had links to international terrorist networks.[11] In 2009, the head of the BKA, Jörg Zierke, publicly stated that there were more than a hundred "primary" investigative targets in Germany consisting of Islamists with terrorist training; there were another three hundred or so "persons of interest" and more than eleven hundred additional individuals who are part of the broader "network" of Islamic extremists.[12]

The Muslim convert Fritz Gelowicz, a twenty-eight-year-old student from the south German town of Ulm, was the leader of the group arrested for targeting the American military installations.[13] Homegrown terrorists like Gelowicz often belong to international networks. Authorities believe that Gelowicz and his group got their orders from an Uzbek splinter group that is said to have its base of operations in Pakistan.

Ulm, a quiet town of 120,000 inhabitants in the state of Baden-Württemberg (adjacent to Bavaria), has been a hub of Islamist extremism in Germany for years. Yehia Yousif, a physician turned Wahhabi imam, lived in Ulm. An Egyptian citizen, Yousif came into contact with the Muslim Brotherhood and the assassins of President Anwar al-Sadat during his studies at the University of Alexandria. In Ulm he preached at a local mosque before fleeing to Saudi Arabia at the end of 2004 to evade detention. Some of his disciples, most of them converts, founded the Islamic Information Center (Islamisches Informationszentrum, or IIZ). This organization operated on a legal basis, offering Arabic language courses, lectures on the "true" Islam, and a German-language newsletter designed to attract converts. But the IIZ was also a cover for other, less legal activities: Fritz Gelowicz was loosely affiliated with the IIZ, and the organization helped other young men from Ulm go to Pakistan for training and to Chechnya for the jihad against the Russians. One twenty-four-year-old German convert died in Chechnya, shot by a Russian army patrol. A naturalized German of Egyptian origin, who had served in the Balkan wars on the side of Mujahedin forces and later was a logistical aide for al Qaeda in Indonesia, he had also moved to Ulm, invited by his fellow countryman Yousif.

The mosque and the IIZ were a perfect cover for radicals seeking contact with other radicals at home and abroad. They facilitated clandestine transport of materiel and men via routes from Istanbul to the North Caucasus and to Pakistan. The detonators obtained by Gelowicz's group, for example, were produced in Syria and then delivered to Turkey, where a fifteen-year-old Turkish boy who had been brought up in Germany obtained the detonators and smuggled them into the country.[14] Iran also was an important intermediate stop for the "peroxide plotters." They traveled by land to Pakistan via Iran, while a person in Iran sent orders by e-mail to the cell in Germany.

The Islamist community in Ulm teaches us many things, not least about the terrorists' ability to operate across borders, even without the leadership or coordination of a mastermind like Ayman al-Zawahiri. It also makes clear the connections among different cells, whose members know each other. For instance, the young man who smuggled the detonators into Germany was acquainted with a Tunisian student who, with three companions, joined an organization of al Qaeda's foreign fighters in Iraq. All four Tunisian men had been living in Germany.[15] In short, while the jihadist community in Germany remains relatively small, the Federal Republic is no longer simply a logistical base. Germany now has its own homegrown terrorists to worry about.

Yet in spite of this change in the nature of the threat, Germans still feel relatively safe from jihad. Accordingly, they strongly disapprove of the metaphor "war on terror." Most Germans still regard counterterrorism as a law enforcement problem to be addressed by the police and prosecutors, not really a matter of national security, and certainly not deserving the attention of German foreign intelligence and the German military. They want to see terrorists captured and prosecuted in conventional criminal trials. Hence the public outcry when two ministers of interior, Otto Schily and Wolfgang Schäuble, expressed their support for the targeted killings of terrorists abroad. Schäuble in particular—who said in an interview that "most of the people would say, 'thank God'" if the Americans found bin Laden and killed him with a missile—came in for heavy criticism from the opposition and even some Social Democratic members of the governing coalition. For them, the interior minister was already far down the slippery slope toward barbarism.[16]

## German Idealism and the War on Terror

The U.S. prison facility at Guantánamo Bay has met with criticism world-wide, but it was the German parliament which established a special panel to investigate the presence of German intelligence officers in the camp.[17] The officers, from both the domestic and foreign intelligence services, had inter-rogated Murat Kurnaz, a Turkish national and long-time resident of Ger-many who had been caught in Pakistan and rendered to the American forces in Afghanistan. The nineteen-year-old man wanted to join the Taliban to fight the multinational expeditionary force. During his detention and inter-rogation, it became clear that he was essentially a loner who had not actu-ally received any military training or even had close contacts to al Qaeda. Nevertheless, because the Turkish government showed no interest in repa-triating Kurnaz and failed to press the U.S. administration for his freedom, it took U.S. authorities four years to release him from Guantánamo Bay.

German public opinion, however, blamed the German government for the young man's fate. Although the interrogation of Kurnaz used standard procedures and the federal agents took no part in controversial practices such as waterboarding, the media lambasted Foreign Minister Frank-Walter Steinmeier, chief of staff in the Chancellery and responsible for oversight of the intelligence community at the time the interrogations were conducted, for mishandling the Kurnaz affair. The opposition demanded the foreign minister's resignation.

The U.S. authorities also came under heavy criticism for the Kurnaz case, as well as for the rendition of Khalid al-Masri, a Lebanese-born German who was arrested in Macedonia and handed over to the CIA. Masri, a member of the Islamist community in Ulm, was flown to Afghanistan and held in cus-tody for five months, until American authorities determined that they didn't have sufficient evidence to warrant his continued incarceration. In Germany, both cases produced widespread uneasiness about counterterrorism cooperation with U.S. agencies. For many Germans, this cooperation is now seen as immoral, and the concept of an "unlawful combatant" considered a violation of the Geneva Conventions and, more generally, the rule of law.[18]

German ethics have often forced the press in Germany to maintain a double standard. The press resolutely opposes torture, extraordinary rendi-tions, and the use of information obtained by foreign intelligence services through controversial means. Yet the arrest of Fritz Gelowicz and his accomplices was based mainly on cooperation with American and Pakistani security services. Information was obtained not only with the interception of an e-mail exchange between the group and its alleged Uzbek masters but also by interrogations conducted by Pakistani police and intelligence.[19] These interrogations undoubtedly did not meet contemporary German ethical standards. However, surprised by the plot itself and taken aback by the enormous loss of life that would have occurred if the attacks had been successful, the press didn't dwell on Pakistani interrogation methods or the propriety of cooperation with Pakistani authorities. Nothing succeeds more than success, even in the land of Kantian idealism.

German and U.S. agencies usually cooperate well, even when German politicians voice moral qualms about U.S.-German liaison work. It is the German public that tends to look with suspicion on American goals and methods. From the American perspective, the Federal Republic is undoubtedly a more difficult partner than either Britain or France. The German distaste for the "war on terrorism" trope is about more than rhetoric, however. With the Cold War ended and Germany reunified, Germans feel safer than at any time in their postwar history. The country is no longer on the front lines. Growing international terrorism, which most Germans believe is primarily aimed at the United States, has not fundamentally changed this disposition. For the German national security community, the attacks of 9/11 were unquestionably a watershed event. But for German society as a whole, this was not the case.

Before reunification, both German states refrained from ambitious foreign policies and overseas military interventions. Since reunification, Berlin has taken a slightly more proactive posture in international politics, but a substantial portion of the German population still believes less is more when it comes to security affairs. Many German citizens are convinced that the withdrawal of German troops from Afghanistan would effectively grant Germany immunity from Islamic terrorism. France and Great Britain, with their own history of deploying armed forces worldwide since World War II, are more tolerant of American interventions overseas than Germany. While the German government has taken tentative steps over the past decade or so toward a more active role outside its borders, the German public is still not convinced that the country really has a geopolitical responsibility to do so.

Germany remains in the shadow of its belligerent past and has hesitated to involve itself in the "war on terror." In the wake of 9/11, the Bundestag expressed its unanimous solidarity with the United States and deployed naval vessels and a limited number of special operations forces to Operation Enduring Freedom. But the bulk of German military deployments to Afghanistan have taken place under the NATO-led, UN-mandated mission of the International Security Assistance Force for Afghanistan. Although the deployment of German forces in Afghanistan may be a historically significant step from the German perspective, that deployment remains limited to Afghanistan's north, and German troops have avoided participation in the allied counterinsurgency campaign against the Taliban in Afghanistan's south and east.

## New Measures and Old Impediments

Given the political situation and history of modern Germany, it has been difficult for Berlin to strike a balance between civil liberties and the prosecution of jihadists. After 9/11, the German legislature and judiciary had more than a few hurdles to overcome in dealing with the new challenges posed by Islamist terrorism. With liberal asylum laws, extensive privacy rights, and an exemption for religious organizations from Germany's ban on hate groups, Germany was a safe haven for international Islamists and their terrorist warriors. Equally problematic was the fact that the German penal code (the relevant provision was section 129) had been designed to combat only domestic terrorism. As long as individuals were not conducting operations in Germany against Germans, they were beyond the reach of the law. Networks only loosely affiliated with each other were not considered terrorist organizations, and their members couldn't be convicted for belonging to a terrorist ring. As a result, the public had to watch the spectacle of an alleged terrorist standing trial for tax evasion.[20] The trials of Abdelghani Mzoudi and Munir al-Motassadeq, both affiliated with Mohammed Atta's cell in Hamburg, lasted for years and showed the German judiciary's weaknesses in prosecuting international terrorism. The indictment of the two Moroccans—the first court proceedings against jihadists anywhere in the world after 9/11—ended with the acquittal of Mzoudi and a fifteen-year sentence for Motassadeq.[21]

Eventually, the legislature enacted changes to section 129 and extended the reach of the statute to terrorist organizations operating outside Germany. In 2001, in an effort to close loopholes in German laws and extend new authority to the police and intelligence services, the Bundestag adopted two major packages of amendments to their penal code and governing statutes. Religious groups were no longer exempted under the ban on hate groups, and alien laws and asylum rules were tightened. In addition, the police and intelligence services were now able to demand information from banks, the post office, telecommunications services, and airlines to better track the financial flows, communications, and travel of suspects, and they had authority to investigate and prosecute terrorist activities or membership even if the terrorism was not directed solely at Germany.[22] Wiretapping became easier for the police, and information sharing between the police and the immigration agency was improved.[23] ID documents, which were already mandatory, could now include biometrical data, such as fingerprints. With the change in immigration laws, the immigration service was now more inclined to deport suspects.[24] And, after years of budget cuts following the Cold War, the intelligence community and law enforcement agencies began to receive additional funding and staff.[25] In 2002 and 2003, for instance, the relevant budgets were increased by more than half a billion dollars.

These improvements notwithstanding, the German public remained reluctant to give its counterterrorism authorities the broad powers and discretion granted in other European states. The counterterrorism packages and related legislation passed in 2001 are far more limited than, for instance, new provisions in the United Kingdom, where authorities may incarcerate a suspect in a precharge detention for up to twenty-eight days. And certainly the oversight mechanism allowing German intelligence to eavesdrop on telephone conversations is unique; whereas in France and Great Britain, the discretion is a matter of executive judgment, under German law, the intelligence agencies must receive prior approval from a specially appointed parliamentary committee.[26] Even though civil rights watchdog organizations rate Germany higher in its defense of privacy laws than most other European countries,[27] conventional wisdom in the German media and political parties regularly decries the "birth of a surveillance society." Hence the effort by Otto Schily as interior minister to give the German federal police the lead role in counterterrorism investigations (over and above state police agencies) failed for lack of political support.[28]

As this failure suggests, Germany has also been bedeviled by a lack of a clear separation of national and state powers and responsibilities within the German federal system. The powers of state governments and legislatures have been much diminished in recent decades due to ever-increasing federal legislation, but at the same time, the German states have developed a variety of mechanisms to modify or undermine the intent of federal legislation. Each of the sixteen German states (*Bundesländer*) is responsible for territorial law enforcement, and every state has its own independent criminal police office and domestic intelligence body, resulting in thirty-two independent state agencies in Germany, in addition to the federal police and security organizations. This structure produces turf battles and is difficult to command, let alone reform, because no supervisory layer or body exists.[29] Although a law passed in 2009 has ameliorated this tension somewhat by giving the Bundeskriminalamt the authority to counter a terrorist threat if the threat affects more than one state or if a state's highest police agency requests the BKA's support, German states in the past have not been shy about challenging the authority of the BKA and the federal prosecutor's office concerning who is in charge of particular cases and investigations.[30]

Complicating matters further is the fact that the ministries themselves enjoy significant autonomy, preventing effective interministry coordination. The Chancellery, which is ostensibly the focal point in the government for counterterrorism, has no security council or comparable staff to direct the different departments. And, finally, there is the problem that some of the states are actually too small to support even minimally competent domestic security agencies. Thus, the federal and large-state security and intelligence agencies do not fully cooperate with the agencies of the small states, creating further analytical and operational weaknesses throughout the country.

Interagency cooperation is also impeded by a regulation stemming from the Allied occupation after World War II. In 1949, the Allied military governors sent a letter to the nascent West German government demanding a strict separation between police and intelligence services. The so-called separation instruction stipulated only that intelligence agencies must not exercise police powers to arrest and search. But many experts regard the sixty-year-old instruction as a legal requirement to keep information sharing between law enforcement and intelligence at a minimum. Although the German government has taken steps to bridge this divide, the political parties have hesitated to bring this matter before the public.[31] As a result, Germany possesses neither fully integrated regional counterterrorism units, as does Great Britain, nor independent, enormously powerful *juges d'instruction,* as does France.

Seeing the weaknesses in federal and interagency cooperation, in late 2004, the German government established the Joint Counterterrorism Center (Gemeinsames Terrorabwehrzentrum, or GTAZ), which represents thirty-nine different agencies and is located in Berlin. Although not an operational entity, the GTAZ was intended to improve the exchange of information among the various German security bodies and to increase the government's overall capacity to produce daily and longer-term threat assessments.[32] Perhaps as important in addressing this problem was the parliament's enactment in December 2006 of legislation creating a centralized, antiterror database that would allow all federal and state police and intelligence agencies to share information through a regulated, multistep process.[33]

Such changes of course have helped facilitate counterterrorist efforts. It has also helped that the German counterterrorism community is relatively small, making it easier for officials to share information with each other informally. Gradually, this has meant that cooperation between the various police and intelligence services has become more routine in the earliest (and often most critical) stages of counterterrorism operations.[34]

One recent step forward was the consolidation of the federal government's domestic signals intelligence collection efforts under the umbrella of the Federal Office of Administration (Bundesverwaltungsamt, or BVA) in Cologne. Previously, all federal and state police and the intelligence service had their own eavesdropping branches. In 2008 the Interior Ministry merged the technical collection branches of the Federal Police (Bundespolizei), the BKA, and the BfV. (The BND and the state police and intelligence services remain outside this new effort.) The BVA collects the signals, however, only as a technical service provider, while the Federal Police, the BKA, and the BfV maintain separate analytic and data-storage capabilities. In devising this arrangement, the government appears to have sidestepped German domestic concerns that the consolidated collection effort might violate the "separation instruction" that is meant to keep police and intelligence functions distinct, or more broadly that this reform would usher in a German *Überwachungsstaat* (surveillance state). This change is an example of the pragmatic—if sometimes overly cautious—approach taken by the German government to addressing the jihadist threat. German authorities, led by the Interior Ministry, go to great pains to implement these changes outside the view of a skeptical public, expanding and adapting the existing legal framework to post-9/11 realities one step at a time.[35]

But old habits die hard. The inquiry into Fritz Gelowicz and the "peroxide plotters" shows the mixed results of the current reforms. On the one hand, the investigation, which lasted for more than eight months and involved several federal and state agencies, was brought to a successful conclusion.[36] Without the knowledge of Gelowicz or the others, the police managed to substitute a harmless substance for the supply of hydrogen peroxide the would-be terrorists had acquired, which meant that the police and intelligence services could continue to gather more evidence as the plot moved forward. On the other hand, after completing the operation, the police authorities complained in a confidential report of various problems that had persisted throughout the investigation. In particular, the flow of information between police and the intelligence community was said to be insufficient. The police alleged that for months, the intelligence agencies deliberately withheld information from U.S. authorities about a planned plot on German soil. The intelligence community denied the accusations, but it was obvious that the lack of a fully integrated federal counterterrorism effort slowed down the investigation. Furthermore, the police forces from different states did not fully cooperate with one another. As the suspects crossed state borders, the surveillance operation stumbled, while federal and state agencies eavesdropped on the cell not knowing of each other's work.[37] The internal report also found that too few surveillance agents were involved in the investigation, that the SWAT team assigned to the case was undermanned, and that there were delays in analyzing wiretapped conversations.

It is significant that German police and intelligence agencies focused on the cell and its outer ring of sympathizers only after receiving warnings from U.S. counterparts—even though the German police and intelligence services had been concerned about the Islamists in Ulm for years. Why were German authorities unable to detect the plotting without help from abroad? The intelligence services are well known for their ability to infiltrate neo-Nazi groups.[38] Did they lack sources from within the radical Muslim community? Was surveillance of the Muslim community hindered by a deficit of officers, or by the fact that two federal agencies and four regional agencies from two states had to be coordinated in the process? As noted earlier, the jihadist community in Germany is relatively small. And the growing number of German converts, most of whom live less secluded lives than Arab or Turkish immigrants, should have made infiltrating the jihadist ranks an easier task. The security services, however, appear reluctant to conduct such operations.[39]

Fortunately, those involved in the bombing plot made astonishing mistakes. They went on with their planning, for example, even after they had learned that they were under police surveillance. Yet pursuit of these four seemingly amateur terrorists stretched the law enforcement system to its utmost. Indeed, some in Germany's national security establishment hint that the agencies involved wouldn't have committed to the case even the resources they did if U.S. authorities—in particular President Bush at the G8 summit in Heiligendamm in June 2007—had not pressed their German counterparts.[40]

Germany's handling of the peroxide plot recalls its handling of the plot to bomb the Strasbourg Christmas market in December 2000. When the French internal security service, the Direction de la Surveillance du Territoire, obtained evidence that a Frankfurt-based terrorist cell with Algerian affiliations was plotting an attack on the market, they informed German intelligence. But the German foreign intelligence service hesitated to disseminate or act on the information, and in the end the French authorities contacted German police directly.[41] That German authorities did not act decisively in dealing with the 2007 plot, some within the German intelligence establishment have suggested, indicates that Germany had not learned as much from 9/11 as one might have hoped—or expected.

## Germany's Divided House

Domestic security is one of the main issues which divide Germany's political parties from each other; this is especially evident when one party is either out of power or a junior partner in the governing coalition. At the same time, each of the country's states also uses security issues as leverage in turf fights with the federal government. Combined, these two divisions create a decision-making process for counterterrorism policy that is exhausting and time consuming for all involved. One of the numerous participants in the process will inevitably express a dissenting voice, and the German desire for achieving a complete consensus before adopting a policy will bring matters to a halt, forcing the participants in the discussion back to square one. Predictably, it took the government in Berlin five years to establish the counterterrorism database after the decision was made to do so. The process of setting up an integrated digital radio network for police and homeland security services has become a never-ending story, lasting some eight years. Every attempt to expand the authorities of the Federal Interior Ministry and the powers of the federal counterterrorism agencies or rationalize the distribution of responsibilities between the police and intelligence authorities at the federal and state levels has been met by German-style inertia.

Even reforms which fall exclusively in the realm of the federal government are difficult to implement. For example, the Bundeskriminalamt and the Bundesamt für Verfassungsschutz were located in Wiesbaden and Cologne after World War II to weaken the possible centralization of executive authority in the newly founded Federal Republic. After 9/11, the Ministry of Interior decided to move these agencies to Berlin to allow for a smoother flow of information between agencies. But the relocation has proceeded slowly because staffs protested the move, and currently both agencies have elements in both Berlin and their original headquarters. As a result, the foreign intelligence service (Bundesnachrichtendienst, or BND), although still located near Munich at the time of this chapter's writing, is the only federal intelligence or policy agency which will completely relocate to Berlin.

This is not to ignore that some changes have been made. For example, the BND is undergoing a major institutional reform to merge its operations and analysis departments. The reform is designed to improve operations and increase analytic relevance. But to date, operational security issues (for example, handling of "need to know" restrictions) have not been adequately addressed, resulting in less cross-discipline cooperation than expected. Moreover, it is arguable that when the BND failed in the past, it did so principally because of a lack of sources abroad, a stifling bureaucracy at home, and an overabundance of conventional wisdom on a variety of pressing issues—all issues that remain to be addressed.

Although the German security architecture remains complicated and German public opinion haunted by the country's past, Social Democratic and conservative governments alike have tried to improve Germany's legal framework for counterterrorism when actually faced with the responsibilities of governing and protecting the population. Since 9/11, every interior minister, whether a Social Democrat or member of the Christian Democratic Union, has called for enhanced capabilities and authorities. Two former interior ministers, Otto Schily and Wolfgang Schäuble, did not hesitate to use the publicity surrounding exposed terrorist plots to press their agenda. They argued for and received an increase in personnel authority to add surveillance teams, for example.[42] Schily, as noted earlier, made efforts to consolidate counterterrorist efforts under the federal umbrella, while Schäuble requested that the government be given the authority to detain individuals suspected of plotting a terrorist attack, even though the police might not have sufficient evidence at the time to bring the individual to trial.[43]

One of Schäuble's significant achievements was passage of a new antiterror law that entered into force in January 2009 and broadened the BKA's powers.[44] While it did not make the BKA the controlling police authority in all counterterrorism investigations, as Schily had previously pushed for, it did give the BKA the controlling authority when cases crossed (or possibly crossed) German state boundaries. Under the new antiterror law, the BKA is now allowed to mount surveillance of a suspect (including monitoring travel, meetings, and conversations) outside his home without court approval; with court approval, it may bug a suspect's apartment, eavesdrop on private conversations, take photographs or record video inside the suspect's domicile without his knowledge, and remotely access a suspect's personal computer.[45]

Schäuble, in the wake of the "peroxide plot" in 2007, also sought to close additional loopholes in Germany's counterterrorism laws. After much debate, a law was passed in the summer of 2009 making it illegal to purchase the ingredients for a bomb.[46] The legislation also makes it illegal to attend a terrorist training camp, a provision that met criticism in the German parliament. As the law was debated, numerous experts expressed their doubts about whether the measure was consistent with the German constitution and the rule of law.[47] A majority in the Bundestag eventually passed the measure, but they also inserted a clause which largely undermines the utility of the law itself. In order to punish someone for visiting a terrorist training camp, the government must prove that a defendant did so with the actual intent of engaging in terrorism. Of course, the original law was premised on the commonsense view that someone who goes to, and stays in, a terrorist camp has, *prima facie*, the intent to become a terrorist. But since attending such a camp generally constitutes an early stage in the life of a terrorist, requiring proof of actual intent makes the law far less useful than it might otherwise have been.

Some of the reforms triggered by 9/11 are still underway, and it is impossible to judge what their long-term effectiveness or adequacy will be. Reforms will always be swimming uphill against the German public's wariness about expanding the government's police and intelligence powers. For example, despite the fact that the two Lebanese "suitcase bombers" were caught on CCTV in Cologne Central Station, efforts to employ cameras more widely in public spaces have met persistent resistance by the public. At times the German security establishment has had to rely on EU directives to overcome limits imposed by politics at home. When, for example, the government was having trouble passing a measure requiring that telecommunications data be retained for use by German security and police, the Federal Republic used a 2006 EU directive—one that required the storage of phone and Internet traffic records for six months—as a legitimating mandate for enacting a German statute a year later.[48]

Currently, perhaps, the main player in the German debate over what the government can and cannot do on the security front is the Federal Constitutional Court (Bundesverfassungsgericht). The court, a watchful sentinel over civil rights, usually rules in favor of personal privacy. While considering the pros and cons of a planned census in 1983, the court formulated the axiom of "informational self-determination" and laid the groundwork for strict data-protection regulations. This has led it to place an injunction on parts of the 2007 law pertaining to the use by German police of retained telecommunications and Internet data and, in 2010, to overturn altogether the law requiring communications providers to store data for six months for possible use by law enforcement authorities.[49] Previously, and even more famously, in 2004 the court banned government eavesdropping that intruded on "core privacy" rights.[50] As a consequence, surveillance teams have to listen carefully and turn off the tape machines when "pillow talk" or other seemingly irrelevant conversations commence, thus making real time analysis of recordings virtually impossible.

On February 27, 2008, the Federal Constitutional Court declared it illegal for the government to use virus-carrying software to remotely gather data from an individual's hard drive.[51] The federal judges expanded the "core privacy" concept, defining a new basic right that guarantees "the confidentiality and integrity of information technology systems." Although the court's president conceded that the new "basic right is not without limits" and that in extreme cases, such as an imminent terrorist threat, the use of remote forensic software would be allowed, how this line will be drawn in practice has German investigators stumped.[52] They are afraid that the ruling will restrict their ability to pursue terrorists via their use of the Internet, just as the court's decision on eavesdropping made bugging operations on private premises virtually impossible. While the court's decision was intended to address the constitutionality of a law on domestic intelligence enacted by the state of North Rhine-Westphalia, the applicability of the decision for a similar provision in the January 2009 antiterror law is obvious. The Federal Constitutional Court is now reviewing the provisions of that law as well.[53]

The court is focused on defending the civil rights–rich German democracy, and has been less attentive to a duty of every democratic government: protecting the lives of its citizens from terrorist attack. In 2006, the court declared that a regulation in the Aviation Security Act, which had authorized the armed forces to shoot down a terrorist-controlled aircraft, was incompatible with the German constitution.[54] It decided that the act violated the fundamental right to life and the guarantee of human dignity as stipulated in the constitution. As noted in the judgment: "By the state's using their [the passengers'] killing as a means to save others, they are treated as mere objects, which denies them the value that is due to a human being for his or her own sake."[55] Only a declaration of war could give the armed forces the right to kill on German soil. Security officials' subsequent call for an amendment to the constitution declaring terrorist attacks an act of war (which would thereby allow the use of force against hijacked aircraft) has little or no chance of finding a majority in today's German legislature.

## Conclusion

Although Germany has not been struck at home by a major Islamist terror attack, since 9/11, more Germans have lost their lives to jihadist terror than to attacks and assassinations carried out by the Red Army Faction.[56] As the threat from Islamist terrorism has become more apparent, the German government has changed laws, introduced new measures, and added resources to deal with it. Nevertheless, there is a kind of "two steps forward, one back" character to what has taken place since 9/11, and there remains a gap between the nature of the threat German officials believe they face and the tools they can employ to combat it. Politics, history, and governing structures have all combined to slow the German government's ability to match its European neighbors in developing the robust counterterrorist regime that its own security officials believe to be necessary.

Of course, all liberal societies must constantly give heed to the extent to which the protection of life can be advanced without undermining rights. However, they must not overlook the right to security—the right not to be killed or maimed by a terrorist attack. German society underestimates the importance of this basic human right while exaggerating the dangers of the "surveillance state." Unfortunately, this attitude will likely remain unchanged until a successful terrorist attack in Germany forces the German public to rethink the balance between security and liberty and demand more from its government.

# 5

## United States:
## Facing the Threat at Home

*Gary J. Schmitt*

The United States did not create the present system for addressing the threat of terrorism de novo in the wake of the attacks of 9/11. Since at least the mid-1980s, terrorism has been a national security concern of some priority, though clearly the counterterrorism regime in place in 2001 was inadequate. Many legislative and policy changes later, what does the U.S. regime consist of, and how effective does it appear to be?

### U.S. Counterterrorism before 9/11

In April 1983, a suicide car bomb aimed at the U.S. Embassy in Beirut killed seventeen Americans and more than fifty others. Six months later, 241 servicemen were killed in a suicide attack on the U.S. Marine barracks in Beirut—until 9/11, the country's largest loss of life to terrorism. What followed, over the next few years, were multiple plane hijackings abroad; bombings in Colombia, Spain, Rome, and Germany; assassinations in Greece; the hijacking of the Achille Lauro cruise liner; the bombing of the LaBelle discotheque in West Berlin; and, most famously, the bombing of Pan Am 103 over Lockerbie, Scotland, resulting in the death of all 259 passengers on board, including 189 Americans.

In the face of this increasing terrorist violence, the two most innovative initiatives undertaken by the U.S. government included the 1986 congressional authorization giving the Federal Bureau of Investigation (FBI) new authorities for conducting and coordinating investigations of overseas terrorist incidents against Americans, and the creation of the Counterterrorism Center (CTC) at the Central Intelligence Agency in the same year.[1] Earlier, a vice presidential task force, led by George H. W. Bush, had noted that "while several federal departments and agencies process intelligence within their own facilities, there is no consolidated center that collects and analyzes all-source information from those agencies participating in anti-terrorist activities."[2] The CTC was designed to address this deficiency. Given the CIA's lead role within the intelligence community, the CTC eventually drew analysts and other officials from across the community, and a senior agent from the FBI's national security division came to serve as the center's deputy director. But perhaps the most significant organizational innovation occurred within the CIA itself: the CTC and its team of analysts were housed within the agency's operations directorate, breaking down the long-time bureaucratic norm at Langley of keeping analysts and operations officers separate. The goal of co-locating the CTC and the operations directorate was to focus analytic efforts more effectively on time-sensitive threats and, in turn, ensure that counterterrorism operations were better informed by all-source intelligence.[3]

The terrorist threat did not lessen in the 1990s. In 1993, Ramzi Yousef, an Islamist terrorist trained in an Afghan camp organized by Osama bin Laden, orchestrated a truck bomb attack on the World Trade Center that came perilously close to killing hundreds or more. Only a few months later, FBI officials thwarted a plot in which the United Nations building and the Lincoln and Holland tunnels in New York were principal targets. In January 1995, Ramzi Yousef was discovered in Manila (after accidently setting off a bomb in his apartment), having hatched a massive plot to bring down a dozen American passenger aircraft in flight over Asia, crash a jet into the CIA headquarters, and bomb the U.S. and Israeli embassies in the Philippines. Then, in April, Timothy McVeigh and Terry Nichols used a truck bomb to tear off the front half of the federal building in downtown Oklahoma City, leaving 168 citizens dead and hundreds injured. In 1996 the attack on the Khobar Towers in Saudi Arabia killed nineteen U.S. military personnel and wounded hundreds of others; and in 1998 al Qaeda carried out truck bombings at the U.S. embassies in Nairobi, Kenya, and in Dar es Salaam, Tanzania, in which more than two hundred were killed, including a dozen Americans, and thousands were wounded. December 1999 was marked by the discovery of two plots designed to cause mass casualties and tied loosely to al Qaeda: Ahmed Ressam's plan (the "Millennium Plot") to attack Los Angeles International Airport, which was foiled by an alert customs official at the U.S.-Canadian border; and an Islamist plan to kill hundreds of American tourists by setting off bombs at select hotels and tourist spots in Jordan, which Jordanian intelligence disrupted. Finally, in October 2000, an al Qaeda suicide attack blew a hole in the side of the USS *Cole* while it was docked in the Yemeni port of Aden, killing seventeen American sailors, wounding dozens, and completely disabling the ship.

In the face of attacks both here and abroad and a rising al Qaeda, the U.S. government took steps to address the terrorist threat. In 1994, Congress passed legislation which, for the first time, outlawed "material support" to terrorism, making it a federal crime to aid and abet terrorist activities and significantly broadening the reach of the law in this area.[4] The legislation also enhanced the FBI's ability to conduct electronic surveillance in the digital age by requiring telecommunications companies and equipment manufacturers to have built-in, inherent surveillance capabilities in their equipment and services—allowing the government to monitor all telephone, broadband Internet, and other traffic in real time if so authorized by court order.[5] This law was followed by an additional act in 1996 that modified and expanded the "material support" provisions in the criminal code.[6] Also that year, the CTC created a unit specifically focused on bin Laden; more broadly, the CIA undertook a significant expansion of its liaison efforts with foreign services in order to develop more intelligence on the al Qaeda threat.[7] As for the FBI, by 1994, the Radical Fundamentalist Unit was set up in the Washington headquarters to oversee intelligence cooperation abroad and monitor investigations domestically. At the same time, the bureau was significantly expanding the number of its offices in overseas embassies. Finally, from 1998 to 2000, the FBI began to take steps to establish counterterrorism as a bureau priority, creating the stand-alone Counterterrorism Division and laying down an ambitious plan to address terrorism and other major security threats in a more proactive fashion. The goal was to move the bureau away from its traditional reactive, law enforcement approach to one that would seek "to deter and prevent—to the maximum extent feasible—criminal activities that threaten vital American interests."[8]

But if the government was not sitting on its hands when it came to counterterrorism, neither was it urgently moving to overcome key legal and bureaucratic hurdles to make its counterterrorism efforts as effective as possible. In 1998, after the bombings of the American embassies in Africa, George Tenet, the nominal head of the U.S. intelligence community as director of central intelligence, issued a memorandum declaring: "We are at war" and "I want no resources or people spared . . . either inside CIA or the Community" in addressing the threat posed by bin Laden and al Qaeda. By one account, however, "Tenet's declaration of war memo had almost no impact [on the U.S. intelligence community]: only a handful of agency heads ever received it, and all of them ignored it."[9] Within the CIA itself, attention given to the CTC waxed and waned.[10] The bin Laden unit had been established but the analysts and the chief assigned to it were not thought to be among the agency's best.[11] More critically, on the operational side, while liaison relations with Middle East powers were beefed up, the agency's own human intelligence (HUMINT) efforts were lacking. As difficult as it might have been to penetrate even the outer rings of an organization like al Qaeda, it was a mistake to rely principally on ties to other intelligence services in the region for timely information the United States needed. As for the FBI, although plans were being laid internally to give counterterrorism a higher priority, the monies for the mission remained flat. The fact is, the bureau's priority remained crime fighting. In July 2001, when concern within Washington's corridors about a potential terrorist attack within the United States was at an all-time high, the FBI's acting director, Tom Pickard, alerted the bureau's major field offices—but, revealingly, his main message to them was to see to it that their respective investigative teams were ready to respond if in fact an attack occurred.[12]

No less important for understanding the state of counterterrorism before 9/11 is that the basic legal and internal guidelines for handling the terrorist threat had not kept up with the changing nature of the threat. In reaction to the abuses by the intelligence community (including elements within the CIA, FBI, and Department of Defense) in monitoring domestic groups and individuals, which came to light in the early and mid-1970s, the standard adopted for monitoring domestic security threats took its cue from the criminal code.[13] In the past, intelligence collection had been about gathering information per se; now, intelligence—gathered either electronically or otherwise against a domestic target—required some level of evidence that a person or group was an agent of a foreign power (or associated with a terrorist group) before an investigation could be started. Although the standard for opening an investigation or conducting surveillance in such cases would not be as stringent as that required for pursuing a more typical criminal investigation, both the Attorney General Guidelines of 1976[14] and the Foreign Intelligence Surveillance Act of 1978 (FISA)[15] nevertheless moved the bar toward that end of the spectrum.

Naturally enough, this sensitivity with respect to domestic intelligence collection began to influence how the bureau, the Department of Justice, the FISA court, and the CIA came to understand their own roles, and how they would interact with each other. The result was the now infamous "wall" between intelligence and law enforcement activities and bureaucracies. In truth, there was more than one wall, and the walls were more like hurdles than walls—but they were indeed hurdles.[16]

Under FISA, for example, the FISA court could issue a warrant for the government to place a phone tap on someone if the government had shown "probable cause" to believe an individual was acting as a spy or terrorist on behalf of a "foreign power" and if the surveillance was being conducted for "the purpose" of collecting foreign intelligence. Because the standard of evidence required to obtain a warrant under FISA was somewhat less stringent than that required by a court in the case of a normal criminal investigation, there was concern that evidence acquired as a result of a FISA tap and used in a criminal trial could be challenged by the defense as not having met the Fourth Amendment prohibition against unreasonable government searches and seizures.[17] (This concern also applied to other types of evidence gathered as a result of counterterrorism and counterespionage investigations.) Rather than risk such challenges, over time, intelligence investigations and criminal investigations were kept further and further apart, with increasing levels of oversight by the Department of Justice to ensure the former did not contaminate the latter.

Compounding this division was the reverse concern by intelligence officials—the concern that key "sources and methods" for collecting intelligence would be exposed at trial as defense lawyers either looked for evidence of misbehavior on the part of prosecutors or the government, or demanded that the government turn over to the defense any possible exculpatory material that it might have uncovered in the course of its investigation. Needless to say, this division between intelligence and law enforcement was also reflected in relations between the CIA and the FBI—with the agency's habit of sharing intelligence on a strict need-to-know basis reinforcing its (then largely correct) view that the FBI was a law enforcement agency, whose principal goal was successful criminal prosecutions.[18] And, finally, there was the long-standing view, grounded in executive orders and practice over the years, that the FBI and CIA had largely distinct missions: Langley was to worry about things abroad, while the bureau was to take care of the home front. Although some progress was made in overcoming these institutional stovepipes—for example, by involving FBI agents in the management and work of the CIA's counterterrorism center in the late 1980s—it was not enough to change the underlying and persistent impediments and traditions that continued to define the American counterterrorism regime.

None of these hurdles to cooperation was insurmountable. Executive orders, Justice Department guidelines, laws, and court findings had created work-arounds that allowed intelligence sharing. That said, the hurdles did exist, and the steps involved in overcoming them were time consuming and often challenging. And with agencies and senior officials burdened with investigations of malfeasance or worse, it was only natural that the American national security bureaucracy would, like most bureaucracies, take two steps back in day-to-day practice to avoid the kind of trouble that they assumed would result if they stepped over a line inadvertently.

This is where things stood in the summer of 2001 when the terrorism warning lights were blinking red.[19] The American counterterrorist system knew enough to be on alert—that something was afoot—but little more. It lacked the human assets that could provide specifics; and its rules and regulations prevented it from aggressively acting on information (flight training by foreigners, for example) which, while potentially telling, was about activities that were legal. Moreover, the bureau was stretched thin, with too few resources to handle ongoing investigations of past terrorist attacks, let alone keep up with new warnings;[20] and, most prosaic of all, Congress and successive administrations had created a bureaucratic culture in which, at the working level, neither the CIA nor the FBI believed it should be routine to pass on intelligence about possible terrorists or terrorist plots.[21] Hence, as unjustifiable as it seems now in hindsight, the CIA was conducting business as usual when it failed to alert the FBI that, by the summer of 2000, two known al Qaeda operatives had U.S. visas and at least one was in the United States. And the FBI was acting in its traditional reactive, law-enforcement mode as it ignored signs of the "possibility of a coordinated effort by Usama bin Laden to send students to the United States to attend civil aviation schools."[22] Al Qaeda's planners and operatives were able to exploit these seams in the U.S. system to devastating effect on 9/11.

## After 9/11: New Laws, Old Laws, and Old Laws Implemented in New Ways

In late October, with the ruins of the World Trade Center still smoldering and the gigantic gash in the Pentagon's outer ring easily seen by Washington-area commuters, Congress passed and President Bush signed the Uniting and Strengthening America by Providing Appropriate Tools Required to Intercept and Obstruct Terrorism Act of 2001 (commonly known as the Patriot Act).[23] A 340-page behemoth, the Patriot Act was less an attempt to provide a new, comprehensive counterterrorist regime than an effort to update and plug holes in the existing system as seen from the necessarily narrow vantage point of a nation that had just suffered its worst terrorist attack ever. It was the legislative equivalent of emergency room triage— which, while never pretty, does have the advantage of making sure the patient is stabilized and, in time, open to more refined treatment.

The act increased the penalties for terrorism and terrorist-related activities, enhanced the government's capacity to deal with terrorist financing, and expanded its ability to exclude foreigners from the United States on the basis of their association with terrorist organizations or support groups. The law also gave the attorney general the authority to hold for up to a week any aliens in the United States suspected of having terrorist ties, without filing charges or initiating deportation proceedings.

But the key elements of the Patriot Act were the measures that increased the government's surveillance authorities and capabilities and lowered the bar for the sharing of information between the law enforcement and intelligence communities. The new law made it easier for information gathered in an appropriately sanctioned terrorism or espionage investigation to be passed to the criminal-investigative side of the street; conversely, if grand jury investigations generated information of value to counterterrorist or counterespionage activities (as was the case after the first World Trade bombings in 1993), this information could now be shared with the intelligence community. No longer was there a bias toward keeping the two realms separate. On the surveillance side, the Patriot Act made some overdue adjustments to account for the changes in communication technology since FISA's passage in the late 1970s. The law now allowed "roving wiretaps"—that is, electronic surveillance targeted at an individual, regardless of whether he or she was using a landline, cell phone, or other telecommunication system, rather than a particular phone number. In addition, it expanded the use of systems ("pen registers" and "trap-and-trace devices") designed to collect transactional (noncontent) data pertaining to landline, cell, or Internet use.

The Patriot Act also clarified the "purpose" standard of FISA, that is, the end for which a FISA warrant could be issued by the FISA court. Over time the courts and the Justice Department had begun to read the FISA statute as allowing a FISA-sanctioned warrant only if the collection's "primary purpose" was gathering foreign intelligence; as noted above, they hoped in the process to preclude Fourth Amendment challenges when an espionage or terrorism case went to trial. Under the new statute, FISA warrants could be issued if a "significant purpose" of the collection was to gather counterterrorist or counterespionage information, signaling to both the courts and the bureaucracy that the need to keep a strict separation between intelligence and criminal investigations had not been Congress's intent when it originally passed FISA. As long as the government could demonstrate that it had asked for a FISA warrant in good faith, any useful information that came out of an intelligence investigation could be shared with prosecutors, and the government's use of the FISA process could not be challenged as an improper circumvention of the more stringent Fourth Amendment warrant requirements for criminal investigations.

Finally, among the more significant (and controversial) measures the Patriot Act put in place was the expansion of FBI and other executive branch authorities to acquire third-party business and transactional information in support of counterterrorism investigations through National Security Letters (NSLs). Requiring only field-level FBI approval and, as originally crafted, not subject to judicial review, an NSL can be issued by intelligence investigators to telecommunication providers, banks, credit card companies, etc., to demand records and data associated with an individual, even if that individual is not the target of a full-blown investigation.[24] In making the case for this new authority, the administration argued that the FBI-issued NSLs would be used to develop cases, generate leads, and provide general data for intelligence analysts; as such, they were analogous to subpoenas issued in the course of grand jury investigations where sometimes broad swaths of information are collected on the basis of general relevance to an investigation. In short, NSLs reflect a post-9/11 view that getting ahead of the curve when it comes to counterterrorism may require collecting information with no precise criminal predicate.

The next major new piece of legislation dealing directly with terrorism was the Intelligence Reform and Terrorism Prevention Act of 2004 (IRTPA).[25] The most significant element in the bill was its restructuring of the U.S. intelligence community, a topic covered below. The act also expanded and strengthened penalties for providing "material support" to terrorists, added new authorities and funding to fight terrorism financing, and modified FISA to allow surveillance warrants for "lone wolf" terrorists. (Prior to this modification, FISA required evidence that a surveillance target was acting on behalf of a "foreign power," which could include terrorist organizations but seemed to ignore terrorist suspects whose ties to a particular organization were still unknown.)

Perhaps the most controversial change to America's laws after 9/11, however, began when one particular law was bypassed—that is, when the president decided he had the authority to circumvent FISA. As noted above, FISA was a response to investigations into intelligence community abuses in the 1970s and to court cases suggesting that there were limits to the president's constitutional authority to engage in surveillance in national security investigations. The 1978 law required the government to convince a special set of judges that there was "probable cause" to believe that the proposed target of the electronic surveillance, if an American or a resident alien, was acting as a spy on behalf of a foreign power or as an operative in a terrorist organization. Only then would the FISA court consider issuing a warrant approving the surveillance. As a result of the "probable cause" standard and the inherent caution that the investigations had instilled in the bureaucracies at both the Justice Department and FBI headquarters, for many years after the measure became law, the FBI and the Justice Department batted a thousand in their petitions to the FISA court.[26] In practice, this meant that wiretaps were being used less to uncover spying or terrorist plots than to confirm that an individual was in fact a spy or a terrorist. This approach certainly lessened the chance that the government might needlessly impinge on the privacy rights of its citizens—which seemed perfectly fine as long as the threats under investigation made erring on the conservative side tolerable.

Whether that calculus was ever the right one is open to debate—especially given the large number of major espionage cases that went undetected in subsequent years—but it seemed particularly dubious in the days and months following the attacks of 9/11, when the priority was to prevent further attacks, not to confirm individual bad behavior on a case-by-case basis. As Benjamin Wittes writes:

> Another fundamental judgment embedded within the statute is that the intelligence agencies have already identified their target, that they already know something about the person about whom they seek information, indeed that they know where this person is and what telecommunication facilities he or she uses. FISA quite deliberately does not contemplate the reverse situation—in which one might identify a surveillance target by processing the very communication traffic the statute meant to shield. The law takes this approach both because the technology of its time did not support such an approach and, probably more importantly, because its drafters actively wanted to preclude domestic intelligence collection in the absence of preexisting evidence against some person.[27]

Believing such an approach would no longer suffice in protecting the country, and also believing it had both the constitutional and legislative authority to do so, the Bush administration determined not long after 9/11 that it would not be bound by FISA's strictures—but did so in secret.

The new surveillance program, dubbed the Terrorist Surveillance Program (TSP) by the administration, has never been described in detail. After a *New York Times* story in 2005 brought its existence to light,[28] however, the president and other senior officials asserted that the program intercepted international communications into and out of the United States where there was a "reasonable basis" to assume that one party to the communication was linked either to al Qaeda or to a related terrorist organization. From news and government accounts, it appears that TSP swept up a vast amount of communication traffic, filtered it with the use of address links and a surface-level, computer-generated survey of the content, and then determined discrete targets for potentially more in-depth and human-monitored surveillance.[29] From the vantage point of FISA, there were two fundamental problems. The first was that the program was conducting surveillance (including possibly of U.S. persons) based initially not on "probable cause" but on something akin to "reasonable suspicion." Second, because of the change in telecommunication technology for most international traffic since the late 1970s, it was tapping into this data stream largely at servers and fiber-optic cables located in the United States; thus these communications, though international in character, were technically "domestic" and hence arguably governed by FISA.

Prompted by the controversial nature of TSP (both outside and inside the administration) and the changed partisan landscape within Congress, the Bush administration began discussions with the FISA court, and later with Congress, to cobble together a new program that would retain the FISA institutional paradigm while updating key provisions of the law. The final result was the FISA Amendments Act of 2008,[30] which gives the government authority to conduct warrantless surveillance (regardless of where the actual physical "tapping" takes places) of targets "reasonably believed" to be outside the United States. The new caveat is that the FISA court is to review and approve at least annually both the general targeting procedures and the government's "minimization" measures to ensure that information inadvertently acquired about Americans who are not targets and not relevant to counterterrorist investigations is purged from government data banks. Next, the law resurrects the "probable cause" standard and individualized warrant requirement from the FISA court when U.S. citizens or legal residents are targets, and, for the first time, applies those requirements when they are outside the country, as well. The act also expands the time allowed for "emergency" surveillances—the period before the government is required to provide the court with the proper paperwork—from two days to seven. And, finally, the law creates a far more elaborate set of congressional reporting requirements.

The Bush administration was criticized not only for bypassing FISA, but also for using existing immigration laws to detain nearly eight hundred aliens who were in violation of these laws in the weeks following the 9/11 attacks. Not knowing if there were remaining terrorist "sleeper" cells with plans to conduct follow-on attacks, and uncertain of who else might have been involved in the 9/11 plots, the Justice Department used "whatever means legally available" to hold individuals until it was reasonably sure that it understood who was behind the attacks and had some idea of what other terrorist plots might be afoot.[31]

From the perspective of civil rights advocates, the sweeps were especially problematic because the immigration hearing for each of the detainees was held in secret and there was no possibility of posting bond. Driving this policy was the Justice Department's determination not to alert terrorist cohorts about the progress of an investigation by allowing information, or the suspect himself, to "hit the streets." In addition, swamped with far more detainees than usual and guided by the Justice Department's initial decision to hold detainees until they had been positively cleared by the FBI, the Immigration and Naturalization Service (INS) was unable to process them in a timely manner or comply with the existing law's ninety-day time limit for deporting immigrants once they had received a formal order to leave or be removed from the country.[32] Nevertheless, some 70 percent of those arrested after 9/11 on immigration violations were released from detention or removed from the country within 150 days, with the average length of confinement being 80 days. With the exception of a handful of suspects thought to have some terrorist links, all detainees were out of detention within a year.[33] None was tied to the 9/11 attacks.

## New Structures, New Guidelines

In addition to the changes made to U.S. statutes, 9/11 resulted in significant and large-scale changes in the country's counterterrorism bureaucracy.

The most massive of the changes was the establishment of the Department of Homeland Security (DHS) in 2002.[34] DHS consolidated into one agency some 180,000 employees and twenty-two different agencies, including the Immigration and Naturalization Service, Customs, Coast Guard, Transportation Security Administration (TSA), Federal Emergency Management Agency, and Border Patrol. Not since the creation of the Department of Defense in 1947 had such a large reorganization in the national security structure taken place at one time. As described by former DHS secretary Michael Chertoff, the four core missions of the new agency were keeping dangerous people out of the country, keeping dangerous materials out of the country, protecting critical infrastructure, and building an agency capable of responding effectively to attacks or disasters.[35]

One advantage of a megadepartment like DHS is its ability to act as a fusion center for intelligence and data that the once-disparate bureaus and agencies contained within in it had in the past failed to share effectively. Customs, the Border Patrol, TSA, INS, and the Coast Guard generate on a daily basis a vast mosaic of who and what is entering the country and who and what is leaving it. As the former head of DHS intelligence has noted, the agency generates a "treasure trove of data" that needs to be reported, collated, and shared if the United States' relatively open borders are to be secured.[36]

To help facilitate the flow of information to and from DHS, the department has placed personnel with other federal and local counterterrorism centers. DHS has also set up liaison relations with the homeland security departments established by the states—at the same time urging the states to create their own fusion centers—so that intelligence from local, state, and federal entities may be collated. Nearly five dozen fusion centers have now been established across the country, with some larger states having more than one.[37]

The other large post-9/11 structural change occurred with the passage of IRTPA in 2004. As noted earlier, George Tenet's 1998 memorandum that the intelligence community should be on a war footing with al Qaeda produced little, if any, reaction. As Director of Central Intelligence, Tenet was head of the intelligence community but commanded few resources outside his role as CIA director. In testimony before Congress, in fact, the then-head of the National Security Agency explained that he took note of Tenet's missive but interpreted it as applying only to CIA staff.[38] Congress, following the recommendations set out by the 9/11 Commission, created the post of director of national intelligence (DNI) to solve this perceived problem.

Whereas the director of the Central Intelligence Agency had in the past also been the nominal head of the U.S. intelligence community, the new "czar" for intelligence would no longer be double-hatted; he would be the head of the intelligence community simply, with new authorities to oversee the community's budget, planning, and personnel as well as several cross-community intelligence centers. To emphasize the DNI's authority over the whole of national intelligence (both foreign and domestic), the budgetary account previously called National Foreign Intelligence Program was renamed the National Intelligence Program to take account of the fact that it now includes the funding stream for both foreign collection and analysis and the FBI's domestic counterintelligence and counterterrorism programs. In addition, the attorney general and FBI director must seek the DNI's concurrence when appointing the head of the bureau's security branch.[39]

Of the centers put under the DNI's immediate direction, the most important was the IRTPA-mandated National Counterterrorism Center (NCTC). The NCTC, housing personnel from across the intelligence community (including the FBI) and cabinet departments (such as Justice, Treasury, Energy, and Transportation), as well as permanent center employees, was established to help fix the pre-9/11 problem whereby terrorist-related information was not shared effectively across the intelligence bureaucracies and disciplines. Staffed by more than five hundred personnel, the center has the statutory task of integrating all terrorist-related information (except that relating exclusively to purely domestic terrorism) from more than two dozen intelligence, military, homeland security, and law enforcement data sources; of continually assessing threats; and of undertaking longer-range analysis. Somewhat uniquely, the center is also responsible for the government's "strategic operational plans" vis-à-vis terrorism, ranging from broad national strategies integrating military, financial, law enforcement, and diplomatic tools available, to more targeted action plans designed to disrupt possible terrorist attacks. In the latter capacity, NCTC's director reports to the president.[40]

Not surprisingly, the FBI has undergone significant changes as well. In the five years after September 11, 2001, with counterterrorism now its top priority, the bureau nearly doubled its number of special agents, assigned a thousand additional special agents to work on counterterrorism, doubled the number of analysts and new translators, and more than tripled personnel assigned to the Joint Terrorism Task Forces (JTTFs).[41]

The FBI also made structural changes and modifications in its chain of command. In particular, in an effort to prevent FBI field offices from drifting from the new national priority given to counterterrorism and focusing once again on more immediate local concerns such as organized crime, the bureau trimmed the field offices' discretionary authority to direct resources and allocate personnel, and gave FBI headquarters in Washington more direct control over field offices' management of counterterrorism programs and investigations. Correspondingly, and following the recommendations of two independent commissions, the Bush administration announced in mid-2005 the creation of a National Security Branch (NSB) within the FBI. Composed principally of the bureau's counterterrorism and counterintelligence units, the NSB was intended to create a more robust domestic intelligence capability, with a bureaucratic culture that would be more attuned to intelligence needs than the bureau, with its historical focus on law enforcement, had been in the past. Those advocating the change hoped NSB would be akin to an in-house MI5, the British domestic intelligence service. At the same time, they argued, keeping the NSB within the bureau would retain the existing synergy between the bureau's national security and law enforcement missions. Reflecting this arrangement, the NSB's chief reports to and receives guidance from the FBI director, the attorney general, and the director of national intelligence.[42]

Prior to the establishment of the National Security Branch, however, the FBI had made changes in the field in response to the attacks of 9/11. Perhaps the most significant of the FBI reforms was the creation of Field Intelligence Groups (FIGs) in 2003. Placed in each of the bureau's fifty-six field offices, the FIGs are "full-service" intelligence cells, with special agents, surveillance specialists, analysts, linguists, and reports officers. The aim is for the FIGs to integrate information from national sources with local intelligence, serve as a conduit for moving investigative information and finished analysis both up and down the national intelligence chain, identify collection gaps, and, generally, be the linchpin in the bureau's effort to integrate more adequately operations and intelligence in the field.[43]

In a similar vein, the bureau has expanded its support for Joint Terrorism Task Forces. Located in the FBI's fifty-six field offices, with another fifty in various U.S. cities, JTTFs are the operationally focused units through which terrorism-related intelligence is passed to local law enforcement officials and locally generated intelligence is passed to the federal level. Led by the FBI and given administrative and policy support by the multiagency National Joint Terrorism Task Force at FBI headquarters and NSB's twenty-four-hour terrorist watch center, the JTTFs primarily conduct field investigations of possible terrorist threats. Modeled after local-federal task forces of the past—which dealt with such hard-target criminal activities as organized crime, drug cartels, etc.—the JTTFs are intended to hone federal-local counterterrorist efforts through enhanced information sharing and better coordination. JTTFs are the federal government's pointy end of the stick when it comes to street-level surveillance, source development, and counterterrorist investigations.[44]

After 9/11, new Attorney General Guidelines were issued governing how the FBI was to conduct its domestic security investigations. The guidelines set out the bureau's responsibilities under existing laws and executive orders and spelled out how its analytical, investigative, and intelligence activities were to be carried out to meet those responsibilities. In general, the changes were designed to give agents more investigative freedom, such as allowing them to attend public events, access information open to the public, or engage in recruiting sources without having a specific intent of detecting or preventing a terrorist activity.

In late 2008, the Bush administration issued, under the auspices of then–attorney general Michael Mukasey, a consolidated set of investigative guidelines; it replaced various separate and overlapping sets of earlier guidelines that had evolved over the years and that reflected the divides between domestic security, criminal, and foreign intelligence investigations. In key respects, the new guidelines simply reflected what had largely become practice as a result of changes in the laws and organizational structures after 9/11. Indeed, the not-so-implicit point in consolidating the guidelines was to address the pre-9/11 problem whereby intelligence and criminal investigations were largely seen as distinct spheres, resulting in a set of bureaucratic norms and rules that restricted and compartmentalized what each could share with the other.[45]

The guidelines also made clear that domestic intelligence collection isn't simply about catching someone breaking a law. Prior to 9/11, the general thrust of guidelines was that the predicate for collecting information would rest on the bureau's having in hand some prior evidence that someone was or might be engaged in criminal activities. But the danger of international terrorism and domestic terrorism alike was simply too grave to risk relying on what had essentially amounted to a reactive collection model. Thus the new guidelines not only emphasized the seamless sharing of information within the bureau and with other relevant law enforcement and intelligence entities; they also, and equally fundamentally, put forward the idea that there might be a need for intelligence collection and analysis that did not have a criminal predicate. Precisely because subversion and terrorism typically involve tight-knit conspiracies, it was understood that leads often come from sources who appear to be law abiding and from surveillance of activities that are in themselves legal. It is not illegal, to take the now-classic examples, to learn to fly a jet; it is not illegal to buy fertilizer or hydrogen peroxide; it is not illegal to travel to and from Pakistan; it is not illegal to buy and use multiple cell phones. Nevertheless, knowledge of each of these activities in context may be precisely the kind of information that the bureau would need in order to head off a terrorist attack.[46]

## Some Concluding Points and Questions

Since the attacks on 9/11, the United States has made significant changes to its counterterrorism regime. But have those changes made the country's ability to counter the terrorist threat appreciably better?

This is not an easy question to answer. In part, this is because we don't actually know everything about the nature of the threat we face. Certainly, the United States doesn't have to contend with the same level of terrorist threat that, for example, Great Britain does at home. At any one time, MI5 and the Special Branches are trying to keep track of literally hundreds of individuals whom they believe are actively engaged in terrorist plots, while having to worry about thousands more who routinely travel back and forth between the United Kingdom and countries that are home to jihadist cells. Nevertheless, the United States remains the primary target for Islamist terrorists. Moreover, answering the question of the effectiveness of the changes made to U.S. counterterrorist policies and practices must be laid against the stringent goal of preventing further catastrophic attacks like those that took place here on September 11, 2001, or in Spain on March 11, 2004. It is possible to make a lot of improvements but still fall short of that goal. Preventing all surprise attacks by a determined foe—be it a terrorist or a state—is a standard not likely to be met if history is any guide. In fine, with all the changes that have been made, we might be safer but not safe.

The goal is further complicated by the nature of the threat itself. A terrorist plot can be the creation of a very small number of individuals, working without much detectable infrastructure and possibly guided and instructed by a leadership cadre that never comes in physical contact with the cell itself. Or, even more problematic, a terrorist may operate on his own, seemingly unconnected to any one plot or group.[47] Add to this the fact that the United States is a continent-size country, is open to doing business with the world, has dozens of major metropolitan areas, and is populated by hundreds of millions of ethnically diverse citizens and resident aliens who move about constantly. It is against this cacophony of legitimate hustle and bustle that we want (indeed, we expect) domestic law enforcement and intelligence agencies to pick up the faint signals of a plot. It is like looking for a needle in a haystack—or, more exactly, scores of haystacks.[48]

The restructuring of the U.S. Intelligence Community to create an intelligence community "czar"—the director of national intelligence—will not in all likelihood help solve this problem. In theory, a strong and effective DNI could focus the intelligence effort so as to avoid the deadly inaction that followed Tenet's 1998 call to war against al Qaeda. But in practice, the establishment of the DNI office—responsible for setting priorities for a dozen or more intelligence agencies, managing a large budget, and running both the national estimate and daily presidential brief processes—has meant a new layer of bureaucracy; and the position of DNI is not likely to make the intelligence community more agile or effective. Aping the General Motors corporate management structure of the '50s and '60s in this day and age seems unlikely to create the intelligence effort we need.[49]

The other major restructuring that took place was the creation of a mega-agency, the Department of Homeland Security. As a rule, a bureaucracy's effectiveness is tied to how limited and focused its core mission is.[50] The broader an agency's authorities and responsibilities, the more likely it will suffer from a diffusion of energy and direction, with a resulting inertia in policies and practices. However, it is still too early to draw conclusions in the case of DHS. Still driven by the specter of 9/11, the DHS has after a rocky start made headway in tightening up transportation and critical infra-structure security. DHS has also been a plus in helping sustain state and local security efforts and a positive force in integrating important data from multiple internal agency sources that otherwise would remain unknown or underutilized.[51] Sustaining this momentum as the attacks of 9/11 recede in the nation's memory will be a significant challenge for future administrations and DHS heads.

The one structural change that seemed to promise a clear improvement in counterterrorism efforts was the creation of the National Counterterrorism Center. Moved out from under the CIA, the NCTC has become an all-source, interagency fusion center—what previous terrorism watch offices and counterterrorism centers aspired to be but couldn't, because of the inability or reluctance to share information across agencies, departments, and disciplines. At least when it comes to terrorist threat information, the center appears to have reduced significantly the bureaucratic hurdles that, before 9/11, precluded the sharing of information among agencies.[52] Nevertheless, as evidenced by the terrorist incident involving Nigerian Umar Farouk Abdulmutallab on Christmas Day 2009, the NCTC still apparently lacks the IT capacity to pool, search, and collate information from its various databases in an automatic or readily accessible fashion. While the institutional "skeleton" is in place, the NCTC's "central nervous system" remains, it seems, relatively rudimentary; hence sorting through the large amounts of incoming data NCTC receives to produce timely, targeted counterterrorist leads will be a somewhat serendipitous process.[53] In addition, there is still apparently the lingering impetus within the NCTC, whose working core comes from agencies principally concerned with foreign intelligence, to focus its attention overseas; this meant in the case of Abdulmutallab that analysts were apparently paying more attention to the threat posed to U.S. interests in Yemen by al Qaeda in the Arabian Peninsula (AQAP) than to signals indicating AQAP might be planning an attack on the U.S. domestically.[54]

Nonetheless, information sharing has increased across the board. The FBI, for example, has reduced the once-high hurdle between law enforcement data and intelligence to a small hop through new laws and internal guidelines. Progress has also been made in the vertical sharing of intelligence, with improvements in the flow from federal to local and state sources and vice versa. The fusion centers and the Joint Terrorism Task Forces have been key here. To be sure, there are concerns about unnecessary duplication of effort, and complaints are still heard about the quality of information shared and the systems in place to share it. But the reality is that there are thousands of local and state police entities of all sizes and at all levels of professionalism, and each faces possible terrorist threats of various sorts.[55] Designing a system that takes account of this variety (while recognizing that terrorist plots in the United States have been generated in major metropolitan areas as well as backwater towns) is an extremely difficult task that probably will never be accomplished to everyone's satisfaction.

Information sharing of course presumes there is information to be shared. Outside of the government's technical collection capability—which probably remains the most useful tool available for tracking terrorist activity—the effort to stay ahead of the terrorists will depend in no small degree on the capabilities of the CIA and the FBI. In the case of the CIA, the issue, despite the vast increase in resources, is whether the agency has created a cadre of operations officers capable of collecting information against targets like al Qaeda. During the Cold War, targets were principally another country's diplomats, military officers, or intelligence officials, since it was they who might have access to an adversary's plans, thoughts, or intelligence needs. And it was the CIA officer—acting as a U.S. diplomat, attaché, or some other embassy official—who had access to these personnel either for the purpose of recruitment or for "handling" once they started to provide intelligence.

Terrorists who exist outside the traditional state-centric system are not readily targetable by traditional CIA recruitment methods and practices, and certainly not by embassy-bound intelligence officers. The agency needs operations officers "with the requisite access and relevant business and technical experience to maneuver in a complex operational world outside the diplomatic cocktail circuit."[56] Although getting access to the innermost circle of a jihadist terrorist group is unlikely, establishing important sources in an outer ring is not impossible. To do so, Langley would likely have to increase substantially the number of its clandestine officers who operate under nonofficial cover (the so-called NOCs). They would need to be ethnically diverse, linguistically proficient, highly paid, and capable of running assets (that is, spies) with ties to Islamist organizations—schools or charities, for example. It is unclear whether the CIA's clandestine service has made that change. According to one long-serving member of the clandestine service, it hasn't. "The 'generalist' case officer still thrives [at the agency]. Former case officers train cadres of new recruits to fit the 'jacks of all trades' mold. Currently this formula remains the path to promotion and success in the clandestine service."[57]

The FBI has faced similar questions about its willingness and ability to transform itself to meet the challenge of preventing terrorist attacks. As noted above, prior to 9/11, there were moves afoot within the bureau to change both its priorities and its operational techniques. But the reality is that this transformational effort never took hold, and the bureau on 9/11 was still by and large a case-based federal investigative agency, where for numerous reasons, HUMINT was not a priority, and FBI field offices were responsible for deciding investigative priorities on a day-to-day basis. The result of all this was a counterterrorism program that lacked direction, resources, and an operational culture designed to head off threats.[58]

Following the attacks on 9/11, the issue was whether the bureau could change or a new entity was needed, designed along the lines of Britain's MI5 or Canada's Security Intelligence Service: a wholly domestic intelligence service, with no law enforcement responsibilities. And the issue remains on the table because of the slow pace of reform initially taken by the FBI. Resources were poured into the bureau to enhance its counterterrorism efforts, but report after report suggested that the FBI ethos remained largely unchanged and that efforts to create a real domestic intelligence service within the bureau were going poorly. Finally, in June 2005, the White House stepped in and ordered the bureau to establish a new national security service, combining the counterterrorism, counterintelligence, and intelligence elements within the FBI into one unit, the National Security Branch, whose special agents and personnel would follow a tailored career path.[59]

Those favoring this step argue that it creates the best of both worlds: a true domestic intelligence organization but one that will have close ties with the law enforcement half of the FBI. And the bureau has established better management, training, and personnel structures within the NSB, which suggest a more serious attempt at reform.[60] If the number of domestic terrorist plots detected by the bureau in the relatively early stages of their planning is indicative, then, it might be that the reform effort is taking hold.

Others, however, doubt the bureau can really change its spots. They point to the tenuous control of the DNI over the NSB's actual activities, the fact that the real reporting chain still goes through the senior management of the FBI and the Department of Justice, and the continuing problems the bureau has apparently had in integrating technology, analysts, and reports officers into a coherent, intelligence-driven counterterrorist program.[61] Indeed, the cases of army major Nidal Hasan, the Fort Hood shooter, and of Umar Farouk Abdulmutallab, the would-be Christmas terrorist, suggest that the FBI's law enforcement mentality still retains something of a hold in its approach to terrorism.

In the first instance, the FBI knew Major Hasan was in email contact with Yemeni-American jihadist cleric Anwar al-Awlaki. But rather than explore how this contact might be exploited to further counterterrorist objectives,[62] the bureau's JTTF review was apparently focused on whether the contact between Hasan and al-Awlaki could be explained as legitimately tied to the major's research on the mind-set of Muslim soldiers. Once the contact was deemed legitimate and not in violation of any law, the matter of Hasan's contact with the known terrorist supporter was apparently dropped. In the case of Abdulmutallab, the FBI followed traditional law-enforcement procedures, including advising him of his Miranda rights. FBI headquarters and the Department of Justice assumed that once Abdulmutallab was in bureau custody, his case would be treated principally as a crime to be prosecuted. In addition, the administration-authorized, FBI-managed terrorist interrogation team (the "High-Value Interrogation Group") had not actually been assembled. This approach suggests a lingering difficulty within the bureau in reconciling its intelligence and law-enforcement functions. To be fair, the approach taken with Abdulmutallab reflected administration policy, as well.[63] Nevertheless, it doesn't appear that the bureau argued for taking a different course.

While much of the focus on collection of intelligence has been directed at national-level entities, such as the FBI, NSA, and CIA, in fact the United States has a virtual million-man army of local and state law-enforcement officials who have a key role to play in keeping the country safe. They have the eyes and ears on the street—and in the jailhouses and prisons where radicalization first occurs and plots are first hatched. And there have been some important local efforts, such as in New York City and in Los Angeles, to develop precisely the kind of capabilities needed on the counterterrorism front.[64] Yet issues of sustainability and professionalism remain in some cities and locales, as do concerns over exactly what privacy and investigative guidelines should govern this street-level police work. None of these issues of course is a showstopper, but if local law-enforcement efforts are seen as overreaching—especially if they result in bad publicity or lawsuits—these local "intelligence" units may be weakened or shut down altogether.[65]

One final development not to be overlooked is the potential impact on domestic security of the Obama administration's decision to foreclose the use of interrogation techniques that go beyond the Army Field Manual in the case of high-value terrorist detainees.[66] Putting aside the (admittedly important) debate over the morality and legality of the CIA's use of "enhanced interrogation techniques" under the Bush administration, there is little question that they led to timely and extremely important intelligence on al Qaeda plots and plans for attacking the United States. Former director of central intelligence George Tenet has said as much: "I know that this program has saved lives. I know we've disrupted plots. I know this program alone is worth more than [what] the FBI, the [CIA], and the National Security Agency put together have been able to tell us."[67] And even though appointed by the very president who has ordered that such techniques no longer be used, current DNI Denis Blair has acknowledged that "high value information came from interrogations in which those methods were used."[68] If it is true, as former CIA director Michael Hayden and Attorney General Michael Mukasey have argued, that "as late as 2006 . . . fully half of the government's knowledge about the structure and activities of Al Qaeda came from those interrogations," then the decision to end them represents perhaps the most significant modification to the U.S. counterterrorist regime since the attacks of 9/11.[69]

In spite of all the questions that can be raised about reforms and changes made to America's counterterrorism regime since 9/11 and the anthrax attacks that followed, the United States has not suffered a significant terrorist incident since 2001, with the exception of the shootings at Fort Hood by army major Hasan in November 2009. This is not for a lack of individuals and groups trying; in some instances it was only dumb luck that spared us from major casualties, as was the case on Christmas day 2009. There have been a number of plotters arrested, and plots and cells disrupted (Richard

Reid, the Lackawana Six, Christopher Paul, Dhiren Barot, the Portland cell, the Virginia Jihad, the Toledo cell, Iyman Faris, Mohammed Jabarah, the California prison plot, Assem Hammoud, Ahmed Omar Abu Ali, Jose Padilla, the JFK Airport plot, the Fort Dix Five, the North Carolina jihadists, and Najibullah Zazi, to list some of the best known in chronological order). As one study noted, from September 11, 2001, to June of 2009, the government filed 119 cases involving Islamist terrorism and charged 289 defendants.[70] And while most cases have been tried in district courts in Virginia's eastern district and New York's southern and eastern districts, cases have arisen in virtually every area of the country, and have involved not only Muslims directed from abroad, but also (in seemingly increased numbers) jihadists of the homegrown stripe.[71] In short, whatever one's final judgment about the ultimate effectiveness of the changes made to the domestic counterterrorism regime, there seems to be little question that America has learned to lean forward—and that the need to do so is still very much a reality.

# 6

# U.S. Counterterrorism in Perspective

*Gary J. Schmitt*

The United States has been at war with Islamist terrorists for more than two decades. With high-profile and devastating attacks in the 1980s and 1990s on American embassies, facilities, and even a U.S. Navy warship, it was understandable that most Americans saw this as a war being waged overseas until the attacks of September 11, 2001. However, this view was not accurate. During the 1990s, the World Trade Center was attacked by a truck bomb (February 1993), and there were subsequent plots to attack major sites around New York City (June 1993) and the Los Angeles International Airport (December 1999). The reason we peg 9/11 as the decisive moment, of course, is that the other plots produced only a few casualties or none at all, whereas some three thousand lost their lives to the attacks on the World Trade Center towers and the Pentagon, and to the hijacking of United Airlines Flight 93.

That the other attacks produced fewer casualties was not for lack of trying. In each case, if the terrorist plans had been ably executed, the number killed and the chaos created would have been significant. In fact, if not for technical miscues in how the bomb was built and placed, it is possible that the first World Trade Center attack would have caused just as many casualties as the hijackings on 9/11.[1]

Nevertheless, 9/11 was clearly the galvanizing event in forcing the U.S. counterterrorist regime to change. In retrospect, the attacks perhaps should not have been a surprise—but they were. The immediate response was not only shock but also the realization of just how little information was on hand to prevent further surprises. Today, terrorism tends to be considered an event of low probability but high consequences. In the immediate days and months that followed the attacks on 9/11, however, that was not how the threat was understood. Lacking any real insight into what al Qaeda was planning to do or could do, and not having in place an effective system for countering the threat itself, the government had to assume that the security problem it faced was one of both high consequence and high likelihood. Combine that assumption with the "needle-in-the-haystack" nature of discovering who might be a terrorist and where he or she might strike next in a country as open and large as the United States, and one can appreciate the urgency with which changes were made to America's counterterrorist posture.

On the home front, this was seen in the rapidity with which the Patriot Act, all three hundred–plus pages of it, was passed by Congress. Less than two months after the attacks on 9/11, the measure was given approval with wide margins in both the House and the Senate.[2] This sense of urgency was also exhibited in how some of the new tools made available by the act were used by the bureaucracy.

Consider specifically the FBI's use of national security letters. NSLs are administrative subpoenas (letters of demand issued by executive branch agencies, most often the FBI) to obtain transactional information from third parties—such as a person's credit record, travel history, or use of the Internet (specifically Web sites visited and email addresses that email was sent to or received from). They do not require judicial sanction on the theory that individuals have less expectation about the privacy of such transactions than, say, about the content of an email or what one actually did on one's vacation. Under pre-9/11 laws, NSLs could be issued in connection with investigations tied to specific espionage and terrorism cases, and where there were "specific and articulable facts" supporting the investigation of a targeted individual. Under the Patriot Act, a broader range of officials could issue letters if the information sought was relevant to an "authorized investigation" to protect against international terrorism or clandestine intelligence activities.[3] NSLs could now be used to collect information to determine if further investigation was warranted; before, they could be employed only after sufficient facts were already in hand to justify a national security investigation of an individual. In short, the Patriot Act made NSLs easier to use by broadening both the justification for their use and who was authorized to issue them.[4]

Given the fact that the FBI had been blamed, at least in part, for the failure to prevent the attacks on 9/11, it was predictable that the bureau would use this new authority to its maximum. In 2000, eighty-five hundred NSL requests were issued. By 2004, the annual number of NSL requests was over fifty-six thousand, and it was just short of fifty thousand in the following two years. But this number would continue to decrease as subsequent internal reviews revealed that the letters were being requested and used improperly, and as the Patriot Act provision was itself scrutinized. FBI personnel had, for example, failed to connect requests with authorized investigations; they retained data beyond what was requested; and they sometimes claimed "exigent" circumstances in issuing letters and then failed to back up that claim with relevant paperwork and information.[5] Not surprisingly, Congress, the courts, and internal FBI and Justice Department auditors all weighed in to create more rigor and oversight in how this investigative tool is used.[6] By 2008, the number of NSLs issued had fallen to less than twenty-five thousand.[7]

This sense of urgency in response to 9/11 was also exhibited in President Bush's decision to engage in warrantless electronic surveillance.[8] Believing that the Foreign Intelligence Surveillance Act of 1978 was dramatically out of date, that continuing to adhere to it put the country at risk, and that the president had an inherent constitutional authority to conduct warrantless surveillance in times of war, the White House moved to a system that sought to answer this core question: to whom is al Qaeda talking? But as they did in the case of NSLs, both the court and Congress began to peel back this discretion, and new legislation eventually devised a new electronic surveillance regime that all three branches of government appear able to live with.

To better understand America's response to 9/11, however, we need to put it in perspective—to compare it both to the response by earlier presidents to earlier crises, and to the response by European governments to the same terrorist threat as that the United States now faces.

## The Energetic Executive

The fact that the president (and the bureaucracy that answered to him) would push as they did following the attacks of 9/11 should not be a surprise. In many respects, the history of the presidency—or, more specifically, the history of the presidency that we best remember—is of chief executives taking action during times of crisis, especially national security crises.[9] Indeed, it is arguably what one would expect from an office designed, as the Framers said, to act with decision and dispatch.[10]

A decade (1776–87) of unstable state governments and ineffective governance at the federal level led many in the founding generation to rethink their initial bias against an independent and energetic chief executive. Under the Articles of Confederation, for example, Congress exercised a variety of powers, some legislative and others concerned with directing the new republic's foreign and defense affairs. It was these latter concerns— which Congress consistently and explicitly described as being "executive" in nature—that in fact took a considerable bulk of the members' time. They repeatedly found the lack of an independent, single executive to be debilitating. Negotiations with foreign powers were needlessly prolonged and muddled, decisions were poorly executed, the war effort was complicated by the constant meddling of Congress, and keeping secrets proved difficult. As a result, by the time the Constitutional Convention met in the spring of 1787, a priority was to establish an executive that could, in the words of *Federalist* 70, act with "decision, activity, secrecy, and dispatch." Unlike the Articles of Confederation, which had collapsed legislative and executive powers into a single body (Congress), the new constitutional system, based on the separation of powers, was intended primarily not to check executive power but actually to free it up.[11]

Of course, for a number of years, especially after the War of 1812, when the country's attention had largely turned to domestic affairs and the settlement of lands to the west, there was far less need to draw on the unique capacities of the president. As a result, the casual observer of the time saw the office as one of little import. Yet as Alexis de Tocqueville, perhaps the most discerning analyst of the American regime, noted at the time he visited the United States in 1830:

> If the executive power is less strong in America than in France, one must attribute the cause of it perhaps more to circumstances than laws. It is principally in relations with foreigners that the executive power of a nation finds occasion to deploy its skill and force. If the life of the Union were constantly threatened, if its

great interests were mixed every day with those of other powerful peoples, one would see the executive power grow larger in
opinion, through what one would expect from it and what it
would execute.[12]

Tocqueville concluded by noting that "the president of the United States
possesses almost royal prerogatives, which he has no occasion to make use
of, and the rights which, up to now, he can use are very circumscribed: *the
laws permit him to be strong, circumstances have made him weak.*"[13] For
Tocqueville, then, the Whiggish view of the presidency as weak is mislead-
ing. To the contrary, the president's authorities are inherently substantial—
needing only the right conditions to be drawn out and exercised. And there
are plenty of examples of presidents responding to crises of one sort of
another that put President Bush's own decisions in perspective.

First and foremost is the example of Abraham Lincoln during the country's greatest crisis, the American Civil War. Lincoln, on his own authority
and guided by his presidential oath "to preserve, protect and defend the
Constitution," spent monies never appropriated by Congress, created military commissions to try civilians, issued the Emancipation Proclamation,
suspended the writ of habeas corpus, and openly defied the Supreme Court
(by refusing to abide by Chief Justice Roger Taney's order to uphold the
habeas corpus writ in the case of Marylander and Southern sympathizer
John Merryman).[14]

During World War I, Woodrow Wilson made no attempt to suspend the
writ of habeas corpus, but he did create a national censorship board and
authorized on his own executive authority the surveillance of phones, cable
traffic, and the mail. He also oversaw an aggressive enforcement of the Espionage Act of 1917—a law which made it a crime to say or write anything
that might be judged to undermine the war effort. Although the war lasted
for the United States a little longer than a year and half, more than two
thousand people were prosecuted domestically under the act. Wilson's
administration also sanctioned the use of an army of more than two hundred thousand volunteers, the American Protective League, which
"assisted" the government in surveillance and investigations of individuals
(often just neighbors) they suspected of domestic subversion. Following the
war, a series of terrorist bombings, combined with fear of communist and

anarchist subversion, led the Wilson administration to conduct large-scale roundups (the Palmer Raids) of suspected radicals, mostly aliens. Thousands were arrested, many were held for months, and several hundred were eventually deported.[15]

Later, the prospect of general war and the attack on Pearl Harbor led Franklin Delano Roosevelt to an equally aggressive posture in protecting the home front. Where "the defense of the nation" was involved, FDR authorized the attorney general to ignore both the 1934 Communications Act and the Supreme Court's decision in *United States v. Nardone II* (1939) prohibiting government wiretaps. In addition, Roosevelt by presidential order alone expanded the FBI and military intelligence's writ to conduct domestic intelligence and countersubversive investigations. And once war broke out, he approved the suspension of the writ of habeas corpus throughout Hawaii and interned over a hundred thousand Japanese immigrants and Japanese-American citizens in "war relocation camps."[16]

One doesn't have to agree with all these decisions, of course, to understand that presidents worried about a direct threat to American liberties and safety will take maximum advantage of the authority they believe is vested by the Constitution in the presidency. In this respect, President Bush was hardly any different from the majority of presidents who occupied the office before him and also faced serious domestic security problems.[17]

### The European Experience

By virtually any yardstick, France has had the most effective domestic counterterrorist regime of all of America's allies.[18] Of course, it hasn't always been that way. For a number of years, France faced a significant terrorist problem at home. But by the mid-1980s the French public had had enough, and the government began to put in place the laws and institutions that, since the mid-1990s, have kept France from suffering a major terrorist incident at home.

To become this counterterrorist powerhouse, however, France took steps that make the measures taken by the United States since 9/11 seem mild. For example, France's investigative magistrates (*juges d'instruction*)—the cornerstone of the French counterterrorist system—combine the powers of intelligence, investigation, prevention, and deterrence in one person. The office runs roughshod over any American concept of separation of powers in its mingling of executive, prosecutorial, and judicial functions. There are some judicial checks, but they appear to be minimal. The only American office that bears even a slight resemblance to the *juges d'instruction* is that of the independent counsels. But unlike an independent counsel, whose mandate is tied to a particular case and is a temporary appointment, *juges d'instruction* often stay in their position for more than a decade. Jean-Louis Bruguière, France's most famous *juge,* stayed on the counterterrorism beat for over a quarter of a century.

Nor have French magistrates been shy about using their powers of arrest and detention preemptively to disrupt possible terrorist plots. Suspects can be sequestered for days, without access to lawyers. Once charged, they can be held without bail or even being brought to trial for several years. And, once in court, they are tried sans jury.

Finally, the French seem tolerant of a system that is relatively intrusive. As privacy advocates point out, the French government has considerable leeway in retaining all kinds of data and giving agencies within the French security and police services access to these data. Moreover, French police and security services are also aggressive in monitoring speech, especially sermons and literature coming from Salafist mosques—with the result that dozens of Islamic fundamentalists in France, including imams, have been sent packing since 9/11.[19] Nor is the criterion for the government to engage in electronic surveillance especially onerous; and independent oversight of the government's practice is minimal. As with most French investigative methods, the criterion is pretty straightforward: is the investigative tool thought to be reasonably necessary to gather information in furtherance of national security? A specific criminal predicate for surveillance is not required.

While the French appear to be on top of the Islamist terrorist threat at home, the British acknowledge they are playing catch-up. Hoping in part that a relaxed approach to Islamist asylum seekers would keep the United Kingdom from being a target, England became home to some of the most virulent anti-Western imams and mosques anywhere in the world. By 2003, British police and security officials were seeing citizens who, having been trained and recruited as terrorists, were willing to carry out attacks against

Israel and the United States. By 2004, they began to see signs that British citizens were traveling abroad to receive training, coming home, creating cells, and then plotting to strike Britain itself. The terrorist attack on London's transport system on July 7, 2005, confirmed the government's worst fears—the United Kingdom was not immune from attacks; even worse, the number of potential jihadist terrorists operating in the United Kingdom numbered in the hundreds, with hundreds more moving in and out of those circles.[20]

Of course, the United Kingdom is no stranger to the threat of terrorism—having had to deal with the problem of Irish-inspired plots off and on for more than a century. But what makes the current threat different, as others have pointed out, is that the Irish operated in a tightly structured network, worked to avoid capture, and had an agenda that, while broad, was nevertheless potentially negotiable. None of this holds true in the case of Islamist terrorists. Add the fact that thousands upon thousands of British citizens of Pakistani descent travel back and forth to Pakistan each year, where some small but dangerous percentage comes in contact with radical elements and schools, and one begins to understand just how large a problem Britain's police and security forces have on their hands.

The capacities the British government brings to bear on the threat are significant and, like those of the French, put America's own counterterrorist efforts in perspective. To start, the British cop on the beat is unconstrained by Fourth Amendment jurisprudence, and for counterterrorist purposes has been authorized "to stop and search" vehicles and persons without a specific suspicion.[21] Moreover, the British acknowledge openly that such stops will fall more heavily on ethnic minorities. As one senior British constable put it, "We should not waste time searching old white ladies. [Searches are] going to be disproportionate. It is going to be young men, not exclusively, but it may be disproportionate to ethnic groups."[22] Rights groups have also taken notice of the British government's pervasive use of closed-circuit television cameras to monitor public spaces, its creation of the world's largest national DNA database, and the easy sharing of records and intelligence collected by the police and security services. Telephone taps and electronic surveillance are easier to authorize in Britain than in the United States; under the British system, numerous senior police officials may apply for warrants, which do not need to be approved by the judiciary but are issued by the state secretary after being judged both "proportionate" (that is, only as intrusive as the circumstances require) and "necessary" to meet "the interests of national security."[23] All of which has led Privacy International to give the United Kingdom the lowest score among the world's major democracies in its privacy-ranking system.[24]

The British government has also been aggressive in prohibiting provocative speech. The 2006 Terrorism Act made it a criminal offense to encourage or glorify terrorism—it required Internet providers to remove any materials that did the same—or to disseminate terrorist publications publicly or privately.[25] In scope, it is not altogether different from the French law prohibiting speech or the use of various media that incite or condone terrorism. And like the French, the British have instituted a system of detentions. In the case of the United Kingdom, a terrorist suspect can be held in jail, with the court's approval, for up to twenty-eight days before being charged. And, even more controversial, under the Prevention of Terrorism Act 2005, individuals suspected of involvement in terrorist activity who cannot be tried or repatriated may be subjected by the home secretary to "control orders" that put them in a state of virtual house arrest.[26] This provision applies to citizens and noncitizens alike. Although limited in practice to around a dozen or so individuals at any given time, and now facing increased judicial scrutiny,[27] the control-order regime is analogous to the ambiguous state of detention facing individuals at Guantánamo.[28]

While for strategic, political, and historical reasons, neither Madrid nor Berlin has been as forward-looking as London or Paris in changing laws or counterterrorism practices, they have not entirely avoided adopting harder-edged measures. Again, this should hardly be a surprise. Both countries have had to deal with serious domestic terrorism problems in the past, and their police and security agencies still draw on that experience to help manage the current threat from the jihadists.

In Germany, for example, "a computer-aided search of the type that had proven successful in profiling and eventually dismantling the Red Army Faction in the 1990s" was used after 9/11 to expose "a number of radical Islamic 'sleepers.'"[29] According to Manfred Klink, who headed the post 9/11 review in Germany, German authorities "reactivated the *Rasterfahndung*"—a system designed to connect the dots between individuals with similar backgrounds—and applied it to the new situation.[30] As a RAND study notes, "despite the prominence of data protection as a national issue, Germany has historically relied on data processing, data mining, and the use of profiling to identify potential terrorists or their support elements."[31] Similarly, since the 1990s, the German foreign intelligence service has been able to collect "strategic intelligence" without a warrant; the service can collect international communication traffic, sifting through it with keyword searches and grid analysis, with no specific suspect person or target in mind. While the German constitutional court in 1999 found parts of the law allowing this broad surveillance unconstitutional, its finding focused on how and when the data could be passed on to other elements within the German government, not on its actual collection.[32]

For Madrid, of course, the fight against ETA, the Basque terrorist organization, produced laws and policies that are still employed today. Under Spain's Code of Criminal Procedure, for instance, terrorist suspects can be held incommunicado (in isolated detention) for up to thirteen days. And an individual charged with a terrorist-related crime can be held in pre-trial detention for up to four years. While being held incommunicado, the detainees do not have right to their own counsel. Court-appointed attorneys are provided, but suspects are not allowed to consult with them in private and, in turn, the attorneys are not allowed to address suspects directly or provide legal advice. Further, an examining magistrate can impose a total restriction on the availability of information (*secreto de sumario*) about the investigation, the initial judicial proceedings, and the specific information justifying an individual's detention, with that restriction applying to the defense lawyers until virtually the start of a trial.[33]

### Comparing and Contrasting

A particular country's approach to meeting the terrorist threat at home, of course, cannot be isolated from that country's geostrategic approach more generally.

The United States has considered itself at war with al Qaeda. And it has been: eliminating the regime in Afghanistan supporting al Qaeda, continuing to strike at its leadership in Pakistan, and attacking its various allied elements in places as dispersed as the Philippines, Indonesia, and the Horn of Africa. The United States has taken this approach in part because the threat comes from abroad, but also in part because it has the military capability to take this fight to the terrorists. Having such a capability gives Washington options other governments simply do not have. For all the talk about the sea change in American domestic security arrangements since the attacks of 9/11, the reality is that laws and guidelines have been changed far more modestly than in previous times when the country has been at war. Taking the fight to al Qaeda is a luxury that U.S. policymakers have and that, in turn, has kept the balance between safety and liberty at home within reasonable bounds.

It is often said that the United States has treated Islamic terrorism since 9/11 under the paradigm of war, while Europe remains committed to dealing with it as a crime.[34] And there is little doubt that the most contentious issues dividing America and Europe in these matters—the status of detainees as "illegal combatants," Guantánamo, interrogations, and the application of the Geneva Accords to detainees—stem largely from that distinction.[35] Nevertheless, the broad brush of "war versus crime" probably confuses as much as it helps explain the real differences (and similarities) between the United States and Europe. First, as Benjamin Wittes and others have pointed out, while the Clinton administration dealt with terrorism mainly through the criminal justice system, some elements of its policy even then implied the country was on something approaching a war footing. How else to explain the use of renditions (capturing terrorist suspects abroad and sending them to third countries for interrogation) and the White House approval of targeted assassinations?[36] Conversely, after 9/11, the United States did not abandon the use of the criminal justice system to address terrorist threats. There have been numerous trials (and convictions) of terrorists here. The United States, under the Obama administration, retains both policy paradigms.

As for the countries of Europe, while it is certainly true that they address the problem of terrorism principally through law and law enforcement, it is also the case that each of the countries examined in this volume has military forces involved in Afghanistan, and, equally important, that the laws they rely on to combat terrorism domestically are often more hard-hitting than those tied to more typical crimes. It would be a mistake to conclude that because "Europe approaches the problem of terrorism in the context of crime, not war,"[37] it treats counterterrorism as just another crime. The

French, for example, make much of the fact that, unlike the United States, they reacted to the attacks on 9/11 with equanimity. However, this ignores the revolution in law and institutions that France had adopted when faced with terrorists attacks on its streets in the 1980s and 1990s. Although the United Kingdom, France, Germany, and Spain are not in a position to make preemptive military action a central element in their country's counterterrorism policy, for each government, the preferred policy is preemption. The tools and rhetoric may differ, but the principal goal is the same: stop terrorist attacks before they can occur.

To this end, the United Kingdom has adopted a number of measures designed to get out in front of the terrorist threat, which it recognizes is substantial. According to senior security officials, British intelligence and police are, at any given time, attempting to keep track of hundreds suspected of terrorist-related planning and activities.[38] And this, they admit, may well be just the tip of the iceberg; for example, those involved in the July 2005 bombings were not on any of the security or police primary-watch lists.[39]

From 2001 to March 2008, UK police have made nearly 1,500 terrorism-related arrests (with approximately two out of three suspects eventually released). Of the remaining third that have been charged with some crime, 340 (or a little over 20 percent of the total number arrested) were charged with a specific, terrorism-related offense. The conviction rate since September 2001 for those actually charged in terrorism-related cases has been around 60 percent, which includes convictions both under specific terrorism laws and under other legislation.[40] Since the bombings in 2005, more than seven hundred have been arrested.[41] These numbers should be set against the fact that there were only three (failed) attacks carried out during that same period: in June 2007, two car bombs failed to explode in central London; the next day, a vehicle loaded with gas cylinders failed to explode at Glasgow's international airport; and in May 2008, a bomb prematurely went off in an Exeter shopping mall, injuring only the terrorist himself. When the number of arrests is compared with the actual number of attacks, it is clear that British authorities are determined to preempt Islamist-inspired terrorism.

In the past, when the British were dealing with the IRA, waiting until an attack was about to unfold was more feasible: the security service was increasingly able to penetrate the IRA's operational cells, the cells did not operate as independent suicide bombers, and they often issued warnings before the bombs they had planted exploded. Waiting today is seen as too risky. In this sense, despite the differences between France's and Britain's counterterrorist efforts, London's view of Islamist terrorism is now similar to that held in Paris.[42]

Accordingly, the French story is similar to the British when it comes to arrests and successful attacks. From 2006 through 2008, French authorities arrested 308 Islamist terrorist suspects, but France did not experience an attack—successful or failed. During this period Spain, too, made many arrests of suspected jihadists (160) but suffered no attacks.[43] As a Europol report makes clear, the arrests made in both countries "were related to attack planning activities."[44]

In the case of Germany, admittedly, the situation is different. The German government arrested only twenty-two Islamist terrorist suspects over the same three-year period.[45] This low number notwithstanding, the government believes that it has a serious problem on its hands. For example, in the 2009 report of the Federal Office for the Protection of the Constitution, the government took special note of the "considerable Islamist potential" within the country. German authorities believe there are some thirty-three thousand Muslims in Germany—about 1 percent of the country's total Muslim population—who have ties to one Islamist organization or another.[46] In addition to the overt threats from al Qaeda and related organizations for Germany's participation in the NATO mission in Afghanistan, the report also took note of the increasing number of German Muslims who had traveled to the border region between Pakistan and Afghanistan.[47] In the words of former interior minister Wolfgang Schäuble: Germany is increasingly in the "crosshairs of Islamist terrorism."[48]

Of course, Germany (like France, the United Kingdom, and Spain) is especially worried about attacks that could cause mass casualties: the September 2007 arrest of three young men—a Turkish national and two Germans—is a reminder that such attacks are not out of the question for Germany, as well. If the plotters had been able to carry out their planned coordinated attacks, the explosive effect would have been greater than that seen in the Madrid train attacks in 2004, where nearly two hundred were killed and nearly two thousand injured.[49] And, indeed, the increase in jihadist Internet propaganda aimed at Germany (and written in German) is almost certainly designed to put pressure on the German government to withdraw its military from the NATO mission in Afghanistan. The hope no doubt is to repeat with Germany the jihadist success in Spain, where a newly elected government pulled its troops from Iraq after the Madrid bombings. As one German official noted, "Islamists aim to attack what they see as the weakest link in the chain."[50]

In the face of the changing threat, successive German governments have tried to expand the reach of the law and its tools. To start, following the attacks on 9/11, German authorities engaged in a large-scale profiling operation—*Rasterfahndung*—to generate leads on possible, still-extant terrorist cells using a set of personal characteristics derived from individuals who had been involved in the attacks or had been members of the so-called "Hamburg cell," to which Mohammed Atta belonged.[51] In addition, Germany attempted to close some major loopholes in its approach to Islamic terrorism following the attacks of 9/11, when it came to light that three of the hijackers had lived and conspired in Hamburg for several years prior to the attack. In particular, the immunity of religious groups and charities from investigations was revoked, and membership in foreign terrorist organizations was criminalized. Shortly thereafter, the government banned several Islamic organizations, began proceedings against some twenty religious groups, and conducted more than two hundred raids—which included raids on nearly six dozen mosques.[52] More recently, the German parliament enacted two new measures: the first (passed in December 2008) makes it a crime to furnish texts (by hard copy or the Internet) which either serve as textbooks for terrorist planning or are intended to incite others to commit terrorist acts, while the second (passed in May 2009) gives the federal police new physical and electronic surveillance powers.[53]

Even more far-reaching was the government's attempt to address the problem posed by the expanding number of Germans who had "visited" terrorist camps and returned home. In this instance, the German government attempted to craft a law which would have made receiving training in a camp a crime in and of itself, with the implicit goal of getting ahead of any operational planning for a terrorist attack that might follow those stays. Ultimately, as the chapter on Germany in this volume notes, the bill was amended to require that prosecutors also prove a suspect has the "intent" to commit a terrorist crime; the change waters down the preemptive capacity of the new law by forcing the government in effect to also show specific planning activities. In short, although Germany has edged more and more closely to the preemptive models employed by other European nations, features of the German constitution, rulings by the German constitutional court, and German domestic politics have so far kept it from taking more forward-leaning measures. Whether those impediments would remain should Germans suffer a serious terrorist attack at home is a question that has yet to be answered. But if Germany's past reaction to the Red Army Faction is any guide, the answer is probably "no."[54]

Finally, there is no question that the democratic states on both sides of the Atlantic have expanded their criminal codes or the application of existing laws in a fashion that attempts to address the terrorist threat before that threat is actualized. In short, no one is waiting for a bomb to go off. For example, new laws on "material support" for terrorism (which can cover a broad range of activities, such as incitement, possession of bomb-making "cookbooks," funding, training, advising, reconnoitering targets, providing lodging, engaging in identity theft) are intended to give governments the capacity to investigate potential conspiracies much earlier than before and allow them to look at a broader range of suspects. Of course, laws that more broadly define terrorist-related crimes also make it easier for government investigators to justify surveillance, raids, and even arrests. In no small number of cases, this has led not to actual prosecutions for terrorism but to charges of easier-to-prove crimes (such as the illegal possession of weapons or credit card fraud), or it has allowed the government to deport individuals under immigration laws that require a lesser evidentiary burden than a major felony would. All of which has the effect of enabling governments under the color of law to get an earlier jump on terrorist-related activities.

How this strategy plays out in terms of actual convictions will vary of course from country to country. Given the potential lethality of the Islamic threat the British face at home and the size of that threat—with more than 2,000 suspects to follow and more than two dozen active plots at any given time to track—it's no surprise that the United Kingdom has made nearly 1,500 terrorist-related arrests between 9/11 and early 2008. It's also no surprise, given the concern with preempting attacks, that many of these arrests have occurred earlier than prosecutors would theoretically like and before a completely convincing evidentiary base for a prosecution has been firmly established. As a result, more than half of those arrested in the United Kingdom are not charged with a crime, and less than a quarter are finally charged with a specific terror-related offense. Of those charged with an offense of one sort or another, a little over four out of ten are acquitted at trial, although the new antiterrorism laws have tended to raise the rate of convictions over the past few years.[55] Such release and acquittal rates appear tolerable to the British to the degree they judge terrorist plots are being disrupted.

Comparing those figures with those in the United States is difficult because of the differences in the prosecutorial system. By and large, arrests are not made in the United States until there is sufficient evidence for an indictment and accompanying detention. In contrast, in the United Kingdom, pressure to prevent attacks, combined with the authority to arrest and detain a suspect before charges are brought, may result in police making arrests earlier than they would otherwise and then using the extended detention period to build (they hope) a more conclusive body of evidence with which to go to trial.[56] Further complicating prosecutions in Britain are the facts that post-charge questioning of an individual is allowed only in limited circumstances, plea bargaining is not formally permitted, and prosecutors are generally prohibited from using intelligence gained from wiretaps and electronic surveillance.[57] These differences probably help account for the difference between the rate of arrests to convictions in the United Kingdom and in the United States.

Although there are differences in how cases are counted,[58] different studies appear to confirm that 80 to 90 percent of terrorist-related prosecutions in the United States since 9/11 have been successful.[59] However, according to one study, of the nearly seven hundred individual terror-related indictments undertaken by the U.S. government between September 2001 and September 2008, slightly more than two out of three were ultimately tried on grounds other than specific terror-related offenses. And where cases were successfully prosecuted as terrorism cases, more than seven of ten convictions were based on violations of the "material support" statutes, while only one of ten successful prosecutions was tied to cases where individuals were found guilty of either committing an actual act of terror or conspiring to do so.[60] The material support laws have become "a pillar of the government's post-9/11 strategy of preventive prosecutions."[61]

As Robert Chesney has pointed out in his study of terrorism cases, the Bush administration, having established prevention as its highest priority, pursued that goal "not only through its intelligence-gathering powers but also [through] its prosecutorial capacities," which involved "at least three tiers of targeted and untargeted methods." Tier one, the "most traditional," was "prosecution for inchoate or completed crimes of violence." A second tier involved more "diffused" prevention methods, such as enforcing laws "relating to activities that may be integral to the preparatory and logistical stages of terrorist attack," including "various illegal but relatively innocuous precursor activities such as immigration fraud, identity fraud, and money laundering." A third tier was preventive in character: where the government suspected that someone had ties to terrorism but lacked evidence to try him on terrorism or terrorism-related charges, charges were brought on wholly different grounds than terrorism with the intention to take potentially dangerous individuals off the street.[62] Examined in totality, the United States, like France in particular, is using its criminal-law process not simply to investigate and punish terrorist acts that have already occurred, but to anticipate their occurrence.

## Conclusion

Drawing significant lessons for the United States from how Germany, France, the United Kingdom, and Spain have addressed the terrorist threat domestically is a complicated task. The underlying variations between the five countries are substantial. First, there is the fact that the United States and the United Kingdom have common-law systems, while France, Germany, and Spain are civil-law regimes. The different systems influence how laws are made, how flexible they are likely to be, how cases are tried, and what role judges play. For example, German judges are given far greater leeway in allowing hearsay into evidence—no small matter in trying terrorist conspiracies.[63] Yet even the two common-law countries, the United States and the United Kingdom, are different, in part because the former has a Bill of Rights and the latter does not. Under current First Amendment jurisprudence, for example, Britain's ban on glorifying terrorism or speaking on behalf of terrorist organizations would likely fail constitutional scrutiny here.[64] In addition, as has been pointed out already, the two countries rely on different rules of evidence and have different procedures for issuing warrants and trying cases in court.

There is also the matter that only the United States is governed under a system whose underlying constitutional principle is separation of powers. The fact that Germany, the United Kingdom, Spain, and France are parliamentary systems, or a mix of parliamentary and presidential, affects not only the discretion allotted the government but also political decisions about the balancing of security and civil liberties, including the level of oversight exercised by the legislature, the courts, and within the executive itself.. Each of the five countries also differs in the degree to which authority is centralized, with the United States and Germany retaining strong federal structures. And, finally, there is the fact that Spain, France, the United Kingdom, and Germany are members of the European Union, a constitutional body that has increasingly weighed in on counterterrorism policies and on how member states have balanced counterterrorism measures with guaranteed liberties.[65]

Equally important is the scale of the domestic jihadist threat each country faces. Although the United States has had its recent share of "home grown" jihadists, the Muslim population in the United States is a significantly smaller percentage of the total population than found in the United Kingdom, Germany, or France and, according to polls, is "highly assimilated" and less prone to radicalization than in many European states.[66] And finally, there is the matter of history, with each country having different experiences with terrorism and internal subversion, and two countries with memories of having lived under a dictatorship. These unique histories have undoubtedly shaped institutional arrangements, intelligence capacities, and police powers.[67]

Take, for example, the question of whether the United States should create a distinct national security court to handle terrorism-related cases. Both France and Spain have established centralized counterterrorism courts. They did so to better protect the officials involved in trying those cases and to create, over time, an expertise among the prosecutors and judges handling these oftentimes difficult trials. Both goals, of course, are worth pursuing in the United States as well. But the principal drivers in the American debate for creating such a court are the need to supervise and legitimize the long-term detention decisions for captured Taliban and al Qaeda fighters and, possibly, the desire to create a trial system for captured terrorists that would have less burdensome standards for evidence and conviction than those imposed by normal Article III courts. These are not issues Spain and France necessarily face, and the possible utility of a national security court must therefore be debated on its own merit in the United States; it is not simply a lesson learned from the Spanish or French experience.[68]

Similarly, there is the issue of whether, like France, Germany, and Britain, the United States should establish a truly distinct domestic security service.[69] Should we take the counterintelligence, counterterrorism, and countersubversion elements within the FBI, separate them from the bureau's law enforcement functions, and create a new agency altogether? Certainly, among the leading democracies, the United States appears to be the odd man out in lacking a domestic intelligence service that can focus on gathering preventive intelligence and has no law enforcement authorities. There is a degree of focused professionalism that results from an agency's having a singular task rather than multiple ones; and intelligence collecting is perhaps more safely undertaken by an agency that does not have an arrest authority. On the other hand, American civil libertarians of both the left and the right have long worried that a separate domestic intelligence service would be more likely to abuse its powers than one tied to a law enforcement agency which operates under the general supervision of the Justice Department and which ultimately has to present its evidence in a court of law.[70] Moreover, if a key fault line prior to 9/11 was the division between the realms of intelligence and law enforcement, and if the passing of information between the two has been a problem, there is an argument to be made that it is operationally useful to have those two functions under one roof.

Nor are the examples of the benefits of a separate domestic intelligence agency so clear. For instance, although French domestic intelligence seems to have been highly successful in recent years in tackling jihadist-sponsored terrorism, that was hardly the case in the past; and certainly the record of the other countries' internal intelligence services has been mixed as well. And, indeed, on the information-sharing front, all have been accused at one time or another of not cooperating fully with colleagues in the law enforcement community. In the case of France's DST and Britain's MI5, a change in resources, policies, and laws probably contributed to their improved record as much as their status as distinct intelligence services did.

As I and my former AEI colleague, Reuel Gerecht, have written else-where, France is Europe's counterterrorist powerhouse. Yet "it is unclear what practical lessons Americans can draw from the French encounter with Islamic terrorism, given the two countries' different histories of interaction with the Muslim world and the significant differences between the two when it comes to legal systems and the domestic purview of the state." French authorities have a unique capacity to focus the combined resources of the state quickly and under a single guiding hand—a facility that "the messier U.S. system of separated powers, judicial independence, and pre-sumptive rights held by individuals against the government" could not possibly duplicate.[71]

All of which leads one to conclude that the "lessons learned" from com-paring the counterterrorism practices of these democracies are less about simply adopting this or that practice, law, or institution than they are about recognizing the underlying fundamental issues or questions each system has had to deal with to be effective. Virtually everyone is working to solve simi-lar problems—how best to share information between intelligence agencies and law enforcement authorities; how best to develop and integrate HUMINT into targeted investigations; how best to keep up with the jihadists' use of modern technology, like the Internet; how best to track ter-rorist financing to choke off resources before serious plotting can begin; and how long an interrogation period to allow police before formal charges are brought. How these problems are solved will be determined by the level and nature of the threat, and by the history, governing framework, and institu-tional capabilities of each country.

That said, it would be wrong to conclude that a comparison of domes-tic counterterrorist regimes across democracies has no practical value. But the value mostly lies in gaining a broader perspective on America's own struggle to deal with the threat from Islamist-inspired terrorism. As the country studies in this volume show, there will always be a trade-off of sorts between the scope of citizen liberties and the powers a state needs to fight certain threats. Yet it is a paramount duty of any liberal democracy not only to protect the rights associated with a decent political order but also to protect the lives of its citizens. Exercising power in the name of secu-rity, therefore, is not necessarily illiberal. And doing so in the face of the unique threat posed by al Qaeda and its allies has required democracies to establish capacities that are generally designed to preempt attacks, not react to them. Although there are differences in how individual countries have sought to meet that strategic goal, it underlies virtually every new law, institution, or (in the case of the United States) military campaign that has been set in place.

Finally, the most valuable lesson to be learned from the comparison of democratic counterterrorist regimes is this: for all the legitimate debate in the United States about whether certain changes in our laws or institutions are necessary to deal with our Islamist enemies, it is clear that the United States is generally no more aggressive in pursing domestic counterterrorism than a number of other democratic allies—and indeed, may arguably be considered less aggressive than either France or the United Kingdom. Yet no objective observer would classify either France or the United Kingdom as anything but free and liberal.[72]

Nor has America's reaction to the attacks on 9/11 produced, as one bestselling author suggests, an unprecedented "war against American ideals," a wholesale attempt to subvert the constitutional order.[73] Indeed, when one examines the various criticisms made about the "war on terror," it is striking how few have to do with the changes made to the American domestic counterterrorism regime. Most concern issues such as rendition, interrogation techniques, Guantánamo, and the like. These are all serious matters, to be sure, but none has an impact on the exercise of American civil liberties directly.

Other issues—such as warrantless wiretapping, data mining, and watch lists—of course could. And there is little question that there were abuses and mistakes made in issuing requests for information with national security letters and using the "material witness" statute in the immediate aftermath of 9/11.[74] Data mining and data sharing on the scale required to find the terrorist "needle in the haystack" can undoubtedly lead to overreaching and bureaucratic stumbling. No one who has worked in government would think otherwise. On the other hand, the introduction of expanded reporting requirements to Congress and the courts, coupled with a system of executive branch inspectors general, civil liberty boards, freedom of information requests, and an aggressive press, makes the likelihood that real abuses will go undetected for any length of time quite small.[75] The American system of separated powers and checks and balances has worked fairly well in allowing the executive to act expeditiously and decisively to meet the threat, and the other branches and institutions to modify and moderate as they deem necessary.

The fact is, the war on terror has produced, and appropriately so, far fewer violations of, and challenges to, individual freedoms than a number of past major U.S. military conflicts. And certainly American Muslims face nowhere the discrimination—either official or private—faced by German-Americans during World War I or Japanese-Americans during World War II. In short, to make an obvious but important point: when it comes to core American liberties (political, press, religion, association, etc.) and practices (dissent, voting, travel, etc.), nothing has really changed here at home. If it is true, as the Obama administration's *Quadrennial Homeland Security Review* states, that "homeland security is as much about protecting the American way of life as it is about protecting this country from future attacks," then what has been put in place domestically to deal with Islamist terrorism has been a success.[76] As far as security and liberty are concerned, America's post-9/11 government has not been perfect, but it has, on the whole, done a remarkably good job of providing for both.

# Notes

## Introduction

1. Reuel Marc Gerecht and Gary Schmitt, "France: Europe's Counterterrorist Powerhouse," *European Outlook* no. 3, American Enterprise Institute, November 2007, http://www.aei.org/docLib/20071101_22370EuO03Gerecht_g.pdf.

2. Organizing for America, "Obama Statement on Today's Supreme Court Decision," http://www.barackobama.com/2008/06/12/obama_statement_on_todays_supr.php.

3. "Obama's Speech on National Security," *New York Times,* May 21, 2009, http://www.nytimes.com/2009/05/21/us/politics/21obama.text.html.

4. The executive order on interrogation and CIA detention facilities is White House, "Ensuring Lawful Interrogations," http://www.whitehouse.gov/the_press_office/EnsuringLawfulInterrogations/. The executive order on the closing of Guantánamo is White House, "Closure of Guantanamo Detention Facilities," http://www.whitehouse.gov/the_press_office/closureofguantanamodetentionfacilities/.

5. See Peter Baker, "Obama's War on Terror," *New York Times Magazine,* January 17, 2010, http://www.nytimes.com/2010/01/17/magazine/17Terror-t.html.

6. For a brief overview of these points, see Jack Goldsmith, "The Cheney Fallacy: Why Barack Obama Is Waging a More Effective War on Terror than George W. Bush," *New Republic,* May 18, 2009, http://www.tnr.com/article/politics/the-cheney-fallacy.

7. President Barack Obama's Inaugural Address, January 20, 2009, http://www.whitehouse.gov/blog/inaugural-address/.

8. John O. Brennan, "A New Approach to Safeguarding Americans" (speech, Center for Strategic and International Studies, Washington, DC, August 6, 2009), http://www.whitehouse.gov/the_press_office/Remarks-by-John-Brennan-at-the-Center-for-Strategic-and-International-Studies/.

9. Ibid. For example, the administration supported the reauthorization of three somewhat controversial elements of the Patriot Act: provisions for obtaining "roving wiretaps," access to business records, and dealing with "lone wolf" terrorist suspects. See the statement of David Kris, assistant attorney general, before the U.S. Senate Committee on the Judiciary, September 23, 2009, http://judiciary.senate.gov/pdf/09-09-23%20Kris%20Testimony.pdf. On February 27, one day before the provisions would have expired under the law, President Obama signed legislation reauthorizing each for a one-year extension. "Obama Extends Patriot Act Provisions," Associated Press, February 28, 2010, http://www.latimes.com/news/nationworld/nation/la-na-patriot28-2010feb28,0,176068.story?.

10. See, for example, Richard C. Leone and Greg Anrig Jr., eds., *The War on Our Freedoms: Civil Liberties in an Age of Terrorism* (New York: PublicAffairs, 2003); and Glenn Greenwald, *How Would A Patriot Act? Defending American Values from a President Run Amok* (San Francisco: Working Assets Publishing, 2006).

11. For a discussion of the use and misuse of NSLs, see chapters 5 and 6.

12. The conviction rate for terrorism-related cases appears to range from 85 percent to just over 90 percent—rates only slightly lower than the overall percentage for convictions under other federal felony laws. See Richard B. Zabel and James J. Benjamin Jr., *In Pursuit of Justice: Prosecuting Terrorism Cases in the Federal Courts, 2009 Update and Recent Developments* (New York and Washington, DC: Human Rights First, 2009), preface, http://www.humanrightsfirst.org/pdf/090723-LS-in-pursuit-justice-09-update.pdf. See also Center on Law and Security, "Terrorist Trial Report Card: September 11, 2008," New York University School of Law, 2, http://www.lawandsecurity.org/publications/Sept08TTRCFinal.pdf.

13. For an overview of these arrests, see Lorenzo Vidino, "The Homegrown Terrorist Threat to the US Homeland," Real Instituto Elcano, December 18, 2009, http://www.realinstitutoelcano.org/wps/portal/rielcano_eng/Content?WCM_GLOBAL_CONTEXT=/elcano/Elcano_in/Zonas_in/ARI171-2009; "Spate of terrorism arrests not connected, analysts say," CNN, September 25, 2009, http://www.cnn.com/2009/CRIME/09/25/terrorism.cases/index.html; and Mary Beth Sheridan and Spencer S. Hsu, "Arrests Suggest U.S. Muslims, Like Those in Europe, Can be Radicalized Abroad," *Washington Post,* December 12, 2009, http://www.washingtonpost.com/wp-dyn/content/article/2009/12/11/AR2009121104404.html.

14. For example, although the Congress passed and the president signed legislation reauthorizing several of the more controversial elements of the Patriot Act in late February 2010 (see note 9 above), the reauthorization was only for one year. This

will allow members of the two judiciary committees to revisit the matter next year and possibly reattach amendments they had originally sought in the past year but backed away from in the run-up to the reauthorization. Because the amendments were understood to be putting greater restrictions on the use of these authorities by the FBI and the Justice Department, some analysts believe the members' decision to drop the amendments was due to worries that they would be seen as being soft on terrorism in the wake of the Fort Hood shootings and the Christmas bombing attempt. See "NSJ Analysis: Obama Signs Bill Extending PATRIOT Act Provisions without Changes," *Harvard National Security Journal,* February 28, 2010, http://www.harvardnsj.com/2010/02/nsj-analysis-obama-signs-bill-extending-patriot-act-provisions-without-changes/.

15. The language quoted is from Karen J. Greenberg, executive director of the Center on Law and Security at the NYU School of Law, in Jane Mayer, "The Trial: Eric Holder and the Battle over Khalid Sheikh Mohammed," *New Yorker,* February 15, 2010, http://www.newyorker.com/reporting/2010/02/15/100215fa_fact_mayer.

16. For an overview of these reforms, see Frank Foley, "Reforming Counterterrorism: Institutions and Organizational Routines in Britain and France," *Security Studies* 18, no. 3 (July 2009): 455–70.

17. U.S. Department of Justice, Office of Justice Programs, Bureau of Justice Statistics, "Law Enforcement Statistics," http://www.ojp.usdoj.gov/bjs/lawenf.htm.

18. Gregory R. Treverton, "Terrorists Will Strike America Again," *Los Angeles Times,* January 19, 2010, http://articles.latimes.com/2010/jan/19/opinion/la-oe-treverton19-2010jan19. Treverton is a former vice chairman of the National Intelligence Council and directs the RAND Corporation's Center for Global Risk and Security.

### Chapter 1: United Kingdom: Once More unto the Breach

1. Louise Richardson, *What Terrorists Want: Understanding the Enemy, Containing the Threat* (New York: Random House, 2006), 22.

2. See K. R. M. Short, *The Dynamite War: Irish American Bombers in Victorian Britain* (Atlantic Highlands, NJ: Humanities Press, 1979).

3. Lord Lloyd of Berwick, *Inquiry into Legislation against Terrorism* (London: Stationery Office, 1996), ix.

4. For terrorism by Scottish, Welsh, foreign, and animals rights groups, see ibid, 2–4.

5. See John Newsinger, *British Counter-Insurgency: From Palestine to Northern Ireland* (Houndsmill, Basingstoke: Palgrave, 2002).

6. See Frank Kitson, *Low Intensity Operations: Subversion, Insurgency, Peacekeeping* (Harrisburg, PA: Stackpole Books, 1971); and Robert G. K. Thompson, *Defeating Communist Insurgency: Experiences from Malaya and Vietnam* (London: Chatto and Windus, 1966).

7. Desmond Hamill, *Pig in the Middle: The Army in Northern Ireland 1969–1984* (London: Methuen, 1985), 136.

8. Prime Minister Harold Wilson, quoted in Peter Neumann, *Britain's Long War: British Strategy in the Northern Ireland Conflict 1969–1998* (Houndsmill, Basingstoke: Palgrave, 2003), 52.

9. Newsinger, *British Counter-Insurgency,* 161.

10. Neumann, *Britain's Long War,* 51.

11. Newsinger, *British Counter-Insurgency,* 162.

12. Neumann, *Britain's Long War,* 57.

13. For interrogation of prisoners, which involved techniques such as hooding, wall-standing, subjection to white noise, withholding of food and water, and sleep deprivation, see Donald Jackson, "Prevention of Terrorism: The United Kingdom Confronts the European Convention on Human Rights," *Journal of Terrorism and Political Violence* 6, no. 4 (Winter 1994): 509. For the events of January 30, 1972, see Newsinger, *British Counter-Insurgency,* 166.

14. Neumann, *Britain's Long War,* 79; and Newsinger, *British Counter-Insurgency,* 168.

15. Paul Wilkinson, *Terrorism and the Liberal State,* 2nd ed. (New York: New York University Press, 1986), 160.

16. See Robert White, "From Peaceful Protest to Guerrilla War: Micromobilization of the Provisional Irish Republican Army," *American Journal of Sociology* 94, no. 6 (May 1989): 1277–1302.

17. Reginald Maudling, the Conservative Northern Ireland secretary, quoted in Neumann, *Britain's Long War,* 57–58.

18. Keith Jeffery, "Security Policy in Northern Ireland: Some Reflections on the Management of Violent Conflict," *Journal of Terrorism and Political Violence* 2, no. 1 (Spring 1990): 23.

19. Laura Donohue, *Counter-Terrorist Law and Emergency Powers in the United Kingdom 1922–2000,* (Dublin: Irish Academic Press, 2001), 155; and Brendan O'Duffy, "The British Approach to Ethnic Conflict in Northern Ireland," in *The Politics of Ethnic Conflict Regulation,* ed. John McGarry and Brendan O'Leary (London: Routledge, 1993), 139.

20. Donohue, *Counter-Terrorist Law and Emergency Powers,* 207.

21. The last being the Prevention of Violence (Temporary Provisions) Act 1939, introduced to combat the mainland bombing campaign launched by the IRA in January 1939.

22. Donohue, *Counter-Terrorist Law and Emergency Powers,* 306.

23. Ibid., 216. The period of review would be extended to twelve months in 1976.

24. See Dermot Walsh, *The Use and Abuse of Emergency Legislation* (London: Civil Liberties Trust, 1983), 63; and Donohue, *Counter-Terrorist Law and Emergency Powers,* 178. The slang term "supergrass" refers to an informer reporting on especially important crimes.

25. Donohue, *Counter-Terrorist Law and Emergency Powers,* 179.

26. Ibid.

27. See Tony Gifford, *Supergrasses: The Use of Accomplice Evidence in Northern Ireland* (London: Cobden Trust, 1984); Steven Greer, *Supergrasses: A Study in Anti-Terrorist Law Enforcement in Northern Ireland* (Oxford: Oxford University Press, 1995); and Donohue, *Counter-Terrorist Law and Emergency Powers,* 179.

28. See Mark Urban, *Big Boys' Rules: The SAS and the Secret Struggle Against the IRA* (London: Faber and Faber, 1993).

29. Ibid., 253.

30. The case was *McCann and Others v. the United Kingdom,* 324 Eur. Ct. H.R. (1995). The ruling is available at: http://cmiskp.echr.coe.int/tkp197/view.asp?action= html&documentId=695820&portal=hbkm&source=externalbydocnumber&table= F69A27FD8FB86142BF01C1166DEA398649.

31. Louise Richardson, "Britain and the IRA," in *Democracy and Counter-terrorism: Lessons from the Past,* ed. Robert J. Art and Louise Richardson (Washington, DC: United States Institute of Peace Press, 2007), 90, 94.

32. The first step toward putting the agencies on a statutory footing was taken in the Interception of Communications Act 1985 passed in the wake of *Malone v. United Kingdom,* 82 Eur. Ct. H.R. (ser. A) (1984), which found that the mechanisms governing the interception of communications by the police were sufficiently ill defined legally to place Britain in breach of article 8 (respect of privacy) of the European Convention on Human Rights.

33. Resolution DH(90) 36 [December 13, 1990], 1990 Y.B. Eur. Conv. on H.R. 206–207.

34. The Security Service Act was amended in 1996 to add support of law enforcement agencies involved in the prevention and detection of serious crime to the service's list of responsibilities.

35. Stella Rimington, "Intelligence, Security and Law" (James Smart Lecture, City of London, November 3, 1994).

36. MPSB, or rather the Special Irish Branch from which MPSB evolved, had been created in March 1883 specifically in response to the threat posed by Fenian terrorism. See Rupert Allason, *The Branch: History of the Metropolitan Police Special Branch, 1883–1983* (London: Secker and Warburg, 1983).

37. Rimington, "Intelligence, Security and Law." However, the Security Service did take the lead in pursuing Irish targets overseas and in gathering intelligence on international terrorist groups. A joint Security Service–Secret Intelligence Service section had been established to run agents against Middle Eastern terrorism. MI5 also maintained an operational station in the province and played a pivotal role in maintaining a back channel for secret negotiations with the Provisional IRA.

38. Ibid.

39. BBC News, "Secret State: Timeline," October 17, 2002, http://news.bbc.co.uk/2/hi/programmes/true_spies/2337091.stm.

40. For the regional conference, see Home Office and Scottish Office, *Guidelines on Special Branch Work in Great Britain*, July 1994, par. 17; for the joint Security Service–MPSP training, see ibid., par. 19.

41. Rimington, "Intelligence, Security and Law."

42. BBC-h2g2, "MI5 – The British Security Service," July 15, 2003, http://www.bbc.co.uk/dna/h2g2/A1080136.

43. Rimington, "Intelligence, Security and Law."

44. Brendan O'Leary and John McGarry, *The Politics of Antagonism* (London and Atlantic Highlands, NJ: Athlone Press, 1993), 387.

45. Newsinger, *British Counter-Insurgency*, 192; and Richard English, *Armed Struggle: The History of the IRA* (Oxford: Oxford University Press, 2003), 280.

46. Richardson, "Britain and the IRA," 95. For the resumption of hostilities, see Newsinger, *British Counter-Insurgency*, 193; and Neumann, *Britain's Long War*, 167. For the British formula that led to peace, see Neumann, *Britain's Long War*, 167.

47. Of course, violence did not cease entirely in Northern Ireland with the coming of the peace process. Indeed, the worst single terrorist incident of the entire "troubles," the August 1998 Omagh bombing which killed twenty-nine civilians, occurred after the Good Friday Agreement was signed and ratified by popular referendums on both sides of the border. Nevertheless, the violence has subsided to what might be described, in Reginald Maudling's phrase, as an "acceptable level."

48. Donohue, *Counter-Terrorist Law and Emergency Powers*, 259.

49. Lord Lloyd of Berwick, *Inquiry into Legislation against Terrorism,* 5, 10.

50. Diplock Courts, introduced in Northern Ireland in 1972 to address the problem of jury intimidation, suspended jury trials for certain "scheduled offenses" related to terrorism. Trials are overseen instead by a single judge acting alone. Between 1974 and 1986 the acquittal rate for those who pleaded "not guilty" in Diplock courts was 33 percent—compared to 55 percent in Crown Court cases. Although the Diplock Court legislation was finally repealed in July 2007, the power to hold nonjury trials in exceptional circumstances anywhere in the United Kingdom still exists through provisions enshrined in the Criminal Justice Act 2003.

51. See Donohue, *Counter-Terrorist Law and Emergency Powers,* 263.

52. Lord Lloyd of Berwick, *Inquiry into Legislation against Terrorism,* 23–24.

53. Donohue, *Counter-Terrorist Law and Emergency Powers,* 265.

54. Ibid., 276.

55. Both the Prevention of Terrorism Act and the Northern Ireland (Emergency Provisions) Act were renewed by Labour until such time as more permanent legislation could be introduced.

56. Donohue, *Counter-Terrorist Law and Emergency Powers,* 283.

57. Ibid., 287.

58. Regulation of Investigatory Powers Act 2000, c. 23, http://www.opsi.gov.uk/acts/acts2000/ukpga_20000023_en_1. See also Home Office, *Interception of Communications: Code of Practice* (London: Stationery Office, 2002), available at http://security.homeoffice.gov.uk/ripa/publication-search/general-publications/ripa-cop/interception-cop?view=Binary; and Victoria Williams, *Surveillance and Intelligence Law Handbook* (Oxford: Oxford University Press, 2006).

59. Prevention of Terrorism (Temporary Provisions) Act, 1989, c. 4.

60. Home Office, Office for Security and Counter Terrorism, "Proscribed Terrorist Groups," http://security.homeoffice.gov.uk/legislation/current-legislation/terrorism-act-2000/proscribed-groups.

61. Where a suspect faced a threat to life or freedom if deported, deportation would be in violation of article 3 of the European Convention on Human Rights and of the international law principle of nonrefoulement. Nonrefoulement is a *jus cogens* principle forbidding the expulsion of a refugee to a country "where his life or freedom would be threatened on account of his race, religion, nationality, membership in a particular social group, or political opinion." This language is found—and the principle is enshrined—in the 1951 Refugee Convention, the 1967 Protocol to the Refugee Convention, and the 1984 Torture Convention.

62. See Madeleine Shaw and Vaughne Miller, *Detention of Suspected International Terrorists—Part 4 of the Anti-Terrorism, Crime and Security Act 2001,* House of Commons Library, research paper 02/52, September 16, 2002.

63. Philip Thomas, "Emergency and Anti-Terrorism Power: 9/11: USA and UK," *Fordham International Law Journal* 26 (April 2003): 1217.

64. Ibid., 1218.

65. Shaw and Miller, *Detention of Suspected International Terrorists,* 27.

66. David Bonner, *Executive Measures, Terrorism and National Security: Have the Rules of the Game Changed?* (Aldershot: Ashgate Publishing, 2007), 232, 292.

67. House of Lords, "Judgments—Secretary of State for the Home Department (Respondent) v. AF (Appellant)(FC) and another (Appellant) and one other action, UKHL 28 (2009)," 4, http://www.publications.parliament.uk/pa/ld200809/ldjudgmt/jd090610/af-1.htm..

68. BBC News, "Cleric Stripped of Citizenship," April 5, 2003, http://news.bbc.co.uk/2/hi/uk_news/2919291.stm. Abu Hamza appealed the decision and temporarily remained in the United Kingdom. He was arrested pending a U.S. extradition request and subsequently charged in the United Kingdom with a variety of terrorism-related offenses. He was convicted in February 2006 on eleven charges, including "soliciting to murder" and "stirring up racial hatred." He was sentenced to seven years in prison.

69. To ensure that national priorities and objectives were effectively pursued at the local level, the Security Service introduced the annual Statement of Joint Working Objectives, and in early 2004 the Association of Chief Police Officers created the position of national coordinator of special branches to promulgate Special Branch policy and best-practice standards. See David Blakey, *A Need to Know: HMIC Thematic Inspection of Special Branch and Ports Policing,* HM Inspectorate of Constabulary, January 2003, available at http://inspectorates.homeoffice.gov.uk/hmic/inspections/thematic/antk/; and Intelligence and Security Committee, *Report into the London Terrorist Attacks on 7 July 2005,* May 2006, 36–37, http://www.globalsecurity.org/security/library/report/2006/isc_7july_report.pdf.

70. Peter Clarke, *Learning from Experience: Counter-terrorism in the UK since 9/11* (London: Policy Exchange, 2007), 27, http://www.policyexchange.org.uk/publications/publication.cgi?id=15; and BBC News, "Five Get Life over UK Bomb Plot," April 30, 2007.

71. Richardson, "Britain and the IRA," 98. Of the suspects detained, only ninety-eight were charged and six convicted of terrorist offenses.

72. Intelligence and Security Committee, *Report into the London Terrorist Attacks,* 33.

73. Ibid., 5.

74. HM Government, *Countering International Terrorism: The United Kingdom's Strategy* (London: Stationery Office, 2006), 1–2.

75. Ibid., 3.

76. Ibid., 29.

77. See, for example, Lord Carlile of Berriew QC, *Report on the Operation in 2006 of the Terrorism Act 2000,* June 2007, 45. Information on the JTAC is available on the MI5 Web site at https://www.mi5.gov.uk/output/joint-terrorism-analysis-centre.html.

78. Cabinet Office, "Government Publishes the Civil Contingencies Bill," CAB 001/04 (press release), January 7, 2004.

79. Paul Cornish, "The United Kingdom," in *Europe Confronts Terrorism,* ed. Karin von Hippel (New York: Palgrave MacMillan, 2005), 155–56.

80. Intelligence and Security Committee, *Report into the London Terrorist Attacks,* 10. The Joint Intelligence Committee sits at the apex of the British intelligence and security community and has since 1957 operated as an organ of the Cabinet Office. The committee meets weekly and consists of the heads of the three intelligence agencies (or their proxies) as well as senior members of other government departments.

81. Intelligence and Security Committee, *Report into the London Terrorist Attacks,* 11; and Bonner, *Executive Measures, Terrorism and National Security,* 211.

82. HM Government, *Countering International Terrorism,* 30.

83. The text of the bill is at http://www.publications.parliament.uk/pa/cm200506/cmbills/055/06055.1-7.html. The Public Order Act 1986 was also amended by the Racial and Religious Hatred Act 2006, which created a new criminal offense of using "threatening words" with the intention of stirring up "religious hatred."

84. The recommendations were appended to a letter from Andy Hayman, assistant commissioner of the Metropolitan Police, to Rt. Hon. Charles Clarke, MP, London, October 6, 2005, http://www.privacyinternational.org/issues/terrorism/library/ukterrorbillmetreport.pdf.

85. Sarah Lyall, "Blair Dealt Stunning Defeat in Parliament," *International Herald Tribune,* November 9, 2005.

86. BBC News, "Blair Defeated over Terror Laws," November 9, 2005.

87. The text of the announcement is available at BBC News, "In Full: Statement on Home Office Split, March 29, 2007, http://news.bbc.co.uk/2/hi/uk_news/politics/6506801.stm.

88. Kevin Sullivan, "Brown Seeks Tougher Anti-Terrorism Laws," *Washington Post,* July 26, 2007.

89. For an overview of the original bill's history, see "Counter-Terrorism Act of 2008," *Guardian,* January 19, 2009, http://www.guardian.co.uk/commentisfree/libertycentral/2009/jan/19/counter-terrorism-act. For the Counter-Terrorism (Temporary Provisions) Bill, see Jacqui Smith, "Statement on Counter-Terrorism Bill," October 13, 2008, at http://www.labour.org.uk/jacqui_smith_statement_on_counter-terrorism_bill. For the text of the bill, see www.icj.org/IMG/J13_CT_Temp_Provisions_Bill.pdf.

90. Police officers had previously been allowed to interview defendants only if earlier statements needed clarification, if public safety was at risk, or if the defendant agreed to be interviewed regarding newly discovered evidence. The amendment allows defendants to be questioned on any aspect of the offense with which they have been charged.

91. See Home Office, UK Border Agency, "Identity Cards for Foreign Nationals," www.bia.homeoffice.gov.uk/managingborders/idcardsforforeignnationals/.

92. Eliza Manningham-Buller, "The International Terrorist Threat to the UK" (speech, Queen Mary University, London, November 9, 2006).

93. Intelligence and Security Committee, *Report into the London Terrorist Attacks,* 8.

94. Manningham-Buller, "International Terrorist Threat to the UK."

95. Sarah Lyall, "British Intelligence Chief Sharpens Terrorism Warning," *New York Times,* November 6, 2007, A3.

96. Intelligence and Security Committee, *Report into the London Terrorist Attacks,* 7.

97. Manningham-Buller, "International Terrorist Threat to the UK."

98. Intelligence and Security Committee, *Report into the London Terrorist Attacks,* 16.

99. Ibid., 39.

100. Ibid., 37.

101. Security Service, "Security Service Work on Serious Crime," https://www.securityservice.gov.uk/output/news/security-service-work-on-serious-crime.html. The Security Service had been given the responsibility for dealing with organized crime under the Security Service Act 1996.

102. Intelligence and Security Committee, *Report into the London Terrorist Attacks,* 34.

103. The size and makeup of the MI5 staff are in Manningham-Buller, "The International Terrorist Threat to the UK."

104. Prime Minister Gordon Brown, "National Security Statement," November 14, 2007, http://www.number10.gov.uk/output/Page13757.asp.

105. Rosie Cowan, "Yard Merger Creates New Anti-terror Department," *Guardian,* October 3, 2006.

106. National Policing Improvement Agency, "Leeds Has New Counter Terrorism Unit" (press release), December 11, 2007; Vikram Dodd, "Shake-up for Anti-Terror Policing," *Guardian,* September 15, 2006; and BBC News, "Regional Anti-terror Unit Formed," April 2, 2007.

107. Dean Godson, introduction to *Learning from Experience: Counter Terrorism in the UK since 9/11,* by Peter Clarke (London: Policy Exchange, 2007), 15.

108. Clarke, *Learning from Experience,* 23.

109. Ibid., 24.

110. BBC News, "Borders Policing Body Begins Work," April 3, 2008. See also Cabinet Office, *Security in a Global Hub: Establishing the UK's New Border Arrangements,* London, November 2007, http://www.cabinetoffice.gov.uk/media/cabinetoffice/corp/assets/publications/reports/border_review.pdf.

111. Home Office, *From the Neighbourhood to the National: Policing our Communities Together,* July 2008, 6.36.

112. Gabrielle Garton Grimwood, *Policing: A Separate Police Force for UK Borders?* House of Commons Library, SN/HA/5122, July 8, 2009, 2. There is some precedent for this approach—British Transport Police are responsible for policing the country's internal transport infrastructure.

113. Ibid.

114. For services to British Muslims going to Mecca, see Foreign and Commonwealth Office, "Assistance for UK Muslims Performing the Hajj," October 6, 2003, http://www.fco.gov.uk/en/news/latest-news/?view=News&id=1549874. For legislation and monthly meetings, see HM Government, *Countering International Terrorism,* 15, 22.

115. HM Government, *Countering International Terrorism,* 22; and Brown, "National Security Statement."

116. HM Government, *Countering International Terrorism,* 14.

117. John Burns, "Muslims in Britain Propose Code for Civic Life," *New York Times,* November 30, 2007, A11.

118. Brown, "National Security Statement."

119. Clarke, *Learning from Experience,* 25.

120. Manningham-Buller, "International Terrorist Threat to the UK."

121. Intelligence and Security Committee, *Rendition,* July 2007, 11, http://www.cabinetoffice.gov.uk/media/cabinetoffice/corp/assets/publications/intelligence/20070725_isc_final.pdf.

122. Eliza Manningham-Buller, statement on behalf of the Secretary of State, A and Others (FC) v. Secretary of State for the Home Department, September 20, 2005.

123. Ibid.

124. Richard Norton-Taylor, "30 Years in Jail for Real IRA Trio," *Guardian,* May 8, 2002.

125. BBC News, "Extradited Bomb Suspect Charged," September 22, 2005, http://news.bbc.co.uk/2/hi/uk_news/4265572.stm.

126. Intelligence and Security Committee, *Rendition,* 12–13.

127. The United Kingdom has attempted a rendition operation on only one occasion. In 1989 SIS facilitated the "rendition to justice" of an Irish Republican terrorist suspect in Zimbabwe, Nicholas "Peter" Mullen. Mullen's subsequent conviction in a British court was overturned by the Court of Appeal, which ruled that his deportation had involved a clear abuse of process. Ibid. 7.

128. The remark is cited in ibid., 47.

129. Ibid.

130. Quoted in ibid; the remark is from oral evidence given on November 7, 2006.

131. Prime Minister Tony Blair, "PM's Press Conference," August 5, 2005, http://www.number10.gov.uk/output/Page8041.asp; and Brown, "National Security Statement."

132. Amnesty International, "UK Must Stop Deportations to Torture States," March 1, 2007, http://www.amnesty.org/en/news-and-updates/featurestories/uk-must-stop-deportations-torture-states-20070301.

133. Manningham-Buller, statement on behalf of the Secretary of State.

134. "Torture evidence inadmissible in UK courts, Lords rule," *Guardian,* December 8, 2005.

135. *A and Others (No. 2) v. Secretary of State for the Home Department* [2005] UKHL 71, 145.

136. Lindsay Clutterbuck, "Law Enforcement," in *Attacking Terrorism: Elements of a Grand Strategy,* ed. Audrey Kurth Cronin and James M. Ludes (Washington, DC: Georgetown University Press, 2004), 157.

137. See Bonner, *Executive Measures, Terrorism and National Security.*

138. Clutterbuck, "Law Enforcement," 143.

139. See Prime Minister Tony Blair's address to the World Affairs Council in Los Angeles on August 1, 2006, at BBC, "In Full: Tony Blair Speech," http://news.bbc.co.uk/2/hi/uk_news/politics/5236896.stm.

140. Christopher Caldwell, "After Londonistan," *New York Times,* June 25, 2006.

141. Patrick Sawer, "Young Muslims 'Are Turning to Extremism,'" *Daily Telegraph*, June 22, 2008, http://www.telegraph.co.uk/news/uknews/2171300/Young-Muslims-%2527are-turning-to-extremism%2527.html?tr=y&auid=3770513.

142. Richardson, "Britain and the IRA," 99.

## Chapter 2: France: In a League of Its Own

1. Hijackers took command of Air France Flight 8960 from Algiers to Paris on December 24, 1994. Based on intelligence gathered about the hijackers' intention to crash the plane into a Paris building or structure, French authorities forced it to land at a Marseille airport, where the hijackers were neutralized by commandos from the Groupe d'intervention Gendarmerie Nationale. The prime minister at the time said that armed fighter jets were ready to take off from Dijon and Creil. It is not known whether President François Mitterrand gave orders to shoot down the Air France plane with hundreds of passengers on board if attempts to make it land failed.

2. In Karachi, on May 8, 2002, eleven employees of DCN (the French naval ship-builder then known as the Direction des Constructions Navales) were killed by a suicide car bomber. Off the Yemen coast, on October 6, 2002, Islamic terrorists struck against the *Limburg*, a French oil tanker. In Madrid, on March 11, 2004, terrorists conducted a series of coordinated bombings against the commuter train system of Madrid, killing 191 people and wounding 1,755. In London, on July 7, 2005, British Islamic extremists conducted a series of coordinated bomb blasts that hit London's public transport system during the morning rush hour. The bombings killed 52 commuters and injured 700.

3. Dominique De Villepin, *Prevailing Against Terrorism: White Paper on Domestic Security against Terrorism* (Paris: La Documentation Française, 2006), http://www.ambafrance-dk.org/IMG/pdf/livre_blanc_english.pdf.

4. Ibid., 5.

5. Although the white paper discusses "worst case" scenarios like 9/11 or attacks involving chemical, biological, or nuclear elements, it suggests that for the time being the more likely threat is attacks using conventional explosives, designed nevertheless to produce as many casualties as possible. See 9, 31, 32, 36–37, 41–43. For al Qaeda's political goals, see ibid., 10, 15–16.

6. Ibid., 29ff.

7. Ibid., 5.

8. Ibid., 45.

9. For an overview of this policy and period, see Douglas Porch, *The French Secret Services: From the Dreyfus Affair to the Gulf War* (New York: Farrar Strauss and Giroux, 1995), 49–54, 431–37.

10. For an excellent overview of the changes made by the French in counterterrorism policy and institutions, see Jeremy Shapiro and Benedicte Suzan, "The French Experience of Counter-terrorism," *Survival* 45, no. 1 (Spring 2003): 67–98.

11. Following attacks by Algerian radicals—the Armed Islamic Group (GIA)—against the Paris metro system in 1995, the government took additional steps to increase street-level security. These included the creation of no-stop zones around key government buildings; new traffic regulations to reduce the number of trucks (and hence potential vehicular bombs) in central Paris; more police surveillance of vulnerable "soft" targets such as schools and houses of worship; and increased deployment of armed police and gendarmes at airports, train stations, and other public places. Peter Chalk and William Rosenau, *Confronting the "Enemy Within": Security Intelligence, the Police, and Counterterrorism in Four Democracies* (Santa Monica, CA: RAND, 2004), 20. As the study notes, these measures remain in place.

12. Ibid., 75.

13. Richard Warnes, "France," in *Considering the Creation of a Domestic Intelligence Agency in the United States: Lessons from the Experiences of Australia, Canada, France, Germany, and the United Kingdom*, ed. Brian A. Jackson (Santa Monica, CA: RAND, 2009), 73–74.

14. Shapiro and Suzan, "French Experience of Counter-terrorism," 77. In addition, to address further the hodgepodge of French police and intelligence activities, the French government has established over the years various policy-coordinating bodies, foremost among them the Conseil de Sécurité Intérieure (Domestic Security Council), chaired by the French president or his representative, which "defines the orientation for domestic security policy and establishes priorities." The prime minister chairs the Comité Interministériel du Renseignement (Interministerial Intelligence Committee), which brings together all of the ministers involved in counterterrorism. And, finally, the Interior Ministry leads the Comité Interministériel de Lutte Antiterroriste (Interministerial Counterterrorist Committee), which coordinates actions at the ministerial level. Chalk and Rosenau, *Confronting the "Enemy Within,"* 21.

15. Two years later, the French also established the Service pour Coordination de la Lutte Anti-Terroriste (SCLAT) within the Justice Ministry to increase working-level cooperation among the various agencies and bureaus involved in the counterterrorism effort.

16. Loi No. 86-1020 (September 9, 1986), http://www.legifrance.gouv.fr/affich Texte.do;jsessionid=487?7828.3B6CC10C322D4B48E11298CE.tpdjo11v_2?cid Texte=JORFTEXT000000693912&dateTexte=.

17. In addition to the specialized investigative magistrates, the law also provided for an equal number of judges. Under French law, there is no requirement for a trial by jury, with France's Constitutional Council finding a bench trial a legitimate adaption to the judicial process in light of the pressures and threats that members of a jury might face in terrorist cases. See Olivier Dutheillet de Lamothe, "French Legislation against Terrorism: Constitutional Issues," November 2006, http://www.conseil-constitutionnel.fr/conseil-constitutionnel/root/bank_mm/pdf/Conseil/constitutional terrorism.pdf. It is worth noting here that, from the early 1960s until 1981, most national security cases were handled by the State Security Court, a special tribunal that was composed of three civilian judges and two military officers. The proceedings took place in secret and there was no right of appeal.

18. In 1998, the DST created a unit—the Unité Enquête Judiciare—which could assist *juges d'instruction* in investigations once they had become law enforcement matters, and which was separate from the DST's intelligence collection function. Nevertheless, according to one senior police official, while the units are formally separated, "they depend on the same boss. They are of the same house, of the same doctrine, of the same culture." Cited in Frank Foley, "Reforming Counterterrorism: Institutions and Organizational Routines in Britain and France," *Security Studies* 18, no. 3 (July 2009): 459. See also Reuel Marc Gerecht and Gary Schmitt, "France: Europe's Counterterrorist Powerhouse," *European Outlook* no. 3, American Enterprise Institute, November 2007, http://www.aei.org/docLib/20071101_22370Eu O03Gerecht_g.pdf.

19. The quotation is from a French magistrate interviewed by Frank Foley in February 2007; cited in Foley, "Reforming Counterterrorism," 458.

20. De Lamothe, "French Legislation against Terrorism: Constitutional Issues," 7.

21. See Shapiro and Suzan, "The French Experience of Counter-terrorism," 78.

22. See Ben Hall, "Sarkozy to Reform Judicial Probe System," *Financial Times,* January 7, 2009, http://www.ft.com/cms/s/0/6dc595f0-dce4-11dd-a2a9-000077b0 7658,dwp_uuid=0e3b4494-227d-11dd-93a9-000077b07658.html. One popular reason for considering the change is the "Outreau Affair," a well-publicized 2005 case in which more than a dozen individuals were falsely accused of pedophilia as the result of a magistrate's investigation. Then minister of the interior, Sarkozy called for the office's abolishment.

23. *Rapport du Comité de Réflexion sur la Justice Pénale,* September 1, 2009, http://www.elysee.fr/download/?mode=press&filename=Rapport_Leger.pdf. The report was the product of an ad hoc government committee, headed by Philippe Léger, former advocate general in the European Court of Justice, and tasked with examining the issue.

24. Mathieu Delahousse, "Suppression du juge d'instruction: l'avis de six professionnels," *Le Figaro,* January 8, 2009, http://www.lefigaro.fr/actualite-france/2009/01/07/01016-20090107ARTFIG00633-suppression-du-juge-d-instruction-l-avis-de-six-professionnels-.php.

25. Cited in Foley, "Reforming Counterterrorism," 460.

26. In July 2008, the DST and RG were merged into one organization, the Direction Centrale du Renseignement Intérieur (DCRI), and tasked with countering terrorism, espionage, cybercrime, and domestic subversion. The creation and mission of the DCRI are explained on the Web site of the interior minister at http://www.interieur.gouv.fr/misill/sections/a_la_une/toute_l_actualite/archives-actualites/archives-securite/creation-dcri/view and http://www.interieur.gouv.fr/misill/sections/a_l_interieur/la_police_nationale/organisation/dcri/folder_contents.

27. Chalk and Rosenau, *Confronting the "Enemy Within,"* 18–19.

28. Author's interview in Paris with French security official, June 2006.

29. Loi du 29 juillet 1881 sur la liberté de la presse, article 24, available at http://www.legifrance.gouv.fr/affichTexte.do?cidTexte=LEGITEXT000006070722&dateTexte=20091031#LEGISCTA000006117631.

30. See *Kruslin v. France,* 176-A, Eur. Ct. H.R. (ser. A) (1990).

31. Loi no. 91-646 du 10 juillet 1991 relative au secret des correspondances émises par la voie des communications électroniques, available at http://www.legifrance.gouv.fr/affichTexte.do?cidTexte=LEGITEXT000006077780&dateTexte=20081003.

32. See the scoring by Privacy International. Only the United States and the United Kingdom score lower than France among transatlantic countries. Privacy International, "Leading Surveillance Societies in the EU and the World 2007," http://www.privacyinternational.org/article.shtml?cmd[347]=x-347-559597.

33. See, for example, Human Rights Watch, *Preempting Justice: Counterterrorism Laws and Procedures in France* (New York: Human Rights Watch, 2008), available at http://hrw.org/reports/2008/france0708/.

34. In late June of 1995, 131 individuals thought to be associated with the Sheik Salem jihadist network were arrested. Over sixty individuals thought to be connected to the so-called Chechen network were detained by French police between 2002 and 2005. On the issue of French pre-trial detention practices, see United Nations Human

Rights Committee, "Concluding Observations on Report Submitted by France under Article 40 of the ICCPR (2008)," CCPR/C/FRA/CO/1, July 31, 2008, 3–4. The report can be found at http://www.legislationline.org/topics/country/30/topic/5.

35. "Suspects are allowed to see a lawyer for the first time only after three days in custody (four days in some cases), and then only for 30 minutes. The lawyer does not have access to the case file, or information about the exact charges against his or her client." Human Rights Watch, *Preempting Justice*, 2.

36. While serving as interior minister, Nicolas Sarkozy stated that some 367 individuals had been detained on suspicion of involvement in terrorist-related activities between 2002 and 2005. Of these, fewer than a hundred were formally charged and incarcerated. To note an earlier example, in early November 1993, French authorities detained nearly ninety individuals in a counterterrorist sweep known as Operation Chrysanthemum. Of that number, only three were judicially detained and became formal investigative targets. See Human Rights Watch, *Preempting Justice,* 27; and Shapiro and Suzan, "French Experience of Counter-terrorism," 84.

37. National Assembly, Report No. 3125, June 6, 2006, 223.

38. The statement is from a Human Rights Watch interview with a French judge; cited in Human Rights Watch, "Preempting Justice," 31.

39. The legislation is article 421-2-1 of the French criminal code, inserted by Act No. 2001-1062 of November 15, 2001, art. 33 *Journal Officiel de la République Française* [J.O.] [Official Gazette of France], November 16, 2001, available at http://195.83.177.9/code/liste.phtml?lang=uk&c=33&r=3794#art16570.

40. Human Rights Watch, *Preempting Justice,* 21–22.

41. "Les prisons françaises comptent 358 detenus pour activisme," *Le Monde,* September 9, 2005.

42. Act No. 2001-1062 of November 15, 2001, on everyday security (Loi no. 2001-1062), available at http://www.legifrance.gouv.fr/affichTexte.do;jsessionid=C18426C7A8C6907593C7E3C8563AC494.tpdjo05v_1?cidTexte=JORFTEXT000000222052&dateTexte=&oldAction=rechJO.

43. Act No. 2003-239 of March 18, 2003, on internal security (Loi no. 2003-239), available at http://www.legifrance.gouv.fr/jopdf/common/jo_pdf.jsp?numJO=0&dateJO=20030319&numTexte=1&pageDebut=04761&pageFin=04789. Act No. 2004-204 of March 9, 2004, on adapting the judicial response to new forms of criminality (Loi no. 2004-204), available at http://www.legifrance.gouv.fr/affichTexte.do;jsessionid=C18426C7A8C6907593C7E3C8563AC494.tpdjo05v_1?cidTexte=JORFTEXT000000249995&dateTexte=20081015.

44. Act No. 2006-64 of January 23, 2006, on action against terrorism (Loi no. 2006-64), available at http://www.legifrance.gouv.fr/affichTexte.do;jsessionid=C184 26C7A8C6907593C7E3C8563AC494.tpdjo05v_1?idSectionTA=LEGISCTA000006 096028&cidTexte=JORFTEXT000000454124&dateTexte=20081015. Some key authorities in the law were set to expire in 2008 unless renewed. On December 1, 2008, at the request of the French government, the National Assembly extended the law authorities until the end of December 2012.

45. For a variety reasons (costs, personnel, privacy), the actual implementation of the national video-protection plan initiated by the French government has been relatively modest. For example, of the 230 French towns equipped with surveillance systems, only 53 have developed a system for transferring the images to the national police. For an overview of this issue and other issues related to the 2006 law, see Éric Diard and Julien Dray, "Rapport d' Information, No. 683," National Assembly, February 5, 2008, http://www.assemblee-nationale.fr/13/rap-info/i0683.asp.

46. According to the government and news reports, the French government has established its own data collection platform, giving it an independent capability to collect communications data (excluding content) related to text messages, mobile phones, or the Internet. The system is overseen and managed by UCLAT. "L'anti-terrorisme espionne aussi mails et textos," Le Figaro, May 28, 2007, http://www.lefigaro.fr/france/20070528.WWW000000165_lantiterrorisme_espionne_aussi_mails _et_textos.html. According the report of the National Assembly, in a seven-month period in 2007, over twenty-seven thousand requests for particular communications data were made to UCLAT by the domestic intelligence services and counterterrorist units of the police and gendarmerie; most requests concerned subscriber identification, although increasingly requests are made concerning relational data and Internet access. UCLAT rejected less than 7 percent of the requests, most for insufficient application information. See Diard and Dray, "Rapport d' Information, No. 683."

47. See "Keeping an Ear to the Ground," Intelligence Online, March 4, 2005; and Piotr Smolar, "Terrorisme: la mise en oeuvre des procédures d'éloignement est critique," Le Monde, June 7, 2007.

48. De Villepin, Prevailing Against Terrorism, 61.

49. Ibid., 113–14.

50. Although the distinction between the two legal systems is not hard and fast, the civil-law system is principally an all-encompassing code that can be adjusted over time by legislatures, whereas the common-law system gives more priority to judicial decisions and precedents—in theory making the law less malleable.

51. Human Rights Watch, *Preempting Justice,* 13. Or as Olivier Dutheillet de Lamothe has argued ("French Legislation against Terrorism," 11), the French legal system allows for "permanent adaptation," a capacity "which is especially important in the fight against radical Islamic terrorism." Given the nature of the threat (decentralized command and operational structures), it "raises a challenge to institutions, which are static by nature. This explains the importance of fluidity between institutions in the rapidity of responses, circulation and implementation," and why "counterterrorism bodies now need flattened flow charts, shortened perhaps even un-hierarchic chains of command, and networking operations that copy those of terrorist organizations."

52. For example, in response to the likely passage of Perben II in 2004, hundreds of lawyers in cities across France went on strike and demonstrated against the proposed measure on the grounds that it would damage fundamental procedural liberties. This was only the third time since World War II that lawyers and lawyers' organizations had called for a national strike.

53. De Villepin, *Prevailing Against Terrorism,* 53. Emphasis added.

## Chapter 3: Spain: From 9/11 to 3/11 and Beyond

1. ETA stands for *Euskadi Ta Askatasuna,* which is Basque for "Basque homeland and freedom."

2. See Rut Bermejo and Fernando Reinares, "Visiones del terrorismo internacional en la opinión pública española," Real Instituto Elcano, *ARI* 32, March 2007; the study is available in English at http://www.realinstitutoelcano.org/wps/portal/rielcano_eng/Content?WCM_GLOBAL_CONTEXT=/elcano/elcano_in/zonas_in/international+terrorism/ari+32-2007 .

3. See Carlos Echeverría, "Lecciones del proceso judicial por la Operación Nova," Grupo de Estudios Estratégicos, March 6, 2008, available at http://www.gees.org/articulo/5220/20; Grupo de Estudios Estratégicos, "Las dificultades de percibir el terrorismo jihadista," October 27, 2007, available at http://www.gees.org/articulo/4630/20; and Al Goodman, "Spain: 11 Guilty of belonging to terror group," CNN, December 14, 2009, http://edition.cnn.com/2009/WORLD/europe/12/14/spain.terror.trial/index.html?eref=rss_world&utm_source=feedburner&utm_medium=feed&utm_campaign=Feed:+rss/cnn_world+(RSS:+World). According to the annual Europol report on terrorism, in 2008, nearly 50 percent of the verdicts reached in Spanish courts resulted in acquittals. Europol, *TE-SAT: EU Terrorism Situation and Trend Report*

*2009* (The Hague: Europol, 2009), 16, http://www.statewatch.org//news/2009/apr/europol-te-sat-2009.pdf.

4. The Civil Guard is the Spanish gendarmerie and has military status, while the National Police is a civilian police force.

5. The National Court also handles other important matters, including crimes against the Crown or members of the government, as well as organized crime, drug trafficking, and counterfeiting.

6. Terrorist offenses are gathered in articles 571–79 of the Spanish criminal code. "Terrorist offenses are structured within the Criminal Law Code according to one presupposition: that of belonging to, acting for the sake of, or collaborating with armed bands, bodies or groups whose aim lies in subverting the constitutional order or in seriously altering public peace." Committee of Experts on Terrorism, "Profiles on Counter-Terrorist Capacity: Spain," Council of Europe, December 2006, http://www.coe.int/t/e/legal_affairs/legal_co-operation/fight_against_terrorism/4_theme_files/apologie_-_incitement/CODEXTER%20Profiles%20%282006%29%20Spain%20E.pdf. The code itself can be found at http://noticias.juridicas.com/base_datos/Penal/lecr. html.

7. See articles 17, 18, and 55 of the Spanish constitution. The text can be found at http://constitucion.rediris.es/legis/1978/ce1978.html.

8. Ley de Enjuiciamiento Criminal, articles 509 and 520 bis. The articles can be found at http://noticias.juridicas.com/base_datos/Penal/lecr.html.

9. Under the law, the suspect does have the right to be informed immediately of the grounds for the arrest, the right to remain silent until brought before a judge, the right not to incriminate himself, and the right to an interpreter if needed.

10. "El Supremo cree inapalazable regular el control de teléfonos," *El País*, December 13, 2004.

11. The provisions are Ley Orgánica 7/2000, December 22, and Ley Orgánica 5/2000, January 12.

12. Ley 12/2003, May 21, de prevención y bloqueo de la financiación del terrorismo, http://www.boe.es/g/es/bases_datos/doc.php?coleccion=iberlex&id=2003/10289.

13. The government set a goal of hiring a thousand new agents between 2004 and 2008. See Fernando Reinares, "Do Government and Citizens Agree on How to Combat International Terrorism?" Real Instituto Elcano, July 28, 2006, http://www.realinstitutoelcano.org/wps/wcm/connect/e088df804f01871dbc34fc3170baead1/1020_Reinares_Government_Citizens_International_Terrorism.pdf?MOD=AJPERES&CACHEID=e088df804f01871dbc34fc3170baead1.

14. See Committee of Experts on Terrorism, "Profiles on Counter-Terrorist Capacity: Spain." The directorate was established in 2006.

15. The organization, mission, and tasks of CNI are set out in Ley 11/2002, May 6, available at http://www.boe.es/g/es/bases_datos/doc.php?coleccion=iberlex&id=2002/08628.

16. "La dotación del CNI se eleva un 17% para luchar contra el terrorismo" [CNI budget increases by 17% to fight terrorism], El Pais, September 29, 2004, http://www.elpais.com/articulo/economia/dotacion/CNI/eleva/luchar/terrorismo/elpepieco/20040929elpepieco_12/Tes; and "Presupuestos. el cni tendrá menos dinero" [Budget: The CNI will have less money], EcoDiario, September 29, 2009, http://ecodiario.eleconomista.es/espana/noticias/1575778/09/09/Presupuestos-el-cni-tendra-menos-dinero.html. According to the latter article, the CNI budget for 2010 has been cut to €241.

17. "Spain arrests suspected Islamic extremists," CNN, February 14, 2008, http://www.cnn.com/2008/WORLD/europe/02/14/soain.terror/index.html.

18. Ley Orgánica 4/2005, of October 10, modifying Ley Orgánica 10/1995, of November 23, Penal Code, relative to crimes related to risks caused by explosives.

19. Law 16/2006, of May 26, regulating the statute for a national member of Eurojust.

20. See European Council Decision 2002/187/JAI and European Council Decision 2005/187/JAI.

21. Law 25/2007, October 18, concerning the preservation of data related to electronic communications. The law followed the March 2006 decision by the European Union to issue Directive 2006/24/EC, which required member states to have communication service providers retain communications data for a period of between six months and two years in order to harmonize requirements throughout the EU and ensure that data would be available for investigative purposes in cases of serious crimes. The directive can be found at http://eur-lex.europa.eu/LexUriServ/LexUriServ.do?uri=CELEX:32006L0024:EN:NOT.

22. Europol's establishment was agreed to under the Maastricht treaty (the Treaty on European Union) in 1992. It was not until 1998, however, that the Europol Convention was ratified by all member states, and not until 1999 that Europol began to fulfil its broader mandate—to help the member states share intelligence effectively in order to combat international organized crime. Europol has no executive powers. It is a support service for the law enforcement agencies of the EU member states.

23. Established in 2002, Eurojust was designed to help member states' judicial and investigative authorities deal more effectively with serious cross-border and organized crime, specifically by helping to coordinate investigations and prosecutions.

24. See Gijs de Vries, "The Fight Against Terrorism—Five Years After 9/11" (speech, Annual European Foreign Policy Conference, London School of Economics and King's College, London, June 30, 2006), http://www.consilium.europa.eu/uedocs/cmsUpload/060630LondonSchoolEconomics.pdf. For an overview of the EU counterterrorism efforts, see EU Counter-terrorist Coordinator, "EU Action Plan on Combating Terrorism," Council of the European Union, November 26, 2009, http://register.consilium.europa.eu/pdf/en/09/st15/st15358.en09.pdf.

25. Europol, TE-SAT: EU Terrorism Situation and Trend Report 2009 (9, 17).

26. Europol, Terrorist Activity in the European Union: Situation and Trends Report, October 2004–October 2005 (The Hague: Europol, 2006), http://www.statewatch.org/news/2006/may/europol-terr-rep-2004-2005.pdf.

27. Europol, EU Terrorism Situation and Trend Report 2007 (The Hague: Europol, 2007), http://www.europol.europa.eu/publications/EU_Terrorism_Situation_and_Trend_Report_TE-SAT/TESAT2007.pdf.

28. Europol, TE-SAT: EU Terrorism Situation and Trend Report 2008 (The Hague: Europol, 2008), http://www.europol.europa.eu/publications/EU_Terrorism_Situation_and_Trend_Report_TE-SAT/TESAT2008.pdf. The report notes that the number of individuals arrested for Islamic terrorist activities in Europe dropped in 2007 to 201 from 257 in 2006 (11). Nevertheless, this figure remains high and the nature of the threat extremely dangerous. According to the report, the "Netherlands, Portugal and Spain reported that the general threat of an attack by Islamist terrorists on their territory increased during 2007. In France and Italy, the threat remains high. The UK has estimated the risk of an attack as highly likely. In addition, France, Italy, Spain and Portugal consider the increasing activities of al Qaeda in the Islamic Maghreb (AQIM) aiming at international targets have an impact on the threat level in their member state" (17). According to the 2009 Europol report, the majority of the arrests of suspected Islamists in Europe took place in France and Spain, with some sixty-one arrested in Spain alone. TE-SAT: EU Terrorism Situation and Trend Report 2009 (9).

29. Such a threat was made on March 11, 2007, on al Qaeda's Internet television channel (known as "The Voice of Caliphate").

30. On March 8, 2007, al Qaeda released a new video recording in which Ayman al-Zawahiri reiterated his hostility toward al-Andalus.

31. Ayman al-Zawahiri first mentioned Ceuta and Melilla in December 2006, when he announced the creation of al Qaeda in the Maghreb; a more recent reference to the two Spanish cities in North Africa can be found in an interview released by As Sahab, the media arm of al Qaeda, on April 2008. See http://www.nefafoundation.org/miscellaneous/FeaturedDocs/nefazawahiri0508-2.pdf.

32. See for instance "El brazo juvenile de Hamas pide que Andalucía vuelva a manos de los musulmanes," ABC (Spain), February 13, 2006, http://www.abc.es/hemeroteca/historico-13-02-2006/abc/Nacional/el-brazo-juvenil-de-hamas-pide-que-andalucia-vuelva-a-manos-de-los-musulmanes_132252042633.html, noting that the Hamas text for primary school students refers to reconquering al-Andalus.

33. See Overseas Security Advisory Council, "OSAC Activity Report: September 2007," https://www.osac.gov/Reports/report.cfm?contentID=74488.

34. Instituto Nacional de Estadística INE [National Institute of Statistics], "National Immigrant Survey 2007. Results Preview" (press release), May 22, 2008, http://www.ine.es/en/prensa/np499_en.pdf. See also "La inmigración en tiempos de crisis" [Immigration in times of crisis], in *Anuario de la inmigración en España.* [Immigration in Spain Yearbook], 2009 ed. (Barcelona: Barcelona Centre for International Affairs, 2010).

35. See Interior and Justice Ministries, "La Comunidad musulmana de origen inmigrante en España 2007," http://www.mir.es/EDSE/informe_musulmanes.pdf.

## Chapter 4: Germany: The Long and Winding Road

1. For an account of German left-wing terrorism, see Butz Peters, *Tödlicher Irrtum: Die Geschichte der RAF* [Fatal error: The history of the RAF] (Frankfurt am Main: Fischer, 2007).

2. The German civilian intelligence and law enforcement community consists of a foreign intelligence service (Bundesnachrichtendienst, BND), a federal domestic intelligence service (Bundesamt für Verfassungsschutz, BfV), a federal investigative police agency (Bundeskriminalamt, BKA), and separate state-level domestic intelligence, and investigative bureaus.

3. Quoted in Harry De Quetteville, "'Massive' Terror Plots Foiled in Berlin," *Telegraph,* September 6, 2007, http://www.telegraph.co.uk/news/worldnews/1562379/Massive-terror-plots-foiled-in-Germany.html.

4. On this issue see Christina Hellmich and Amanda J. Redig, "The Question Is When: The Ideology of al Qaeda and the Reality of Bioterrorism," *Studies in Conflict and Terrorism* 30, no. 5 (2007): 375–96.

5. For a brief overview of what the law was and how it was modified, see Oliver Lepsius, "Liberty, Security and Terrorism: The Legal Position in Germany," *German Law Journal* 5, no. 5 (2004): 440.

6. In January 2003, the Federal Ministry of Interior banned the Islamist organization Hizb ut-Tahrir for anti-Semitic propaganda and hate speech. The al-Aqsa Foundation, an Islamic charity based in Aachen, was banned in the summer of 2002, after it was determined that the organization was raising funds for the Palestinian terrorist group Hamas. In 2004, Metin Kaplan, the leader of Cologne-based Turkish Islamist group Kalifatstaat ("caliphate state"), was expelled to Turkey, and his organization was banned for promoting Islamist and jihadist ideologies. For more information, see "Germany Bans Islamic Group," *San Francisco Chronicle*, January 16, 2003; and "Germany Deports Radical Long Sought by Turks," *New York Times*, October 13, 2004.

7. For an account of the German integration debate and in the context of counterterrorism, see Guido Steinberg, *In al-Qaeda's Sights: Germany Needs an Anti-Terrorism Strategy*, Koerber Policy Paper No. 9, Hamburg, January 2010, http://www.koerber-stiftung.de/fileadmin/user_upload/internationale_politik/pdf/2010/Koerber_Policy_Paper_No_9.pdf.

8. For an overview of trends in European homegrown terrorism, see Edwin Bakker, "Jihadi Terrorists in Europe, Their Characteristics and the Circumstances in which they Joined the Jihad: An Explanatory Study," Netherlands Institute of International Relations, Clingendael, December 2006, http://www.clingendael.nl/publications/2006/20061200_cscp_csp_bakker.pdf.

9. Werner Schiffauer, *Die Gottesmänner: Türkische Islamisten in Deutschland* [The men of God: Turkish Islamists in Germany] (Frankfurt: Suhrkamp, 2000).

10. Craig Whitlock, "Converts to Islam Move Up In Cells," *Washington Post*, September 15, 2007, http://www.washingtonpost.com/wp-dyn/content/article/2007/09/14/AR2007091402265.html.

11. Oliver Schroem, "Überforderte Ermittler" [Overextended investigators], *Die Zeit*, May 6, 2004, http://www.zeit.de/2004/20/Islam-Kasten.

12. Jost Mueller-Neuhof, "Es gibt keine Entspannung. Im Gegenteil" [There is no easing up. To the contrary], *Der Tagesspiegel*, October 28, 2009, http://www.tagesspiegel.de/politik/BKA-Anti-Terror-Gesetze;art771,2934458. For an overview of jihadism in Germany, see Annette Ramelsberger, *Der deutsche Dschihad* [The German jihad] (Berlin: Econ, 2008).

13. For background and details on this terrorist plot, see Simone Kaiser et al., "Operation Alberich: How the CIA Helped Germany Foil Terror Plot," *Spiegel Online*

*International,* September 10, 2007, http://www.spiegel.de/international/germany/0,1518,504837,00.html; Yassin Musharbaslı and Marcel Rosenbach, "Sauerland Cell in the Dock: Germany Prepares for Homegrown Terror Trial," *Spiegel Online International,* April 16, 2009, http://www.spiegel.de/international/germany/0,1518,619381,00.html; and Anne Penketh, "Frankfurt Bomb Plot: Islamic Centre Had 'Calamitous Role,'" *The Independent,* September 9, 2007, http://www.independent.co.uk/news/world/europe/frankfurt-bomb-plot-islamic-centre-had-calamitous-role-401791.html.

14. Marcel Rosenbach and Holger Stark, "Terrorismus: Aladins Erzählungen" [Terrorism: Aladdin's stories]," *Der Spiegel,* vol. 41 (2007), http://www.spiegel.de/spiegel/print/d-53203434.html.

15. In October 2007, coalition forces captured records with the names of some six hundred foreign fighters in a raid near Sinjar, along Iraq's Syrian border. See Combating Terrorism Center, *Al-Qaeda's Foreign Fighters in Iraq: A First Look at the Sinjar Records* (West Point, NY: U.S. Military Academy, 2007), www.ctc.usma.edu/harmony/pdf/CTCForeignFighter.19.Dec07.pdf.

16. Schäuble's remark is in "Spiegel-Gespräch: Es kann uns jederzeit treffen" [It can hit us at any time], *Der Spiegel,* July 9, 2007, 32, available at http://wissen.spiegel.de/wissen/image/show.html?did=52185901&aref=image036/2007/07/07/ROSP200702800310033.PDF&thumb=false. See also *Spiegel Online International,* "Schäuble in Trouble: Interior Minister in Crisis over Targeted Killings Remark," July 16, 2007, www.spiegel.de/international/germany/0,1518,494635,00.html.

17. Focus Online, "Bundestag: BND-Ausschuss eingesetzt" [Parliament: Foreign intelligence service committee appointed], April 7, 2006, http://www.focus.de/politik/deutschland/bundestag_aid_107311.html.

18. For an account of U.S. actions seen from the German perspective, see Wolfgang S. Heinz, *Terrorismusbekämpfung und Menschenrechtsschutz in Europa* [Terrorism and human rights protection in Europe] (Berlin: German Institute for Human Rights, 2007), http://files.institut-fuer-menschenrechte.de/488/d63_v1_file_4641e705b1a84_IUS-032_S_Terror3_ND1_RZ_WEB.pdf .

19. Holger Stark, John Goetz, and Matthias Gebauer, "'Forbidden Fruits' of Torture: Germans Relying on Pakistani Interrogation Methods," *Spiegel Online International,* October 1, 2007, http://www.spiegel.de/international/germany/0,1518,508931,00.html.

20. The Tunisian citizen Ihsan Garnaoui was arrested for possessing explosives manuals and for attempting to organize a terrorist ring in Berlin. He was convicted of tax evasion in April 2005. See Bloomberg.com, "Berlin Court Acquits Tunisian

Garnaoui of Planning Bomb Attacks," April 6, 2005, http://www.bloomberg.com/apps/news?pid=71000001&refer=germany&sid=aEEBt0PGKKxM.

21. The judges in Hamburg criticized U.S. authorities for not providing sufficient evidence, such as uncensored interrogations of detainees in Guantánamo. See "Sentencing in 9/11 Case is German Milestone," *International Herald Tribune*," January 10, 2007.

22. See Shawn Boyne, "Preserving the Rule of Law in a Time of Terror: Germany's Response to Terrorism," in *Law vs. War: Competing Approaches to Fighting Terrorism*, ed. Shawn Boyne, Michael German, and Paul R. Pillar (Carlisle, PA: U.S. Army Strategic Studies Institute, 2005), 17–22, http://www.strategicstudiesinstitute.army.mil/pdf-files/PUB613.pdf. See also Hans-Jörg Albrecht, "Country Report on Germany," Research and Documentation Centre, Netherlands Ministry of Justice, 2006, www.wodc.nl/images/Werkdocument%201%20Germany_tcm44-59194.pdf. New authorities also made it possible to track money laundering, employ security checks for personnel at critical sites, and add air marshals to German flag carriers.

23. Only the wiretapping powers of police authorities were expanded. The foreign intelligence service—the BND—is still not allowed to eavesdrop on German citizens in Germany or abroad. In the spring of 2008 a public outcry arose when it became known that the BND had spied on computers belonging to the Afghan government and unintentionally recorded email exchanges between an Afghan minister and a German journalist living in Kabul.

24. In 2005, for instance, the state of Bavaria deported Yehia Yousif's twenty-two-year-old son, Omar, to Egypt. Omar Yousif had attended a terrorists' training camp in Pakistan in 2001. After returning to Germany he committed some petty crimes.

25. For a first official explanation of the counterterrorism packages, see Federal Ministry of the Interior, "Fakten zur Evaluierung des Terrorismusbekämpfungsgesetzes [Facts about the Terrorism Act]," May 2005, www.bmi.bund.de/cln_012/nn_165104/Internet/Content/Common/Anlagen/Themen/Terrorismus/Fakten__Evaluierung__Terrorismusbekaempfungsgesetz,templateId=raw,property=publicationFile.pdf/Fakten_Evaluierung_Terrorismusbekaempfungsgesetz.pdf. See also Francis T. Miko and Christian Froehlich, "Germany's Role in Fighting Terrorism: Implications for U.S. Policy," Congressional Research Service, Washington, DC, December 27, 2004, 4, http://www.fas.org/irp/crs/RL32710.pdf.

26. The committee, known as the G-10 Commission, consists of four members and is selected by a parliamentary oversight committee for intelligence matters; the commission members may or may not be sitting members of the German Parliament.

In emergencies, German intelligence may operate without prior approval of the G-10 Commission but must seek its retroactive approval shortly thereafter. For a brief overview of the G-10, see German Bundestag, "G-10 Commission," http://web archiv.bundestag.de/archive/2008/0506/htdocs_e/parliament/03organs/05oth comm/othcom5.html.

27. For country rankings, see Privacy International, "Leading Surveillance Societies in the EU and the World 2007," http://www.privacyinternational.org/article.shtml? cmd[347]=x-347-559597.

28. Michael Jacobson, *The West at War: U.S. and European Counterterrorism Efforts, Post–September 11* (Washington, DC: Washington Institute for Near East Policy, 2006), 39. Schily made a similar effort with respect to German domestic intelligence, attempting to place all the state domestic intelligence agencies under the control of one federal institution. The effort failed. See Richard Warnes, "Germany," in *Considering the Creation of a Domestic Intelligence Agency in the United States,* ed. Brian A. Jackson (Santa Monica, CA: RAND, 2009), 105.

29. For example, Germany's domestic intelligence agency, the BfV, cannot give any of the state intelligence bureaus, the LfVs, direct orders. And, as of 2006, the BfV actually had fewer personnel (2,447) than the total in the LfVs (approximately 2,900). Warnes, "Germany," 103–4.

30. Under the law, the BKA is also authorized to take the lead if the jurisdiction of any one state police agency cannot be discerned. The text of the law is at http://bundesrecht.juris.de/bkag_1997/BJNR165010997.html#BJNR165010997BJNG003001377

31. Interior Ministers Schily and Schäuble took steps to circumvent the "separation instruction" by establishing joint oversight of domestic intelligence and police affairs in the Ministry of Interior. Furthermore, the federal government has taken preliminary steps to establish integrated counterterrorism units, expecting that a successful terrorist attack in Germany will tip the balance in favor of more muscular counterterrorism measures.

32. For background, see Federal Ministry of the Interior, "Joint Counter-Terrorism Centre—International Terrorism," http://www.en.bmi.bund.de/cln_028/nn_1016300/Internet/Content/Themen/Terrorism/DataAndFacts/Joint__Counter__Terrorism__Centre__International__Terrorism.html.

33. The text of the Act on Joint Databases of 2006 can be found at http://www.en.bmi.bund.de/cln_028/nn_1016300/Internet/Content/Common/Anlagen/Gesetze/Antiterrordateigesetz__en,templateId=raw,property=publicationFile.pdf/Antiterror

dateigesetz_en.pdf. An overview of its provision can be found at Federal Ministry of the Interior, "Federal Minister of the Interior Wolfgang Schäuble Explained that the Counter-Terrorism Database Is Essential to the Fight against Terror," http://www.en. bmi.bund.de/cln_028/nn_1016300/Internet/Content/Themen/Terrorism/DataAnd Facts/Antiterrordatei__en,templateId=renderPrint.html.

34. Author's interviews with German counterterrorism officials, 2006–2007.

35. Interview with a senior official in the Federal Ministry of Interior, February 2009. On this issue see Günther K. Weisse, "Kompetenzzentrum für Technische Kommunikationsüberwachung" [Competence center for technical communications monitoring], *Der Sicherheitsmelder,* June 8, 2009, http://www.sicherheitsmelder.de/ gate.dll?op=start

36. Simone Kaiser, Marcel Rosenbach, and Holger Stark, "Operation Alberich: How the CIA Helped Germany Foil Terror Plot," *Spiegel Online International,* September 10, 2007, www.spiegel.de/international/germany/0,1518,504837,00.html; and Yassin Musharbash, "Terror Trial: Germany Ends Biggest Case since RAF," *Spiegel Online International,* March 4, 2010, http://www.spiegel.de/international/ germany/0,1518,681833,00.html.

37. Author's interviews with German counterterrorism officials, April 2008.

38. For accounts of infiltration of right-wing extremist groups, see an interview with Heinz Fromm, head of Bundesamt für Verfassungsschutz, in *Frankfurter Allgemeine Sonntagszeitung,* January 28, 2008, available at www.verfassungsschutz.de/de/presse info/interview.

39. Author's interview with a high-ranking officer in the German intelligence community, April 2007.

40. Author's interview with an official in the German Chancellery, May 2008.

41. Author's interview with a German liaison officer based in Paris, March 2001.

42. This development replicates the situation in the 1970s, when the threat of domestic terrorism triggered the growth of the Bundeskriminalamt. In a decade, the number of employees went from nine hundred to three thousand. For the history of BKA see Wolfgang Kraushaar, ed., *Die RAF und der linke Terrorismus* [The RAF and Left-Wing Terrorism], vol. 2 (Hamburg: Hamburger Edition, 2006); and Dieter Schenk, *Horst Herold und das BKA* [Horst Herold and the BKA] (Hamburg: Hoffmann und Campe, 1998). See also Wilhelm Dietl, *Die BKA Story* [The BKA Story], (München: Droemer, 2000); Dorothea Hauser, *Baader und Herold: Beschreibung eines Kampfes* [Baader and Herold: Anatomy of a Struggle], (Berlin: Fest, 1997); and Peters, *Tödlicher Irrtum* [Fatal Error].

43. After the general elections in September 2009, Wolfgang Schäuble was appointed minister of finance. Schäuble's deputy August Hanning, the former head of Bundesnachrichtendienst and for some years the driving force behind the German counterterrorism efforts, went into early retirement. Thomas de Maizière, the former secretary of the Federal Chancellery and Chancelor Angela Merkel's close political ally, became minister of interior. Merkel's new coalition partner, the Free Democratic Party (FDP), opposes any further strengthening of counterterrorism laws for civil liberty reasons. On this topic, Merkel yielded to the FDP. Therefore the new minister, Thomas de Maizière, distanced himself from his predecessors' course of action. See the interview with de Maizière, "Ich kann nicht gegen jede Gefahr ein Gesetz machen" [I cannot draft a law against every threat], *Süddeutsche Zeitung,* November 21, 2009.

44. See *Spiegel Online International,* "Big Brother Worries: German Parliament Passes Anti-Terror Law," November 13, 2008, http://www.spiegel.de/international/germany/0,1518,590198,00.html. The text of the law (Gesetz über das Bundeskriminalamt und die Zusammenarbeit des Bundes und der Länder in kriminalpolizeilichen Angelegenheiten) is at http://bundesrecht.juris.de/bkag_1997/BJNR165010997.html #BJNR165010997BJNG003001377.

45. This last provision—computer spying—met considerable criticism from both ends of the political spectrum. It passed, however, because, although the German media and public are deeply skeptical of giving new authorities to the intelligence services, they seem less reluctant to see an expansion of powers in the field of police and law enforcement; perhaps this is one reason counterterrorism efforts in Germany are principally police driven.

46. Law of July 30, 2009 to Prosecute the Preparation of Serious Violent Crimes Directed against the State (adopted August 3, 2009). See section 89a, (2), 2 and 3, http://www.bmj.de/files/3c0226a343658ac9bedc9c374a4100c1/3826/gesetz_staatsgefaehrdeter_gewalttaten_terror_bundesgesetzblatt.pdf.

47. Florian Gathmann, "Gutachter kritisieren Terrorcamp-Gesetz" [Experts criticize terror camp law], *Spiegel Online,* April 22, 2009, www.spiegel.de/politik/deutschland/0,1518,620555,00.html.

48. See Ministry of Justice, "Bundestag beschliesst Umsetzung der EU-Richtlinie zur Vorratsdatenspeicherung" [German Parliament agrees on implementation of EU directive on data retention] (press release), Berlin, November 9, 2007, http://www.bmj.de/enid/Pressestelle/Pressemitteilungen_58.html?druck=1&pmc_id=4813.

49. N-tv.de, "Vorratsdatenspeicherung: Gesetz teilweise ausgesetzt [Data retention: Law partly suspended for the time being]," March 18, 2008, http://www.n-tv.de/politik/

Gesetz-teilweise-ausgesetzt-article12206.html. The 2010 ruling by the court did not preclude data retention by the government simply. Instead, the court held that the current law was insufficient in ensuring the stored data were itself secure and not precise enough in how the data might be used. The law itself had been drawn up following an EU directive mandating the six-month data retention requirement. Federal Constitutional Court, "Konkrete Ausgestaltung der Vorrats-datenspeicherung nicht verfassungsgemaess" [Concrete design of data retention not constitutional], Press Release No. 11/2010; and court decision 1 BvR 256/08 of March 2, 2010. http://www.bundesverfassungsgericht.de/pressemitteilungen/bvg10-011.html.

50. Federal Constitutional Court, "Verfassungsbeschwerden gegen akustische Wohnraumüberwachung (so genannter Grosser Lauschangriff) teilweise erfolgreich" [Constitutional complaint against audio surveillance of the home (so-called large-scale eavesdropping attack) partially successful]," Press Release No. 22/2004; and court decision 1 BvR 2378/98 and 1 BvR 1084/99. http://www.bundesverfassungsgericht.de/pressemitteilungen/bvg04-022.html.

51. Federal Constitutional Court, "Provisions in the North Rhine-Westphalia Constitution Protection Act (Verfassungsschutzgesetz Nordrhein-Westfalen) on Online Searches and on the Reconnaissance of the Internet Null and Void," Press Release No. 22/2008; and court decisions 1 BvR 370/07 and 1 BvR 595/07. Both sets of documents are available at http://www.bundesverfassungsgericht.de/pressemitteilungen/bvg08-022en.html.

52. Federal Constitutional Court, "Provisions in the North Rhine-Westphalia Constitution Protection Act"; and court decisions 1 BvR 370/07 and 1 BvR 595/07. According to Jörg Zierke, the head of the Bundeskriminalamt, the court's decision, combined with other limitations imposed by the government, will probably result in his agency's using the new instrument in fewer than ten cases each year.

53. "Bundesverfassungsgericht prüft BKA-Gesetz" [Federal Constitutional Court weighs BKA-Law], Handelsblatt, April 23, 2009, http://www.handelsblatt.com/politik/deutschland/bundesverfassungsgericht-prueft-bka-gesetz;2250586.

54. Federal Constitutional Court, "Authorisation to Shoot Down Aircraft in the Aviation Security Act Void," Press Release No. 11/2006, February 15, 2006; and court decision 1 BvR 357/05. Both sets of documents are available at www.bundesver-fassungsgericht.de/en/press/bvg06-011en.html.

55. Federal Constitutional Court, "Authorisation to Shoot Down Aircraft"; and court decision 1 BvR 357/05.

56. Miko and Froelich, "Germany's Role in Fighting Terrorism," 2. By the BKA's count, some seventy Germans have died since 9/11 from jihadist-inspired terrorism. See Mueller-Neuhof, "Es gibt keine Entspannung."

## Chapter 5: United States: Facing the Threat at Home

1. The Omnibus Diplomatic Security and Antiterrorism Act of 1986, Pub. L 99-399, 100 Stat. 853 (1986). For background on the creation of the CTC, see Duane R. Clarridge, *A Spy for All Seasons* (New York: Scribner, 1997), 319–29.

2. *Public Report of the Vice President's Task Force on Combating Terrorism* (Washington, DC: U.S. Government Printing Office, 1986), 25; http://www.population-security.org/bush_and_terror.pdf.

3. The CIA center was, according to one account, preceded by a National Security Decision Directive, issued by President Reagan in April 1984, which authorized pre-emptive strikes and reprisal raids against foreign terrorists. See G. Davidson Smith, *Combating Terrorism* (New York: Routledge, 1990), 63.

4. Violent Crime Control and Law Enforcement Act of 1994, Pub. L. No. 103-322, 108 Stat. 2115 (1994). "Material support" can include money, property, lodging, training, equipment, help with establishing a false identity, weapons, transportation, and so on. To be a crime under the statute, however, the person providing the support has to know that it is to be used by someone who is or will be engaged in the commission of a possible range of crimes, including terrorism.

5. In 1995, shortly after the Oklahoma City bombing, President Clinton issued a Presidential Decision Directive which stated the government's goal: "to deter, defeat and respond vigorously to all terrorist attacks. . . . In doing so, the U.S. shall pursue vigorously efforts to deter and preempt, apprehend and prosecute, or assist other governments to prosecute, individuals who perpetrate or plan to perpetrate such attacks." Presidential Decision Directive-39, White House, June 21, 1995, http://www.fas.org/irp/offdocs/pdd39.htm. Although parts of the PDD remain classified, President Clinton has written that the directive included authorization for carrying out "covert action and aggressive efforts to capture terrorists abroad." Bill Clinton, *My Life: The Presidential Years* (New York: Vintage, 2005), 428–29.

6. Antiterrorism and Effective Death Penalty Act of 1996, Pub. L. No. 104-132, 110 Stat. 1248 (1996). The bill's major addition to the antiterrorism laws was to make it a federal crime to provide "material support or resources" to groups that had been

designated as foreign terrorist organizations by the State Department. Unlike the 1994 act, the 1996 act did not require the government to prove that those providing support knew it would be used in commission of a violent crime. As a result, it became a crime to give support or aid to groups for use even in their ostensibly "charitable" endeavors once those same groups had been formally designated as terrorist groups by the government.

7. U.S. Senate Select Committee on Intelligence and U.S. House Permanent Select Committee on Intelligence, *Joint Inquiry into Intelligence Community Activities before and after the Terrorist Attacks of September 11, 2001,* S. Rpt. No 107-351, H. Rpt. No. 107-92, 107th Cong., 2nd sess., December 2002, 230. See also Amy B. Zegart, *Spying Blind: The CIA, the FBI, and the Origins of 9/11* (Princeton, NJ: Princeton University Press, 2007), 77–78. The FBI would not create a special bin Laden unit until late in 1999. Louis Freeh, "On War and Terrorism" (testimony before the 9/11 Commission, Washington, DC, April 13, 2004), http://govinfo.library.unt.edu/911/hearings/hearing10/freeh_statement.pdf .

8. Federal Bureau of Investigation, "Draft FBI Strategic Plan: 1998–2003, Keeping Tomorrow Safe," May 1998; cited in Zegart, *Spying Blind,* 132.

9. Zegart, *Spying Blind,* 80–81. See also *The 9/11 Commission Report: Final Report of the National Commission on Terrorist Attacks upon the United States* (New York: W.W. Norton and Co., 2004), 357.

10. According to the CIA inspector general's report on the agency's own performance leading up to the 9/11 attacks, DCI Tenet, despite the rhetoric, neither followed up his memorandum with decisive action nor prevented funds from being drained away from the CTC. Office of the Inspector General, Central Intelligence Agency, "OIG Report on CIA Accountability with Respect to the 9/11 Attacks," Executive Summary, viii–xi, https://www.cia.gov/library/reports/Executive%20Summary_OIG%20Report.pdf.

11. According to the report of the CIA inspector general, "most of its officers did not have the operational experience, expertise, and training necessary to accomplish their mission in an effective manner." Ibid, xi.

12. 9/11 Commission, "Threats and Responses in 2001," Staff Statement No. 10, April 13, 2004, 5, http://govinfo.library.unt.edu/911/staff_statements/staff_statement_10.pdf .

13. For an overview of this point, see Abram N. Shulsky and Gary J. Schmitt, *Silent Warfare: Understanding the World of Intelligence,* 3rd ed. (Washington, DC: Brassey's Inc., 2002), 149–58.

14. The guidelines, devised by Attorney General Edward Levi, were actually two sets of guidelines for intelligence investigations, one for foreign intelligence and counterintelligence and a second for domestic security, echoing the prevailing presumption that foreign and domestic security threats were largely distinct problems that might involve different sets of constitutional issues. Although the foreign intelligence guidelines have never been published in full, a sanitized version appears in U.S. Senate, Select Committee on Intelligence, *National Intelligence Reorganization and Reform Act of 1978: Hearings,* 95th Cong., 2d sess., 1978, Committee Print, 774–90. The domestic guidelines, along with the 1983 revision by Attorney General William French Smith, can be found in Roy Godson, ed., *Intelligence Requirements for the 1980s: Domestic Intelligence* (Lexington, MA: Heath, 1986), 225–64. For a useful overview of the Smith changes and the continuity with the Levi guidelines, see John T. Elliff, "The Attorney General's Guidelines for FBI Investigations," *Cornell Law Review* 69, no. 4 (April 1984): 785–815.

15. Foreign Intelligence Surveillance Act of 1978, Pub. L. No. 95-511, 92 Stat. 1783 (1978).

16. See Zegart, *Spying Blind,* 158–59; and Devin Rollis, "The Wall between National Security and Law Enforcement," in *Can't We All Just Get Along? Improving the Law Enforcement–Intelligence Community Relationship,* ed. Timothy Christenson (Washington, DC: National Defense Intelligence College, 2007), 143–62.

17. See, for example, the Reno Justice Department guidelines issued in 1995 that restricted FISA-generated information from being shared with criminal investigators. The text of the guidelines can be found at http://fas.org/irp/agency/doj/doj071995.pdf . On the problem of the government using FISA for purposes other than intelligence matters, see Stewart A. Baker, "Should Spies Be Cops?" *Foreign Policy,* Winter 1994–1995, 36.

18. "Sharing secrets . . . ran against the grain of everything CIA officers had known, believed, and cherished for years," and "the FBI was an informational 'black hole,' repeatedly withholding information . . . on the grounds that sharing relevant counterterrorism information could compromise pending investigations." Zegart, *Spying Blind,* 113, 140.

19. A significant exception to the view that the terrorist threat America faced was principally the threat to U.S. persons and property abroad was contained in the initial report of the United States Commission on National Security/21st Century, also known as the Hart-Rudman Commission. The commission's first major finding was that "America will become increasingly vulnerable to hostile attack on our homeland,

and our military superiority will not entirely protect us"; its first major recommendation was the creation of a cabinet department of National Homeland Security, which would have "responsibility for planning, coordinating, and integrating various U.S. government activities involved in homeland security." See United States Commission on National Security/21st Century, *New World Coming: American Security in the 21st Century, Major Themes and Implications* (September 15, 1999), 4, http://www.au.af.mil/au/awc/awcgate/nssg/nwc.pdf; and *Roadmap for National Security: Imperative for Change* (February 15, 2001), viii, http://www.au.af.mil/au/awc/awcgate/nssg/phaseIIIfr.pdf.

20. U.S. Department of Justice, Office of the Inspector General, *A Review of the FBI's Handling of Intelligence Information Related to the September 11 Attacks,* Washington, DC, November 2004; redacted and unclassified June 2005, 345.

21. See Office of the Inspector General, Central Intelligence Agency, "OIG Report on CIA Accountability with Respect to the 9/11 Attacks," xiii–xvi.

22. *9/11 Commission Report,* 181–82, 272; and Zegart, *Spying Blind,* 104–7.

23. Pub. L. No. 107–56, 115 Stat. 272 (2001).

24. For background on the history of the letters and the changes made by the Patriot Act to the use of the letters, see U.S. Department of Justice, Office of the Inspector General, *A Review of the Federal Bureau of Investigation's Use of National Security Letters,* Washington, DC, March 2007, 7–10, http://www.usdoj.gov/oig/special/s0703b/final.pdf. For an analysis of follow-on legislation and federal court decisions pertaining to NSLs, see Charles Doyle, "National Security Letters in Foreign Intelligence Investigations: Legal Background and Recent Amendments," Congressional Research Service, Washington, DC, September 8, 2009, http://www.fas.org/sgp/crs/intel/RL33320.pdf.

25. Pub. L. No. 108-458, 118 Stat. 3638 (2004).

26. See, for example, the attorney general's annual reports to Congress on FISA applications, available at http://www.fas.org/irp/agency/doj/fisa/index.html. For a balanced account of this prior approach to electronic surveillance under FISA, see Benjamin Wittes, *Law and the Long War: The Future of Justice in the Age of Terror* (New York: Penguin Press, 2008), 219–27.

27. Wittes, *Law and the Long War,* 228–29.

28. James Risen and Eric Lichtblau, "Bush Lets U.S. Spy on Callers Without Courts," *New York Times,* December 16, 2005, http://www.nytimes.com/2005/12/16/politics/16program.html?_r=1&pagewanted=print.

29. See Wittes, *Law and the Long War,* 233; Alberto Gonzalez and Michael Hayden, press release and press briefing, December 19, 2005, http://www.globalsecurity.org/intell/library/news/2005/intell-051219-dni01.htm; and Offices of the Inspectors

General of the Department of Defense, Department of Justice, Central Intelligence Agency, National Security Agency, and Office of the Director of National Intelligence, *Unclassified Report on the President's Surveillance Program,* Report No. 2009-0013-AS, Washington, DC, July 10, 2009, http://judiciary.house.gov/hearings/pdf/IGTSP Report090710.pdf.

30. Pub. L. 110–261, 122 Stat. 2436 (2008).

31. The language ("use whatever means legally available") is that of Michael Chertoff, who was then assistant attorney general for the Criminal Division; quoted in U.S. Department of Justice, Office of the Inspector General, *The September 11 Detainees: A Review of the Treatment of Aliens Held on Immigration Charges in Connection with the Investigation of the September 11 Attacks,* Washington, DC, April 2003, 13, http://www.usdoj.gov/oig/special/0306/full.pdf. Nearly half of the aliens detained came from either Pakistan or Egypt. Ibid, 21.

32. See Daniel B. Prieto, "War about Terror: Civil Liberties and National Security after 9/11," CFR Working Paper, Council on Foreign Relations, February 2009, 21–22, http://www.cfr.org/publication/18373/; and Eric Lichtblau, *Bush's Law: The Remaking of American Justice* (New York: Pantheon Books, 2008), 46–47. Lichtblau writes that the Justice Department decided to "hold until cleared" because "the risk of doing otherwise, officials believed, was simply too great. 'We have to hold these people until we find out what is going on,' Michael Chertoff, head of the Justice Department's Criminal Division, told his deputy. 'If we turn one person loose we shouldn't have,' said David Laufman, chief of staff to the deputy attorney general, 'there could be catastrophic consequences' " (46–47).

33. U.S. Department of Justice, Office of the Inspector General, *September 11 Detainees,* 105, 196; and Lichtblau, *Bush's Law,* 47.

34. The first institutional change of note, however, was the creation of the Transportation Security Administration (TSA) with the enactment of the Aviation and Transportation Security Act in November 2001, Pub. L 107-71, 115 Stat. 597 (2001). With the establishment of TSA, the federal government was charged with all security screening of passengers and baggage at all commercial airports, which necessitated the hiring and training of over fifty thousand individuals.

35. Michael Chertoff, "How America Responded to Terrorism: 2001–2008" (speech, Center for National Policy, Washington, DC, March 3, 2009), http://www.cnponline.org/ht/display/ContentDetails/i/11467.

36. Charles E. Allen, "Address to the Washington Institute for Near East Policy" (May 6, 2008), http://www.dhs.gov/xnews/speeches/sp_1210107524856.shtm.

37. For background on the fusion centers, see Todd Masse and John Rollins, "A Summary of Fusion Centers: Core Issues and Options for Congress," Congressional Research Service, Washington, DC, September 19, 2007, http://assets.opencrs.com/rpts/RL34177_20070919.pdf; and Eileen R. Larence, "Federal Efforts are Helping to Address Some Challenges Faced by State and Local Fusion Centers," testimony before the Committee on Homeland Security and Governmental Affairs, U.S. Senate, April 17, 2008. The testimony by Larence, the GAO director for homeland security and justice issues, and the accompanying GAO report can be found at http://www.gao.gov/new.items/d08636t.pdf.

38. *9/11 Commission Report,* 357. It should be pointed out that Tenet's memo was addressed just to CIA officials and only subsequently was faxed to the heads of the other major intelligence agencies, seemingly as an "FYI" notice.

39. Sec. 1074 of IRTPA.

40. See National Counterterrorism Center, "About the National Counterterrorism Center," http://www.nctc.gov/about_us/about_nctc.html. For a useful explication of the NCTC's history—the original reason for giving it this planning role, the ambiguities in the law governing that role, and the center's slow evolution toward being a more useful generator of interagency counterterrorist planning, see Project on National Security Reform, *Toward Integrating Complex Missions: Lessons from the National Counterterrorism Center's Directorate of Strategic Operational Planning,* February 2010, http://www.pnsr.org/data/files/pnsr_nctc_dsop_report.pdf.

41. For FBI post-9/11 personnel tables, see FBI, "People," http://www.fbi.gov/aboutus/transformation/people.htm.

42. See FBI, "National Security Branch Overview," September 2006, http://www.montana.edu/wwwcp/Virtual%20Library/FBI.pdf.

43. See Alfred Cumming and Todd Masse, "Intelligence Reform Implementation at the Federal Bureau of Investigation: Issues and Options for Congress," Congressional Research Service, August 16, 2005, 21–22, http://www.fas.org/sgp/crs/intel/RL33033.pdf.

44. For an overview of the JTTFs, see FBI, "Protecting America against a Terrorist Attack," http://www.fbi.gov/page2/may09/jttfs_052809.html.

45. For the text of those guidelines, see http://www.justice.gov/ag/readingroom/guidelines.pdf.

46. For an analysis of the new guidelines, see Gary Schmitt, "An 'Intelligent' FBI," *Weekly Standard,* October 10, 2008, http://www.weeklystandard.com/Content/Public/Articles/000/000/015/676zlmni.asp. A redacted version of the FBI's internal "Domestic

Investigations and Operations Guide," issued on December 16, 2008, is now publicly available; see http://graphics8.nytimes.com/packages/images/nytint/docs/the-new-operations-manual-from-the-f-b-i/original.pdf.

47. There have been three cases of likely jihadist-inspired terrorism in the United States since 9/11: the 2002 shooting of customers at an El Al counter in Los Angeles International Airport by Egyptian national Hesham Mohamed Hadayet; the shooting at the military recruitment center in Little Rock, Arkansas, in June 2009 by Muslim convert Abdulhakim Mujahid Muhammad; and the 2009 shooting by Army major Nidal Hasan at Fort Hood, Texas. Each of these shootings appears to be an instance of an individual acting on his own.

48. To get a sense of the task, consider that since 2004, the FBI has been in charge of creating and managing the U.S. government's consolidated terrorist watchlist. According to the bureau and the Justice Department, the list contains over a million "known or suspected terrorist identities." Minus aliases and variations in name spellings, the total number of U.S. persons and foreigners on that list is approximately four hundred thousand. Of that number, the FBI has said that fewer than 5 percent are U.S. citizens or legal resident aliens—still, a figure of approximately twenty thousand. See "Responses of the Federal Bureau of Investigation to Questions for the Record Arising from the March 25, 2009 Hearing before the Senate Committee on the Judiciary," September 15, 2009, 58–59, http://www.fas.org/irp/congress/2009_hr/fbi-qfr.pdf. The FBI's management of the watchlist has been criticized by the Justice Department's Office of the Inspector General, both for failing to keep the list adequately updated and for being tardy in removing unnecessary entries. Given the massiveness of the undertaking and detailed reporting requirements associated with keeping a list of this sort, it is not particularly surprising that these problems would occur. See U.S. Department of Justice, Office of Inspector General, "The Federal Bureau of Investigation's Terrorist Watchlist Nomination Practices," May 2009, http://www.justice.gov/oig/reports/FBI/a0925/final.pdf.

49. On these and related points, see Richard A. Posner, *Uncertain Shield: The U.S. Intelligence System in the Throes of Reform* (Lanham, MD: Roman and Littlefield, 2006), 55–86; and Gary Schmitt, "Truth to Power," in *The Future of American Intelligence,* ed. Peter Berkowitz (Stanford, CA: Hoover Institution Press, 2005), 62–64. See also the report issued by Edward Maguire, "Critical Intelligence Community Management Challenges," Office of the Director of Inspector General, Office of the Director of National Intelligence, November 12, 2008, 2, http://www.fas.org/irp/news/2009/04/odni-ig-1108.pdf.

50. James Q. Wilson, *Bureaucracy: What Government Agencies Do and Why They Do It* (New York: Basic Books, 1989).

51. Charles Allen, "Terrorism in the Twenty-First Century: Implications for Homeland Security," in *Terrorist Threat and U.S. Response* (Policy Focus No. 86), eds. Matthew Levitt and Michael Jacobson (Washington, DC: Washington Institute for Near East Policy, 2008), 29–30, http://www.washingtoninstitute.org/pubPDFs/Policy Focus86.pdf.

52. For a relatively positive early account of the progress made by the NCTC on this front, see House Permanent Select Committee on Intelligence, Subcommittee on Oversight, "Initial Assessment on the Implementation of the Intelligence Reform and Terrorism Prevention Act of 2004," July 27, 2006, 8, 11, 17, http://www.fas.org/irp/congress/2006_rpt/hpsci072706.pdf. According to former DNI John Negroponte, by April 2006, information from twenty-eight different systems were flowing into the NCTC. Negroponte, "Intelligence Reform: Making it Happen" (speech, National Press Club, Washington, DC, April 20, 2006), http://www.dni.gov/speeches/printer_friendly/20060420_speech_print.htm.

53. Ian Millhiser, "'Connecting the Dots' Requires a Commitment to IT Infrastructure," Center for American Progress, January 11, 2010, http://www.americanprogress.org/issues/2010/01/connecting_dots.html. The same general point emerges in the following exchange between the chairman of the Senate Homeland Security Committee, Sen. Joseph Lieberman, and DNI Denis Blair. Lieberman: "Do we not have the capacity within the NCTC to conduct a Google-like search?" Blair: "The search tools that we now have depend on certain characteristics and I don't want to describe them here, but they also have blind spots that don't allow the Google-like idea that we have from our own [personal] computers. Several of those shortcomings came up in this case." Senate Committee on Homeland Security & Governmental Affairs, "Intelligence Reform: The Lessons and Implications of the Christmas Day Attack, Part I," Hearings, January 20, 2010, available at http://hsgac.senate.gov/public/index.cfm?FuseAction=Hearings.Hearing&Hearing_ID=db07fd72-c631-42ea-a514-215127425e3a. NCTC director Michael Leiter testified that "each day NCTC receives literally thousands of pieces of intelligence information from around the world . . . and places more than 350 people . . . on the [terrorist] watchlist—virtually all based on far more damning information than that associated with Mr. Abdulmutallab." Statement before the House Committee on Homeland Security, "Flight 253: Learning Lessons from an Averted Tragedy," January 27, 2010, 4, http://hsc.house.gov/SiteDocuments/2010012 7100923-82356.pdf.

54. "Analytic focus during December was on the imminent AQAP attacks on Americans and American interest in Yemen, and on supporting CT efforts in Yemen." "Summary of the White House Review of the December 25, 2009 Attempted Terrorist Attack," White House, January 7, 2010, 4, http://www.whitehouse.gov/sites/default/files/summary_of_wh_review_12-25-09.pdf. See also Eric Lipton, Eric Schmitt, and Mark Mazzeti, "Review of Jet Bomb Plot Shows More Missed Clues," *New York Times,* January 18, 2010, http://www.nytimes.com/2010/01/18/us/18intel.html.

55. For background, see Masse and Rollins, "A Summary of Fusion Centers"; and Matt A. Mayer, *Homeland Security and Federalism: Protecting America from Outside the Beltway* (Santa Barbara, CA: ABC-CLIO, 2009), 131–34.

56. Joseph W. Augustyn, "Upgrade America's Spy Program: The CIA's National Clandestine Service Urgently Needs Reform," *Christian Science Monitor,* April 7, 2009, http://www.csmonitor.com/2009/0407/p09s02-coop.html.

57. Ibid. See also Reuel Marc Gerecht, "A New Clandestine Service," in *The Future of American Intelligence,* ed. Peter Berkowitz (Stanford, CA: Hoover Institution Press, 2005), 103–38. For a more positive assessment of the CIA, see Karen deYoung and Walter Pincus, "Success Against al-Qaeda Cited: Infiltration of Network is a Factor as Administration Debates Afghanistan Policy," *Washington Post,* September 30, 2009, http://www.washingtonpost.com/wp-dyn/content/article/2009/09/29/AR2009092903699.html.

58. See Zegart, *Spying Blind,* 120–55.

59. Posner, *Uncertain Shield,* 89–93; Cumming and Masse, "Intelligence Reform Implementation at the Federal Bureau of Investigation"; and George W. Bush, "Strengthening the Ability of the Department of Justice to Meet Challenges to the Security of the Nation," memorandum, June 29, 2005, http://www.fas.org/irp/news/2005/06/wh062905-doj.html.

60. See FBI, "National Security Branch Overview" September 2006, http://www.montana.edu/careers/Virtual%20Library/FBI.pdf.

61. See Zegart, *Spying Blind,* 189–93; and Posner, *Uncertain Shield,* 87–117.

62. The email contact between Major Hasan and al-Awlaki potentially could have been exploited in two ways. The first would have been to use a bureau-constructed, online imposter of al-Awlaki to explore whether the major was interested in more than just research. The second path would have been to approach Major Hasan and use his exchanges with the cleric to see whether al-Awlaki might have been willing to put the major in contact with more operational elements within the terrorist network. Obviously, there is no guarantee that either of these efforts would have proved fruitful and,

certainly, in the case of the second, it is extremely unlikely, given the major's own jihadist inclinations, that he would have cooperated with authorities. However, the point here is not whether either effort would have worked but the fact that neither was considered in this instance.

63. Attorney General Eric H. Holder Jr. to Senator Mitch McConnell, February 3, 2010, http://www.justice.gov/cjs/docs/ag-letter-2-3-10.pdf?utm_source=Newsletter &utm_medium=Email .

64. See Mayer, *Homeland Security and Federalism,* 137–39; and Richard Falkenrath, "Defending the City: NYPD's Counterterrorism Operations" (speech, Washington Institute for Near East Policy, Washington, DC, June 23, 2009), http://www.washingtoninstitute.org/html/pdf/falkenrath20090623.pdf.

65. See Mayer, *Homeland Security and Federalism,* 136–37; and Eric Schmitt, "Surveillance Effort Draws Civil Liberties Concern," *New York Times,* April 29, 2009, http://www.nytimes.com/2009/04/29/us/29surveil.html?pagewanted=print.

66. See Executive Order 13491, "Ensuring Lawful Interrogations," January 22, 2009, http://www.whitehouse.gov/the_press_office/EnsuringLawfulInterrogations/; and Department of Justice, Office of Public Affairs, "Special Task Report on Interrogation and Transfer Policies Issues Its Recommendations to the President," August 24, 2009, http://www.justice.gov/opa/pr/2009/August/09-ag-835.html.

67. Quoted in Marc A. Thiessen, *Courting Disaster: How the CIA Kept America Safe and How Barack Obama is inviting the Next Attack* (Washington, DC: Regnery Publishing, 2010), 10.

68. Peter Baker, "Banned Techniques Yielded 'High Value Information,' Memo Says," *New York Times,* April 21, 2009, http://www.nytimes.com/2009/04/22/us/politics/22blair.html.

69. Michael Hayden and Michael B. Mukasey, "The President Ties His Own Hands on Terror," April 17, 2009, http://online.wsj.com/article/SB123993446103128041.html.

70. See Richard B. Zabel and James J. Benjamin Jr., *In Pursuit of Justice: Prosecuting Terrorism Cases in the Federal Courts, 2009 Update and Recent Developments* (New York and Washington, DC: Human Rights First, 2009), 6, http://www.humanrightsfirst.org/pdf/090723-LS-in-pursuit-justice-09-update.pdf.

71. See Mitchell D. Silber, "The Fort Hood Attack: A Preliminary Assessment," testimony before the Senate Homeland Security and Governmental Affairs Committee (November 19, 2009), http://hsgac.senate.gov/public/index.cfm?FuseAction=Hearings.Hearing&Hearing_ID=70b4e9b6-d2af-4290-b9fd-7a466a0a86b6.

## Chapter 6: U.S. Counterterrorism in Perspective

1. For background on the New York plots and the period more generally, see Andrew C. McCarthy, *Willful Blindness: A Memoir of the Jihad* (New York: Encounter Books, 2008). For background on the Millennium Plot, see Gov't. Sentencing Mem. United States v. Ressam, No. CR99-666C (W.D. Wash. April 20, 2005), http://intel files.egoplex.com/ressam-sentencing-memo.pdf. See also PBS, *Frontline,* "Ahmed Ressam's Millennium Plot," http://www.pbs.org/wgbh/pages/frontline/shows/trail/ inside/cron.html.

2. The act became law on October 26, 2001, forty-five days following the attacks of 9/11. The measure passed in the House of Representatives by a vote of 357 to 66; in the Senate the vote was 98 to1.

3. In addition to expanding the authority to use NSLs to other government agencies besides the FBI, the Patriot Act also expanded the range of personnel within the FBI who could authorize their use. Previously, only FBI headquarters could authorize NSLs; however, under the new law, the discretion was given to the heads of the FBI field offices, as well.

4. For background on NSLs, see Charles Doyle, "National Security Letters in Foreign Intelligence Investigations: Legal Background and Recent Amendments," Congressional Research Service, Washington, DC, September 8, 2009, http://www.fas. org/sgp/crs/intel/RL33320.pdf. This broad authority of the Patriot Act was modified in 2007 by the passage of the USA Patriot Improvement and Reauthorization Act, Pub. L. No 109-177, sec. 115 (2006), which explicitly allows the recipient of an NSL to petition a United States district court "for an order modifying or setting aside the request."

5. See U.S. Department of Justice, Office of the Inspector General, *A Review of the Federal Bureau of Investigation's Use of National Security Letters,* Washington, DC, March 2007, http://www.usdoj.gov/oig/special/s0703b/final.pdf; U.S. Department of Justice, Office of the Inspector General, *A Review of the FBI's Use of National Security Letters: Assessment of Corrective Actions and Examination of NSL Usage in 2006,* Washington, DC, March 2008, http://www.justice.gov/oig/special/s0803b/final.pdf; and U.S. Department of Justice, Office of the Inspector General, *A Review of the Federal Bureau of Investigation's Use of Exigent Letters and Other Informal Requests for Telephone Records,* Washington, DC, January 2010, http://www.justice.gov/oig/special/s1001r.pdf. This last report of the inspector general (IG) is only partially related to the use of NSLs. Between 2003 and 2006, the bureau issued requests for information from communication service providers that ignored the NSL process and were said to be justified as time-sensitive, urgent requests. When concerns about the use of "exigent letters"

arose, the bureau issued "after-the-fact" NSLs to give the requests legal "cover" (165–84). Although the FBI ceased the practice of issuing exigent letters in 2006, the IG report notes—but doesn't accept—the bureau's contention that, relying on an Office of Legal Council opinion, it had a statutory basis for this practice (263–68).

6. See the three reviews by the Justice Department's inspector general cited in the previous note. For a brief overview of the amending legislation and the role of the courts in modifying the Patriot Act's provisions regarding NSLs, see Doyle, "National Security Letters in Foreign Intelligence Investigations." Also controversial was that, as originally crafted, the Patriot Act forbade NSL recipients from disclosing to anyone that the government had asked for the information; under a strict reading of the law, a recipient could not consult with others in his company or his lawyer.

7. See the annual report to Congress for 2008 pursuant to sections 1807 and 1862 of the Foreign Intelligence Surveillance Act of 1978 and section 118 of USA Patriot Improvement and Reauthorization Act of 2006, available at http://www.usdoj.gov/nsd/foia/reading_room/2008fisa-ltr.pdf.

8. Jack Goldsmith, *The Terror Presidency: Law and Judgment Inside the Bush Administration* (New York: W. W. Norton and Co., 2007), 71–75.

9. See William H. Rehnquist, *All the Laws But One: Civil Liberties in Wartime* (New York: Alfred A. Knopf, 1998).

10. See Jeffrey Tulis and Joseph M. Bessette, "On the Constitution, Politics, and the Presidency," in *The Constitutional Presidency,* ed. Joseph M. Tulis and Jeffrey K. Bessette (Baltimore: Johns Hopkins University Press, 2009), 1–27.

11. See Joseph M. Bessette and Gary J. Schmitt, "Executive Power and the American Founding," in *Separation of Powers and Good Government,* ed. Bradford P. Wilson and Peter W. Schramm (Lanham, MD: Rowman and Littlefield, 1994), 47–62. See also Jerrilyn Green Marston, *King and Congress: The Transfer of Political Legitimacy, 1774–1776* (Princeton, NJ: Princeton University Press, 1987); and Charles C. Thach Jr., *The Creation of the Presidency: 1775–1789* (Baltimore: Johns Hopkins University Press, 1969), chap. 3.

12. Alexis de Tocqueville, *Democracy in America,* trans. and ed. Harvey C. Mansfield and Delba Winthrop (Chicago: University of Chicago Press, 2000), 118.

13. Ibid., 119. Emphasis added.

14. See Rehnquist, *All the Laws But One,* 11–74.

15. Ibid., 170–83; and Geoffrey R. Stone, *Perilous Times: Free Speech in Wartime, From the Sedition Act of 1798 to the War on Terrorism* (New York: W. W. Norton and Co., 2004), 156–58.

16. See Rehnquist, *All the Laws But One,* 184–202, 212–17; Neal Katyal and Richard Caplan, "The Surprisingly Stronger Case for the Legality of the NSA Surveillance Program: The FDR Precedent," *Stanford Law Review* 60, no. 4 (2008): 1035–61; and Laura K. Donohue, *The Cost of Counterterrorism: Power, Politics, and Liberty* (New York: Cambridge University Press, 2008), 218–19.

17. Undeniably, assertions of presidential authority by the Bush administration could have been handled more adroitly politically, and lessons might have been learned from the examples of George Washington and Lincoln. See Gary J. Schmitt, "The Myth of the (Bush) Imperial Presidency," *National Security Outlook* no. 1, American Enterprise Institute, January 2009, http://www.aei.org/docLib/2009 0113_0123821JanNSOg.pdf.

18. Reuel Marc Gerecht and Gary Schmitt, "France: Europe's Counterterrorist Powerhouse," *European Outlook* no. 3, American Enterprise Institute, November 2007, http://www.aei.org/docLib/20071101_22370EuO03Gerecht_g.pdf.

19. Interviews with French security officials, June 2006. According to a report by Human Rights Watch, "Available government figures indicate that 71 individuals described as 'Islamic fundamentalists' were forcibly removed from France between September 11, 2001, and September 2006. Fifteen of these were described by the government as imams." *In the Name of Prevention: Insufficient Safeguards in National Security Removals* (New York: Human Rights Watch, 2007), 1, http://www.hrw.org/sites/default/files/reports/france0607_0.pdf.

20. See Peter Clarke, *Learning from Experience: Counter-terrorism in the UK since 9/11* (London: Policy Exchange, 2007), 21–22, http://www.policyexchange.org.uk/publications/publication.cgi?id=15. In 2006, Eliza Manningham-Buller, then head of MI5, publicly commented that her agency was tracking close to thirty active terrorist plots and trying to keep abreast of 1,600 suspects, most of whom were British-born and linked to Pakistan-based terrorist groups. Deborah Haynes and Michael Holden, "Britain Facing 30 Terrorist Plots, Says Spy Chief," *Washington Post,* November 10, 2006.

21. For an overview of the "stop and search" powers, see Clare Feikert and Charles Doyle, "Anti-Terrorism Authority under the Laws of the United Kingdom and the United States," Congressional Research Service, Washington, DC, September 7, 2006, http://fas.org/sgp/crs/intel/RL33726.pdf. In January 2010, however, the European Court of Human Rights ruled that the "stop and search" powers violated article 8 (the right to respect for private and family life) of the European Convention on Human Rights. Previously, the British courts had upheld the law as a proportionate measure

in light of the threat faced and the minimal inconvenience to privacy. See *In the Case of Gillan and Quinton v. United Kingdom,* January 12, 2010, http://cmiskp.echr.coe.int/tkp 197/view.asp?item=8&portal=hbkm&action=html&highlight=&sessionid= 47102277&skin=hudoc-pr-en. The United Kingdom has announced it will appeal the ruling to the EU Grand Chamber. Of particular concern to the government is the ruling's impact on ensuring security for the upcoming London Summer Olympics in 2012.

22. Quoted in Feikert and Doyle, "Anti-Terrorism Authority under the Laws of the United Kingdom and the United States," 4. The use of the "stop and search" powers had grown nearly fourfold from 2004 (33,117) to 2008 (117,200), with blacks and Asians more likely to be stopped than whites. Because of growing criticism of how the police were using the powers, the Metropolitan Police announced in July 2009 plans to employ the powers in a more targeted and discrete manner. And, indeed, according to Lord Carlile, the UK government's independent reviewer of the use of the terrorism laws, a kind of reverse discrimination was taking place because of the criticism, with police increasing the number of whites they stopped to lessen the appearance of racial or ethnic bias on their part. See Lord Carlile of Berriew QC, "Report on the Operation in 2008 of the Terrorism Act 2000 and of Part 1 of the Terrorism Act 2006," presented to Parliament pursuant to section 36 of the Terrorism Act 2006 (June 2009), 29, http://security.homeoffice.gov.uk/news-publications/publication-search/general/Lord-Carlile-report-2009/Lord-Carlile-report.pdf?view=Binary.

23. Feikert and Doyle, "Anti-Terrorism Authority under the Laws of the United Kingdom and the United States," 22–26.

24. Privacy International, "Leading Surveillance Societies in the EU and the World 2007," http://www.privacyinternational.org/article.shtml?cmd[347]=x-347-559597.

25. For an overview of these provisions, see Lord Carlile, "Report on the Operation in 2008 of the Terrorism Act 2000 and of Part 1 of the Terrorism Act 2006," 48. In January 2010, the UK Home Secretary announced the banning of Islam4UK and Al Muhajiroun, two Islamist organizations, under the antiterrorism laws proscribing the incitement or glorification of terrorism. BBC News, "Islam4UK Islamist Group Banned under Terror Laws," January 12, 2010, http://news.bbc.co.uk/2/hi/8453560.stm. Under the law, the order banning an organization must be laid before the Parliament, and the organization being proscribed has access to different appeal mechanisms to try and lift the order.

26. See Feikert and Doyle, "Anti-Terrorism Authority under the Laws of the United Kingdom and the United States," 5–13; for a comparison of British detention practices with those of France, see Jerry Shapiro, "Detention of Terrorism Suspects in

Britain and France," testimony before the Commission on Security and Cooperation in Europe, July 15, 2008, http://www.brookings.edu/testimony/2008/0715_terrorism_shapiro.aspx. Among the restrictions placed on the individual are curfews, electronic tagging, and withholding the individual's passport, as well as restrictions on visitors, phone use, and the Internet. The inability of the government to try some individuals is tied at least in part to the fact that, under British law, information derived from signals intelligence cannot be used in court.

27. In June 2009, the Law Lords (now the UK's Supreme Court) ruled that detainees were entitled to be told "sufficient" information about the case against them to enable them to challenge the control finding. The court tied its finding to a 2009 ruling by the EU high court that found an accused individual had a fundamental right to be informed of the evidence against him and that, with Parliament's passage of the Human Rights Act of 1998, such decisions must be taken as controlling. Parliament's account of the ruling is at http://image.guardian.co.uk/sys-files/Guardian/documents/2009/06/10/controlorder.pdf.

28. An independent assessor, Lord Carlile, has reviewed the use of control orders and concluded that he "would have reached the same decision as the Secretary of State in each case a control order has been made." See Lord Carlile of Berriew QC, "Third Report of the Independent Reviewer Pursuant to Section 14(3) of the Prevention of Terrorism Act 2005," February 18, 2008, http://security.homeoffice.gov.uk/news-publications/publication-search/general/report-control-orders-2008?view=Binary.

29. Francis T. Miko and Christian Froehlich, "Germany's Role in Fighting Terrorism: Implications for U.S. Policy," Congressional Research Service, Washington, DC, December 27, 2004, 6, http://www.fas.org/irp/crs/RL32710.pdf.

30. Tessa Szyszkowitz, "Germany," in *Europe Confronts Terrorism,* ed. Karin von Hippel (New York: Palgrave Macmillan, 2005), 44.

31. Richard Warnes, "Germany," in *Considering the Creation of a Domestic Intelligence Agency in the United States: Lessons from the Experiences of Australia, Canada, France, Germany, and the United Kingdom,* ed. Brian A. Jackson (Santa Monica, CA: RAND, 2009), 113.

32. Oliver Lepsius, "Liberty, Security, and Terrorism: The Legal Position in Germany," in *German Law Journal* 5, no. 5 (May 2004): 451. The law was amended in 2001 to include better supervision over the data collected, and the amended law was subsequently upheld by the court as constitutional. See David Banisar, "Speaking of Terror: A Survey of the Effects of Counter-terrorism Legislation on Freedom of the Media in Europe," Media and Information Society Division, Directorate General of

Human Rights and Legal Affairs, Council of Europe, November 2008, 31, http://www. coe.int/t/dghl/standardsetting/media/Doc/SpeakingOfTerror_en.pdf.

33. For an overview of these measures, see Human Rights Watch, *Setting an Example: Counter-terrorism Measures in Spain,* vol. 17, no. 1(D), January 2005, 23–54, http://www.libertysecurity.org/IMG/pdf/HRW_report_Spain.pdf; and James Beckman, *Comparative Legal Approaches to Homeland Security and Anti-terrorism* (Burlington, VT: Ashgate Publishing, 2007), 119 –21.

34. See, for example, Anthony Dworkin, "Beyond the 'War on Terror': Towards a New Transatlantic Framework for Counterterrorism," *Policy Brief,* European Council on Foreign Relations, May 27, 2009, 2, http://ecfr.3cdn.net/1e18727eafdddcceb7_81m6ibwez.pdf.

35. The Europeans have largely avoided this debate by turning captured suspected terrorists and combatants over either to the United States or to the local (Afghan or Iraqi) government. In doing so, they have not had to confront the problems associated with using the traditional laws of war to deal with terrorist suspects or, in turn, the insufficiency of relying instead on the criminal court system for dealing with captured terrorists and illegal combatants.

36. Benjamin Wittes, *Law and the Long War: The Future of Justice in the Age of Terror* (New York: Penguin Press, 2008), 19–33.

37. Karen J. Greenberg, "European Counterterrorism and Its Implications for the U.S. War on Terror," *NYU Review of Law and Security,* Summer 2005, 2, http://www.lawand security.org/publications/specialissueeurope_000.pdf.

38. BBC News, "'Thousands' Pose UK Terror Threat," November 5, 2007, http:// news.bbc.co.uk/2/hi/uk_news/7078712.stm.

39. See Gary Schmitt, "Could 7/7 Have Been Stopped?" *Weekly Standard,* May 29, 2006, http://www.weeklystandard.com/Content/Public/Articles/000%5C000%5C 012%5C248itlib.asp.

40. See Home Office, "Statistics on Terrorism Arrests and Outcomes Great Britain, 11 September 2001 to 31 March 2008," May 13, 2009, 1–2, http://www.homeoffice. gov.uk/rds/pdfs09/hosb0409.pdf.

41. Ibid., 8.

42. On these points, see John Bew and Martyn Frampton, *Talking to Terrorists: Making Peace in Northern Ireland and the Basque Country* (London: Hurst and Co., 2009), 110; Clarke, *Learning from Experience,*. 22–23; and Frank Foley, "Reforming Counterterrorism: Institutions and Organizational Routines in Britain and France," *Security Studies* 18, no. 3 (July 2009): 462–63.

43. For statistics on France, Spain, and other European Union members, see Europol, *TE-SAT: EU Terrorism Situation and Trend Report 2009* (The Hague: Europol, 2009), 12–13, 49, http://www.europol.europa.eu/publications/EU_Terrorism_Situation_and_Trend_Report_TE-SAT/TESAT2009.pdf.

44. Ibid., 17.

45. Ibid., 49.

46. Bundesministerium des Innern [Ministry of Interior], *Verfassungsschutzberichts 2008* [Report on Protection of the Constitution], May 19, 2009, 207–08, http://www.bmi.bund.de/cae/servlet/contentblob/463552/publicationFile/23343/vsb_2008.pdf.

47. Ibid., 4. More recently, the threat profile Germany faces has reportedly expanded to include al Qaeda allied Islamists from North Africa planning attacks on German targets. Matthias Gebauer, "Fears of Election Attack: Germany Bolsters Anti-Terror Measures," *Spiegel Online International,* July 10, 2009, http://www.spiegel.de/international/germany/0,1518,635467,00.html.

48. See Wolfgang Schäuble, "Das Konzept der vernetzten Sicherheit" [The concept of networked security] (speech, seventh Symposium of the Agency for Constitutional Protection, Berlin, December 8, 2008), http://www.wolfgang-schaeuble.de/index.php?id=30&textid=1227&page=1.

49. Europol, *TE-SAT: EU Terrorism Situation and Trend Report 2008* (The Hague: Europol, 2008), 18, http://www.europol.europa.eu/publications/EU_Terrorism_Situation_and_Trend_Report_TE-SAT/TESAT2008.pdf.

50. Gebauer, "Fears of Election Attack."

51. In 2006, the German constitutional court ruled the broad profiling was unconstitutional in the absence of a specific threat. For background on the use of profiling by German authorities and the court's decision, see Gabriele Kett-Straub, "Data Screening of Muslim Sleepers Unconstitutional," *German Law Journal,* November 1, 2006, http://www.germanlawjournal.com/index.php?pageID=11&artID=770.

52. See Miko and Froehlich, "Germany's Role in Fighting Terrorism," 4–6; and Michael Jacobson, *The West at War: U.S. and European Counterrorism Efforts, Post-September 11* (Washington, DC: Washington Institute for Near East Policy, 2006), 36.

53. See paragraph 91 of the German penal code, "Anleitung zur Begehung einer schweren staatsgefährdenden Gewalttat" [Instructions to commit a serious act of violence that endangers the state], available at http://www.gesetze-im-internet.de/stgb/BJNR001270871.html. The amending provisions ("Gesetz zur Abwehr von Gefahren des internationalen Terrorismus durch das Bundeskriminalamt" [Law to counter the threats of international terrorism by the Federal Criminal

Police Office) of the law governing the Bundeskriminalamt can be found at http://www.bgblportal.de/BGBL/bgbl1f/bgbl108s3083.pdf. On the latter law, see "Big Brother Worries: German Parliament Passes Anti-Terror Law," *Spiegel Online International,* November 13, 2008, http://www.spiegel.de/international/germany/0,1518,590198,00.html.

54. Article 10 of the Basic Law of the Federal Republic of Germany states that "the privacy of correspondence, posts and telecommunications shall be inviolable." But it then adds that "restrictions may be ordered only pursuant to a law," suggesting the right to privacy in this instance is not simply inviolable. See p. 17 of the English text, available at https://www.btg-bestellservice.de/pdf/80201000.pdf. As Oliver Lepsius points out, at the height of the concern over the RAF, the German legislature and courts made what they believed were the necessary adjustments in German security laws to deal with the threat. "While security was seen as antagonistic to civil liberties in the 1970s, in the 1980s their relationship changed and was seen as more equal. Security was named a 'basic right' and became a 'state duty' (Staatsaufgabe)." Lepsius, "Liberty, Security, and Terrorism," 435–36. And, indeed, an earlier (1970) Federal Constitutional Court decision on government monitoring of communications described the German state as being a "combative democracy," meaning that the state had an obligation to not allow "opponents of the constitution" to use constitutional rights granted under the constitution "to endanger, harm or destroy the continuing existence of the state." See Paul M. Schwartz, "German and U.S. Telecommunications Privacy Law: Legal Regulation of Domestic Law Enforcement Surveillance," *Hastings Law Journal* 54 (August 2003): 772.

55. See Home Office, "Statistics on Terrorism Arrests and Outcomes," 2, 5–6, 9.

56. The government, in particular, believes this extended detention is required to build an evidentiary case given the following factors: greater use of encrypted computers by terrorist cells, the increasing complexity of the networks themselves, and the possible ties to international networks. For an overview of the logic behind the current system of precharge detention, see Shapiro, "Detention of Terror Suspects in Britain and France," 4.

57. Ibid.; and Feikert and Doyle, "Anti-Terrorism Authority," 5–8, 32–33.

58. For a brief overview of the differing tallies of terrorism-related prosecutions and cases, see Richard B. Zabel and James J. Benjamin Jr., *In Pursuit of Justice: Prosecuting Terrorism Cases in the Federal Courts,* (New York and Washington, DC: Human Rights First, 2008), 21–22, .http://www.humanrightsfirst.info/pdf/080521-USLS-pursuit-justice.pdf.

59. See Center on Law and Security, "Terrorist Trial Report Card: September 11, 2008," New York University School of Law, 2, http://www.lawandsecurity.org/publications/Sept08TTRCFinal.pdf. See also Richard B. Zabel and James J. Benjamin Jr., *In Pursuit of Justice: Prosecuting Terrorism Cases in the Federal Courts, 2009 Update and Recent Developments* (New York and Washington, DC: Human Rights First, 2009), 9, http://www.humanrightsfirst.org/pdf/090723-LS-in-pursuit-justice-09-update.pdf. In the wake of the debate over the Obama administration's decision to try Khalid Sheikh Mohammed and four other 9/11 plotters in a federal court, this latter study has been used by some to suggest the decision rests on solid, empirical grounds and that the criminal court system can effectively handle terrorism cases. Although the study does make that case, it doesn't argue that the detention and military tribunal system for illegal combatants is unnecessary or that the criminal justice system is appropriate for such cases. The study's real targets are proposals for the creation of new, terrorism-specific "national security courts" (1–3).

60. Center on Law and Security, "Terrorist Trial Report Card," 2, 6. The exact number given in the report is 693. According to the study, "'Prosecutions' as used herein are counted per defendant. A proceeding with three co-defendants, for example, counts as three prosecutions. If the same person is prosecuted in two separate proceedings under two separate indictments, they are counted separately." 2. In Zabel and Benjamin's 2008 study of terrorism prosecutions, "almost half of the terrorism cases . . . surveyed have included charges for offenses" against the material support laws. See *In Pursuit of Justice,* 32.

61. Zabel and Benjamin, *In Pursuit of Justice,* 6. Zabel and Benjamin go on to say that "material support cases have been brought against persons who enrolled at terrorist training camps, who acted as messengers for terrorist leaders, who intended to act as doctors to terrorist groups, or who raised money to support terrorist organizations. Although these cases can potentially result in overreaching, and although not all material support cases have resulted in convictions, the government's overall record of success in this area is impressive, and most if not all of the convictions seem sound." Ibid.

62. Robert M. Chesney, "Federal Prosecution of Terrorism-Related Offenses: Conviction and Sentencing Data in Light of the 'Soft-Sentence' and 'Data-Reliability' Critiques," *Lewis and Clark Law Review* 11, no. 4 (Winter 2007): 854–55, http://legacy.lclark.edu/org/lclr/objects/LCB_11_4_Art2_Chesney.pdf..

63. Christoph J. M. Safferling, "Terror and Law: Is the German Legal System Able to Deal with Terrorism?" *German Law Journal* 5, no. 5 (May 2004): 519,

http://www.germanlawjournal.com/pdfs/Vol05No05/PDF_Vol_05_No_05_515-524_special_issue_Safferling.pdf.

64. In *Brandenburg v. Ohio,* 395 U.S. 444 (1969), the Supreme Court held that advocating force or unlawful activity was proscribed only when it was meant to—and likely to—incite imminent, lawless action. For an overview of legislation by European countries curtailing or banning speech or media that incite or condone terrorism, see Guy de Vel, *"Apologie du terrorisme"* and *"Incitement to Terrorism"* (Strasbourg: Council of Europe, 2004).

65. For an overview of the recently adopted Lisbon Treaty and the new EU prerogatives with respect to domestic security and role of the European Court of Justice, see General Secretariat of the Council of the EU, "Background: The Lisbon Treaty's Impact on the Justice and Home Affairs (JHA) Council: More Co-decision and New Working Structures," December 2009, http://www.se2009.eu/polopoly_fs/1.25977!menu/standard/file/111615.pdf; and Brendan Donnelly, "Justice and Home Affairs in the Lisbon Treaty: A Constitutionalising Clarification," *European Institute of Public Administration* 2008 (1), 1–5, http://www.eipa.eu/files/repository/eipascope/20080509184107_SCOPE2008-1-4_BrendanDonnelly.pdf.

66. See "Muslim Americans: Middle Class and Mostly Mainstream," Pew Research Center, May 22, 2007, http://pewresearch.org/pubs/483/muslim-americans; and "Mapping the Global Muslim Population," Pew Forum on Religion and Public Life, October 2009, http://pewforum.org/docs/?DocID=450.

67. For an overview of these points, see Peter Chalk and Walter Rosenau, *Confronting the "Enemy Within": Security Intelligence, the Police, and Counterterrorism in Four Democracies* (Santa Monica, CA: RAND, 2004).

68. See Andrew C. McCarthy and Alykhan Velshi, "We Need a National Security Court," AEI Working Paper 156, Washington, DC, August 20, 2009, http://www.aei.org/paper/100038. See also Jack Goldsmith, "Long-Term Terrorist Detention and Our National Security Court," working paper, Series on Counterterrorism and American Statutory Law, Brookings Institution, Georgetown University Law School, and the Hoover Institution, http://www.brookings.edu/papers/2009/0209_detention_goldsmith.aspx; and Stephen I. Vladeck, "The Case against National Security Courts," *Willamette Law Review* 45 (Spring 2009): 505–25.

69. See Brian A. Jackson, ed., *Considering the Creation of a Domestic Intelligence Agency in the United States: Lessons from the Experiences of Australia, Canada, France, Germany, and the United Kingdom* (Santa Monica, CA: RAND, 2009).

70. This concern seems to ignore the fact that, as the history of the FBI makes clear, housing intelligence and law enforcement under one roof does not necessarily preclude abuses of authority, either.

71. Gerecht and Schmitt, "France: Europe's Counterterrorist Powerhouse," 2, 4.

72. For example, according to Freedom House's annual international survey of country political rights and civil liberties (*Freedom in the World 2009*), France and the United Kingdom—along with Spain, Germany, and the United States—remain in the category of states assessed to be the world's freest. The survey results are in Freedom House, "Combined Average Rankings—Independent Countries," http://www.freedom house.org/uploads/fiw09/tablesandcharts/Combined%20Average%20Ratings %20(Independent%20Countries)%20FIW%202008.pdf .

73. Jane Mayer, *The Dark Side: The Inside Story of How the War on Terror Turned into a War on American Ideals* (New York: Doubleday, 2008). Paraphrasing historian Arthur Schlesinger Jr., Mayer writes, "The Bush administration's extralegal counterterrorism program presented the most dramatic, sustained, and radical challenge to the rule of law in American history" (8).

74. On the use of national security letters, see the discussion in this chapter. Under a 1984 law, the government is authorized, with court approval, to detain individuals who are a flight risk in order to secure their testimony. After 9/11, the law was used to detain possible witnesses but also suspects where probable cause was lacking for an arrest. According to a report issued by Human Rights Watch, some seventy individuals—citizens and aliens—were detained under the law's provision. Of that number, Human Rights Watch believes that forty-two were ultimately released without charges being filed against them, seven were charged with providing support to terrorist organizations, twenty were charged with other crimes, twenty-four were deported, and two were subsequently designated as "enemy combatants." The report states that the government subsequently apologized to thirteen individuals for wrongful detainment. *Witness to Abuse: Human Rights Abuses under the Material Witness Law since September 11,* Human Rights Watch, June 2005, 5, 17–19, http://www.aclu.org/files/FilesPDFs/materialwitnessreport.pdf.

75. Conversely, it may be that such oversight also results in bureaucratic caution. This issue has arisen in both the case involving army major Nidal Hasan, the Fort Hood shooter, and Umar Farouk Abdulmutallab, the Christmas airplane bomber. In the former, there are concerns that analysts and investigators shied away from follow-up questions about the major's behavior and email contacts with a known foreign jihadist out of concern that doing so would be seen as potentially infringing on the

major's First Amendment rights. In the latter case, although Abdulmutallab had been placed on a broad watch list following his father's warning to the U.S. Embassy in Nigeria, his name had not been placed on the much smaller "no-fly" list for lack of any corroborative information. In this case, the concern with expanding the no-fly list to include the likes of Abdulmutallab may be the result of previous complaints by members of Congress and others that the list had grown too large and contained names that obviously did not belong on it.

76. U.S. Department of Homeland Security, *Quadrennial Homeland Security Review Report: A Strategic Framework for a Secure Homeland,* February 2010, 2, http://www. dhs.gov/xlibrary/assets/qhsr_report.pdf.

# Index

# About the Authors

**Rafael L. Bardají** is the founder of the Strategic Studies Group (Grupo de Estudios Estratégicos [GEES]), a Spanish think tank. He served in the Spanish government as national security advisor from 1996 to 2004. He is currently the foreign policy director at the Foundation for Analysis and Social Studies (Fundación para el Análisis y los Estudios Sociales [FAES]) in Madrid, consults widely on international security affairs, and writes regularly in the Spanish press.

**Ignacio Cosidó** is a member of the Spanish parliament and the homeland security spokesperson for Spain's People's Party (Partido Popular). Previously, he served as chief of staff of the Spanish Civil Guard (Guardia Civil) from 1996 to 2004 and was a senator in Spain's upper house from 2004 to 2008. He is a senior fellow at the Strategic Studies Group (Grupo de Estudios Stratégicos) and writes regularly for the Spanish press.

**Eric Gujer** is a longtime journalist and editor for *Neue Zürcher Zeitung* (NZZ), a German-language Swiss daily newspaper. He was a correspondent for NZZ in Berlin from 1998 to 2008. He is the author of *Kampf an neuen Fronten: Wie sich der BND dem Terrorismus stellt* [The Fight on New Fronts: How the BND Is Confronting Terrorism].

**Tom Parker** is Policy Director for Terrorism, Counterterrorism and Human Rights at Amnesty International USA. He is an adjunct professor at Bard College in New York and a former officer in Britain's Security Service (MI5). His chapter in this volume was written in a private capacity and does not reflect the views of Amnesty International.

**Gary J. Schmitt** is a resident scholar and director of Advanced Strategic Studies at the American Enterprise Institute. Previously, he served as staff director of the U.S. Senate's Select Committee on Intelligence and was executive director of the President's Foreign Intelligence Advisory Board during Ronald Reagan's second term. His recent books include *Silent Warfare: Understanding the World of Intelligence* (Brassey's, 2002), *Of Men and Materiel: The Crisis in Military Resources* (AEI Press, 2007), and *The Rise of China: Essays on the Future Competition* (Encounter, 2009).